The Abolition of White Democracy

The Abolition of
White Democracy

Joel Olson

University of Minnesota Press
Minneapolis • London

An earlier version of chapter 2 was originally published as "The Democratic Problem of the White Citizen," *Constellations* 8, no. 2 (2001): 163–83.

An earlier version of chapter 3 was originally published as "Whiteness and the Participation-Inclusion Dilemma," *Political Theory* 30, no. 3 (2002): 384–409.

Published by the University of Minnesota Press
111 Third Avenue South, Suite 290
Minneapolis, MN 55401-2520
http://www.upress.umn.edu

Library of Congress Cataloging-in-Publication Data

Olson, Joel, 1967-
    The abolition of white democracy / Joel Olson.
        p. cm.
    Includes bibliographical references and index.
    ISBN 0-8166-4277-X (hc: alk. paper) ISBN 0-8166-4278-8 (pb: alk. paper)
    1. United States—Race relations—Political aspects. 2. Racism—Political aspects—
United States. 3. Race discrimination—Political aspects—United States. 4. Democracy—
United States. 5. Whites—United States—Politics and government. 6. Whites—
Race identity—United States. 7. United States—Politics and government.
8. Multiculturalism—United States. I. Title.
    E184.A1O4525 2004
    323.173—dc22

                                                    2004005026

Printed in the United States of America on acid-free paper

The University of Minnesota is an equal-opportunity educator and employer.

Today at last we know: John Brown was right.

—W. E. B. Du Bois

Contents

Acknowledgments

Lisa Disch read every chapter—twice. Sometimes more. She corrected errors, made suggestions, and forced me to rethink certain problems. This book is much stronger as a result, and I am especially grateful to her. Lawrie Balfour and Noel Ignatiev also carefully read the entire manuscript and offered excellent advice on revisions, most of which I have tried to take. Mary Dietz, August Nimtz, and David Roediger read an early version of this project and gave me valuable assistance throughout the research and writing process.

Bruce Baum, Samuel Chambers, Luis Fernandez, Ryan Fortson, Traci Harris, Rebecca Hill, Kathleen Iudicello, Laura Janara, Mike Kramer, Joe Lowndes, Jeffrey Lustig, Catherine O'Leary, Ramsey Eric Ramsey, Tom Sabatini, Andrew Sabl, Becki Scola, Andrew Seligsohn, and Stephen White all read one or more chapters and offered helpful criticisms. Dan Gannon came up with the title. Yan Baohua helped prepare the index. Eric Bright, my coworker at a word processing job while I was writing an early draft of the book, didn't actually read any chapters, but he listened to my arguments and kept me on my toes with discussions of Marx, Foucault, feminism, and race while we typed other people's manuscripts. Daniel Kelliher never read a page, but he helped me see history and theory from the bottom up, and for that I am thankful. Malcolm Creed Olson chewed on numerous pages of several drafts, but I don't think he swallowed any.

This book emerged out of questions and interests that arose from my involvement in various grassroots political activities. These influences were as significant as my academic ones and deserve mention. In Minneapolis, the Blast! collective, the Love and Rage Federation, and Minneapolis Anti-Racist Action were central to my political development and my thinking on questions of race and democracy. In Phoenix, the Ruckus collective and Phoenix Copwatch helped me similarly. I owe a debt to my fellow members on the editorial board of the *New Abolitionist*, John Garvey, Beth Henson, Noel Ignatiev, and Chris Niles. The way in which all of these groups merge intellectual work with political agitation has been a model for me.

I learned from working on this project that scholarship is selfish. Reading and writing, its principal elements, are solitary activities. When a research project consumes a scholar, it's far too easy to set aside other tasks, and friends and family pay for the scholar's selfishness. Audrey Creed endured plenty while I worked: she picked up the slack on jobs that should have been equally shared, and all she asked was for me to acknowledge that and to finish this thing in a reasonable amount of time. For everything, Audrey, thank you. This book is dedicated to you.

Introducing the White Democracy

Racial discrimination has no place in a democratic society. There is little disagreement with that. It embodies inequality, intolerance, exclusion, and injustice. Democracy, on the other hand, stands for equality and freedom. Democratic citizenship is inclusive of all members of a polity while racial oppression actively prohibits certain people from exercising their rights as citizens. Yet in spite of these sharp contrasts, racial matters pervade nearly every aspect of life in the United States. Race influences where we live, the schools we attend, the friends we make, the votes we cast, the opportunities we enjoy, even the television shows we watch. As contrary as discrimination and democracy seem to be, they somehow coexist in the American political order.

In his 1940 book *Dusk of Dawn*, the great political theorist W. E. B. Du Bois argues that race is the central problem facing democracy in the United States and the world. One question this problem raises is how can African Americans and people of color throughout the world become part of democracy, which has heretofore been reserved exclusively for whites. Another question is how would the "self-government" of the world's peoples of color, once achieved, change democracy. How might American democracy, for example, be transformed if it was shorn of white supremacy? Would it simply be more inclusive or would its nature be fundamentally altered?[1] Contemporary political theory has had difficulty grappling with both of these questions. Part of the reason is because it has had a hard time figuring out what to do with race. If racial oppression is contrary to democracy, there seems to be little that an analysis of race can contribute to questions of citizenship, participation, or equality. Beyond arguments opposing racism, there does not seem to be much for political theory to do. As a result, it has devoted few resources toward answering either of Du Bois's questions, particularly the latter, even though it is especially suggestive.

Political theory has had little to say about Du Bois's questions because it has not theorized race as a political category. Reflecting American society at large, the discipline has generally treated race as something created prior to or outside the political realm. This "pre-political" conception of race tends to separate racial inequality out from democratic ideals, which makes it difficult to recognize the ways in which race and democracy are interconnected.

I argue that we need a specifically political theory of race. I mean "political" in two ways. First, an effective theory must identify race as a set of relations within a network of power that organizes people into particular groups and/or roles for the purpose of governing the polity. Second, such a theory must consider politics as participation, community, and the initiation of new possibilities, or in Mary Dietz's words, as "the collective and participatory engagement of citizens in the determination of the affairs of their community."[2] The disciplinary aspect of politics must be complemented by its democratic aspirations. A theory of race must take into consideration both senses of the political. It must understand race as produced within the political realm rather than prior to it and therefore as a product of democracy rather than its antithesis. This requires, however, breaking with the dominant theoretical approach toward the American racial order, which tends to bracket race from democracy.

Ideals/Practices

The bracketing of racial discrimination from democracy generally takes the form of an assumed contradiction between the ideals and practices of American democracy. In his classic *An American Dilemma*, Gunnar

Myrdal argues that Americans universally hold to the "American Creed": the belief in progress, equality, the essential dignity and perfectibility of humans, and their inalienable right to freedom, justice, and fair opportunity.[3] The Creed derives from the essential message of the Declaration of Independence: "All men are created equal." The problem, Myrdal continues, is that the ideal of equality is not always lived up to. Numerous disadvantaged groups in the United States, particularly African Americans, are discriminated against daily despite the Creed. The result is a conflict between the ideals of the Creed and those local and individual values, jealousies, parochialisms, prejudices, norms, and folkways that undermine the Creed in practice. The "Negro Problem" is "an American dilemma" because the treatment of African Americans stands as a vivid contradiction between democratic ideals and discriminatory practices.

> From the point of view of the American Creed the status accorded the Negro in America represents nothing more and nothing less than a century-long lag of public morals. In principle the Negro problem was settled long ago; in practice the solution is not effectuated. The Negro in America has not yet been given the elemental civil and political rights of formal democracy, including a fair opportunity to earn his living, upon which a general accord was already won when the American Creed was first taking form. And this anachronism constitutes the contemporary "problem" both to Negroes and to whites.[4]

The great moral and political project of the nation, according to Myrdal, is to make practices consistent with ideals.

Myrdal's influence pervades contemporary attempts to address the racial "dilemma," even among his critics. Rogers Smith, for example, argues that liberal and republican ideals in the United States have always been accompanied by numerous "inegalitarian ascriptive traditions" such as racism, patriarchy, and nativism.[5] Instead of an American Creed pit against discriminatory practices, Smith proposes a "multiple traditions" approach that acknowledges that ascriptive traditions like racism are full-blown ideologies (not just practices) that have always coexisted alongside liberal and republican traditions. "American political actors have always promoted civic ideologies that blend liberal, democratic republican, and inegalitarian ascriptive elements in various combinations designed to be politically popular."[6] For Smith, the "massive inequalities in American life" are not a violation of the Creed so much as they represent a conflict between rival traditions, one emphasizing the fundamental equality and liberty of all, the other insisting on the special status and privileges of a particular group. Rather than distinguish good ideals from bad practices, Smith differentiates between good and bad traditions, specifically the vaunted traditions of liberalism and republicanism versus the "illiberal, undemocratic traditions of ascriptive Americanism."[7]

Despite their differences, Myrdal and Smith both believe that democratic ideals are distinct from racist practices and ideologies. Thus, both bracket race from democracy. Myrdal believes that if more whites had a full awareness of the contradiction between their belief in human equality and the fact of Black subordination, they would act to eliminate the gap between ideals and practices. "There is no doubt," he writes, "that a great majority of white people in America would be prepared to give the Negro a substantially better deal if they knew the facts."[8] Smith's multiple traditions thesis holds that republican and liberal traditions exist alongside and often do battle with ascriptive traditions such as racism and sexism but presumes that each tradition is logically coherent and relatively independent from the others. This formulation leaves the ideals/practices dichotomy essentially intact, only with Smith it is not a conflict between racist practices and egalitarian ideals but egalitarian versus inegalitarian ideological traditions. Thus, the multiple traditions thesis does not overthrow the ideals/practices dichotomy; it just cuts it another way. Both Myrdal and Smith insulate American democratic ideals from the taint of racial oppression, for in each account discrimination contradicts democratic traditions but in no way forms a part of these traditions themselves.[9]

Slavery, the seizure of American Indian lands, Chinese exclusion laws, Jim Crow legislation, Japanese internment, Mexican *bracero* pro-grams. Instead of understanding these as unfortunate episodes in viola-tion of the egalitarian ethos of the democratic tradition, what if we understand these events as perfectly compatible with American democ-racy? Historian Edmund Morgan argues that "The rise of liberty and equality in this country was accompanied by the rise of slavery."[10] There is no contradiction between democratic ideals and practices of slavery; the former depended on the economic base of the latter. This interde-pendence of slavery and freedom, Morgan holds, is "the central paradox of American history."[11] Similarly, Derrick Bell and Preeta Bansal argue that the early American republican notion of a "common good" was de-fined against Black subordination. There was no contradiction between republican ideals and racial oppression; rather, they were intimately linked.[12] What if, as these arguments suggest, racial oppression and American democracy are mutually constitutive rather than antithetical?

This central question drives this book. It is a question that Myrdal's and Smith's models cannot contemplate. The ideals/practices split can-not explain how racial subordination constructs democratic ideals as well as violates them. Yet I argue this is precisely the case. It is not so much that racial discrimination is a "dilemma" for white Americans or that liberal citizenship coexists with ascriptive traditions that exclude people of color. Rather, the very structure of American citizenship is white, to the point where, for most of American history, to be a citizen was to be white and vice versa. Racial oppression makes full democracy impossible, but it has also made American democracy possible. Con-versely, American democracy has made racial oppression possible, for neither slavery nor segregation nor any other form of racial domination could have survived without the tacit or explicit consent of the white majority. American democracy is a white democracy, a polity ruled in the interests of a white citizenry and characterized by simultaneous relations of equality and privilege: equality among whites, who are priv-ileged in relation to those who are not white. The burdens of white citizenship—particularly on efforts to expand democracy—remain with us today.

This is not to say that there is no *possible* contradiction between democratic ideals and the privileged status of whites, only that there is no *necessary* contradiction. Logically, absolute equality and privilege conflict. When equality is reserved only for some, however, it can co-exist with privilege. When this occurs, any contradiction between them must be articulated, as the oppressed challenge the oppressor to "live up to its ideals." As Pierre van den Berghe argues, "Notwithstanding some soul-searching by a few genteel slave-owning intellectuals like Jefferson and Madison in the late eighteenth and early nineteenth centuries, there is little evidence of an 'American Dilemma' during most of the nineteenth century and the first third of the twentieth century. The democratic, egalitarian, and libertarian ideals were reconciled with slavery and genocide by restricting the definition of humanity to whites."[13] Slaves and free Black persons had to point out the contradiction between praising the principles of the Declaration while also holding slaves.[14] Myrdal's inability to see that the contradiction between ideals and practices is not inherent but created by the victims of racial oppression left him stunned by the emergence of the civil rights movement just ten years after his book was published. He could not see that Black agency forced the American dilemma, not the American Creed itself. The contradiction between racial oppression and democracy may seem self-evident today, but it took the deeds of Nat Turner and Ella Baker to make them so.[15]

The ideals/practices dichotomy makes it difficult to study race as a political category because it tends to insulate democratic ideals from criticism. It renders liberty, equality, democracy, and citizenship as pure, unalloyed ideals to aspire to rather than essentially contested concepts.[16] Democracy becomes an unsullied ideal to strive for, albeit always unsuccessfully, rather than a space of action, struggle, contestation, and conflict. The logic of the ideals/practices split is that exclusion and discrimination is the problem, for which equality and democracy is the solution. But democracy is not just a solution; it is a political problem itself. The question is not just democracy for whom but what kind of democracy, not just who is to be made equal but what kind of equality, not just who is to be free but what kind of freedom. Democracy is not a refuge that exists above the fray of interminable political conflict. It is a rough-and-tumble product of such conflict.[17] One of the advantages of analyzing democracy and race as mutually constitutive is that, in addition to providing a better way to understand how race functions, it renders democratic ideals political again. It takes them down from their pedestal, makes them amenable to critical analysis, and reveals how they can foster both equality and privilege, freedom and slavery. It provides new ways of imagining what democracy is and could be. One of the purposes of my critique of the white democracy, then, is to reimagine democracy and its radical potential.

Race as a Political Category

It is widely acknowledged in academia (if not in the general public) that race is a "social construction." To say that race is a product of social forces rather than a biological category, however, tells little about how these forces operate. As David Roediger notes, "[T]he insight that race is socially constructed is so sweeping that by itself it implies few specific political conclusions."[18] An analysis of the relationship between race and democracy illuminates the concept of social construction by understanding race as a relatively autonomous political system in its own right, with its own norms, ideology, power relations, and logic.[19] Race functions by organizing people into particular groups. One group or "race" receives preferential treatment through the social order while the other race or races are subordinated to a status below that of the members of the dominant race. The result is the political docility and economic utility of all races, as the dominant race represses the subordinate one and is itself disciplined by the imperatives of perpetuating the system of privilege. Race, then, is by definition a system of discrimination, hierarchy, and power. As van den Berghe writes, "The existence of races in a given society presupposes the presence of racism, for without racism physical characteristics are devoid of social significance."[20] Further, the racial order functions to preserve the privileges of the dominant race at the expense of the other race or races. The key to understanding race as a political system, then, is through an analysis of the dominant or "white" race. Thus, a critique of whiteness, or the condition of racial privilege in a democratic polity, is crucial to understanding how race functions as a political system.

If Du Bois provides the foundation for a critique of whiteness, as I argue in the next chapter, James Baldwin provides the language and polemical framework. In his powerful essay "On Being 'White' . . . And Other Lies," he argues that white people are not white because of their skin color or European ancestry but through a moral and political choice.

> Americans became white—the people who, as they claim, "settled" the country became white—because of the necessity of denying the Black presence and justifying the Black subjugation. No community can be based on such a principle—or, in other words, no community can be established on so genocidal a lie. White men—from Norway, for example, where they were Norwegians—became white: by slaughtering the cattle, poisoning the wells, torching the houses, massacring Native Americans, raping Black women.[21]

Whiteness, Baldwin argues, is not a genetic inheritance so much as it is a social relation. It is not something one is; it is something one does. As the historian Theodore Allen writes, "For when an emigrant population from 'multiracial' Europe goes to North America or South Africa and there, by constitutional fiat, incorporates itself as the 'white race,' that is no part of genetic evolution. It is rather a political act: the invention of 'the white race.'"[22] "White" or "Caucasian" is not a neutral physical description of certain persons but a political project of securing and protecting privileges in a society whose ideals would seem to forbid them. Yet because whiteness is a decision made, it is also a decision that can be undone. Undoing it does not mean simply refusing to classify people by race; it means abandoning a politics in which the standing of one section of the population is premised on the debasement of another. (This explains why I do not capitalize white throughout the book, but I do capitalize Black. The two terms are not symmetrical. Black is a cultural identity as well as a political category, and as such merits capitalization like American Indian, Chicana, or Irish American. White, however, for reasons I detail in the next chapter and in chapter 4, is strictly a political category and thus, like "proletarian," "citizen," or "feminist," requires no capitalization.)

As Baldwin suggests, race is a form of political power. It confers full citizenship to those who can prove themselves white and guarantees their privileged status over those deemed not-white and therefore less than citizens. The privileges of whiteness, then, include and rest upon the rights and duties of citizenship. Hence, the racialization of citizenship and in particular the citizenship of the dominant race, or *white citizenship*, becomes a central problem for democratic theory. White citizenship is the enjoyment of racial standing in a democratic polity. It is a position of equality and privilege simultaneously: equal to other white citizens yet privileged over those who are not white. It is both a structural location in the racial order and a product of human agency. Individual whites may consciously defend their privileges, reject them, or deny they exist, yet the structure of the racial order makes it difficult for individual whites to "jump out" of their whiteness at any given time. The category does not explain every belief or behavior of every white person but encompasses the structures and social relations that produce white privilege and the ideas that defend it. In this way, the category is similar to the phrases "the white man" or "the Negro" that were common in the civil rights era (as in "What does the Negro want?"). The white citizen is not necessarily coextensive with persons of pale skin or predominant European ancestry. Skin color is but a "badge," as Du Bois writes, that is used to distribute people along the color line.[23] Nor is it coextensive with wealth. As I argue in chapter 1, the distinctive feature of white citizenship is that it crosses class lines.

The white citizen is one who enjoys the status and privileges of a racial polity. The political challenge is to eliminate these advantages in favor of more democratic forms of citizenship. The consequence of doing so, I maintain, would be the dissolution of white democracy.

The Democratic Problem of the White Citizen

This book attempts to bring questions of participation and race together in the context of political theory. The central challenge I confront is how to expand political participation in a society that has been historically marked by racial discrimination. The key to this challenge, I argue, lies in the white citizen, and the task of democratic politics is to abolish him.

Democracy and racial oppression are intimately connected in the United States—the freedom of some has depended on the subordination of others. This connection is sealed through citizenship. Citizenship is a political identity signifying equality in the public sphere and the shared enjoyment of rights and duties, including the all-important right to participate in governing public affairs. American citizenship, however, historically has also been a form of social status that has served to distinguish those who were or could become full members of the American republic from those who could not. In the formative years of American democracy, citizenship was in a very real sense proof that one was not and could not become a slave. Given the racial character of chattel slavery in the United States, its antithesis, citizenship, was also racialized. If the Black race was associated with slavery in the public imagination, the white race was associated with citizenship. The standing of citizens, then, was a *racialized* standing. In the antebellum era, citizenship granted an individual not just political status but a white racial status as well. The two were indissoluble. Whiteness became the political color of citizenship. The significance of racialized citizenship is not that only white persons could become citizens; it is that becoming a citizen effectively made one white.

As I stated above, white citizenship is simultaneously an identity of equality and privilege. The privileges of white citizenship, or what Roediger calls the "wages of whiteness," are public, psychological, and material.[24] They include the enjoyment of all the rights accorded citizens including suffrage, the right to join political parties, access to desired jobs, the ability to compete in an unrestricted market, the capacity to sit on juries, the right to enjoy public accommodations, and the right to consider oneself the equal of any other. Whiteness, legal scholar Cheryl

Harris notes, is a "consolation prize," particularly for poor and working-class whites.[25] It does not guarantee that all whites will be successful but it ensures that no white citizen will ever be thrown down to the absolute bottom of the social hierarchy. In exchange for this prize, working-class whites acquiesce to the domination of the political and economic system by powerful elites. Whiteness grants working-class whites a special status—not quite rich but not quite powerless—that becomes the focus of the white citizen's political energy rather than challenges to elite rule. As a result, the wages of whiteness constrain "any vision of democracy from addressing the class hierarchies adverse to many who considered themselves white."[26]

Only with the victories of the civil rights movement was the linkage between white standing and citizenship formally broken. Nevertheless, the movement was unable to completely eradicate the antidemocratic influence of whiteness. The legacy of white standing remains at the root of advantages whites currently enjoy over African Americans and others in nearly every social indicator, from life expectancy to unemployment rates to net financial assets to incarceration rates to SAT scores. Yet the "wages of whiteness" do more than dole out a set of privileges to whites. They shape how the white citizen understands democracy. The political values and vision of the white citizen bundle racial privilege with democratic ideals. What appears as an obvious unjust advantage to those who are not white appears to the white citizen as a natural right, a normal condition, or a deserved advantage. As a result, the white citizen resists any political vision in which his or her privileges are not respected. The democratic problem of the white citizen is that the tension between the desire for equality and the desire to maintain one's racial standing results in a narrow political imagination that constrains the way white citizens understand citizenship (as status rather than participation), freedom (as negative liberty), and equality (as opportunity rather than social equality). The white imagination exhibits little incentive to expand participation in public affairs because it construes citizenship as an identity to possess rather than a power to employ.

The political challenge, then, is to subvert the privileges of the white citizen and transform his or her democratic imagination. In practical terms, this means eradicating any disparity between whites and people of color in the realms of education, law enforcement, employment, housing, health care, and politics. Thus, my argument refutes growing arguments to replace so-called "divisive" race-based policies such as affirmative action with "universal" or "class-based" policies and insists on defending and strengthening those programs that directly undermine the wages of whiteness. The implications of my argument go beyond public policy, however. Since whiteness is a position of privilege, I argue that the subversion of this privilege amounts to no less than the *abolition* of white citizenship itself. This, of course, is not ethnic cleansing. The white citizen is not a biological or cultural group but a political category. Eliminating the powers of the category eliminates the category itself, much like the end of feudalism abolished the aristocracy and the Civil War abolished the slaveholders. Further, just as these previous forms of abolition paved the way for new, more democratic political orders (representative democracy and Radical Reconstruction, respectively), abolishing the white citizen paves the way for new possibilities in which privilege would be inimical to democracy rather than a functional part of it. In other words, movements against racial domination might not realize liberal democracy so much as suggest a world beyond it.

Historical struggles against white citizenship, then, provide crucial lessons for contemporary democratic theory. Particularly important are the Black freedom struggles. While various groups, from American Indians to the Irish to the Italians to the Jews to the Chinese to the Mexicans, have endured racial oppression in the United States, the archetype of not-whiteness historically has been Blackness. This is due to the original function of the racial order, which was the maintenance of slavery.[27] The system of racial subordination was designed primarily for African Americans for the purposes of exploiting their labor, first under slavery and then under segregation. This is not to say that only African Americans suffered under the domination of a racial state, only that, given their central role in economic production, their unique unfree

status in "the land of the free," an
ing the racial order, the Black expe
relationship between race and den
"America is, in large part, what it i
slave and what the slave did to wh
ican freedom struggles have adva
any other kind of movement in tł
itly challenged the connection bet
overthrow of slavery, the unfulfill

privileges of whiten
in general and b
and relations
in its spe
categ
pol

triumphs of the civil rights movement: all of these efforts expanded and transformed American democracy and thereby provide a guidepost for future struggles. Such is the significance of the abolitionists' condemnation of the Constitution as a "covenant with death and an agreement with hell," the freedmen's insistence on "forty acres and a mule," and the Black Panthers' call for "Power to the people!" All of these efforts in some way imagined a world beyond liberal democracy. In their spirit, I argue for an *abolitionist-democratic* politics that makes the struggle against white privilege central not only in the fight against racial discrimination but also in the effort to expand the participation of ordinary people in those affairs that affect their daily life. Any strategy for a more democratic and participatory society, I insist, must directly confront and undermine the white citizen.

Despite its significance, contemporary political theory has generally not considered the democratic problem of the white citizen. Colorblind approaches do not account for the persistence of racial inequality since the civil rights movement, while multiculturalism and theories of recognition frame racial oppression as a cultural conflict rather than a problem of power. Theories of difference tend to consider race as one form of "difference" among others, isolating it from its historical context. All these approaches misconstrue racial domination as a problem of *exclusion* (for which the solution is inclusion) rather than a problem of *privilege* (for which the solution is abolition). Including the excluded is important, but by itself inclusion does not undermine the passive model of citizenship that white democracy promotes nor does it eliminate the

ss. By concentrating on whiteness rather than race
y connecting whiteness to participation, citizenship,
of power, an abolitionist-democratic politics places race
fic historical context rather than lumping it in the general
ies of difference, identity, or exclusion. It shifts the discourse of
tical theory from the problem of diversity to the problem of privilege, from strategies of inclusion to strategies for abolition, from a
vision of the equal recognition of races to a vision of a world without
whiteness, and from the goal of fulfilling liberal democracy to the possibility of transcending it.

I begin my argument in chapter 1 by using the work of Du Bois
to propose a political definition of race that sets out what whiteness is
and how it is fundamental to the American democratic experience. I
argue that at the foundation of the American racial order is a *cross-class
alliance* between the dominant class and one section of the working class.
This alliance confers privileges to its members, in exchange for which
they guarantee the social stability necessary for the accumulation of
capital. This alliance, Du Bois argues, produces two "worlds" of race, the
white and the dark worlds. It results in a peculiar kind of democracy, a
Herrenvolk democracy, in which the white world enjoys democratic
rights and political equality while the dark world is subjected to the
tyranny of the white majority. I use this definition of race to reinterpret Du Bois's famous concept of "double consciousness," arguing that
it is fundamentally an expression of alienation that results from racial
oppression.

I apply this theory of race to American citizenship in chapter 2.
After providing a brief history of the origins of white citizenship, I turn
to Judith Shklar's conception of citizenship as standing and Du Bois's
critique of the "public and psychological wages" of whiteness to show
that the struggle for citizenship was also a struggle to join the cross-class
alliance. As American workers fought to define themselves as citizens,
they also fought to become white. Through an analysis of coverture and
antimiscegenation law, I distinguish between the processes that created
white and male citizenship and show how white women, including many

of those active in the movements for women's equality, sought and received racial standing. After discussing Tocqueville's chapter on the "Three Races" in *Democracy in America*, in which I argue that democracy and racial oppression were not contradictory in the Jacksonian era until slaves and abolitionists made them so, I return to Du Bois to show how white citizenship thwarts attempts to create a more democratic society.

There are two stages of the white democracy, which are divided by the civil rights movement. Chapter 2 addresses the problem of the white citizen in the first stage, the *Herrenvolk* democracy. Chapter 3 addresses the second, post–civil rights stage, in which whiteness becomes less a form of *standing* and more of a *norm* that sediments accrued white advantages onto the ordinary operations of society. After explaining this shift, I use this analysis to address the "participation-inclusion dilemma" in contemporary democratic theory. The dilemma is that in a racial polity, the quest for greater participation may actually serve to strengthen the tyranny of the majority race. The quest for inclusion, on the other hand, may undermine racial tyranny but does little to increase participation. Through a critique of William Connolly's *Ethos of Pluralization*, I argue that political theories based on a strategy of inclusion perpetuate normalized white privilege even as they seek to resolve the problem of difference. I then contrast Connolly's argument with Iris Marion Young's *Justice and the Politics of Difference* and Lani Guinier's *Tyranny of the Majority*. Through an interpretation of these texts I argue that an effective democratic theory must go beyond inclusion by redefining the problem from exclusion to privilege and the lack of participation. The best way to undermine the tyranny of the white majority and to expand democratic participation, I contend, is through a politics aimed at the elimination of white privilege.

Whiteness also persists in the ways in which Americans have come to understand race and the proper resolution of its disorders. In chapter 4 I address the two principal racial paradigms since the civil rights movement, color blindness and multiculturalism. I argue that while both repudiate the essential principles of *Herrenvolk* democracy, neither effectively undermines whiteness. Through a critique of Justice John

Harlan's dissent in *Plessy v. Ferguson* and Stephan and Abigail Thernstrom's *America in Black and White*, I show how whiteness persists in the color-blind ideal through its narrow, formal conception of race as a politically irrelevant physical attribute. Turning to multiculturalism, I analyze Charles Taylor's work on the "politics of recognition" and its influence on scholars such as Nancy Fraser and many of those working in the area of "whiteness studies." The key flaw of the multicultural ideal is that its political objective of achieving the "equal recognition" of cultures requires that it redefine race as culture. Understanding whiteness as one culture among others rather than a category of privilege, however, obscures its power. Ultimately, the color-blind and multicultural ideals perpetuate the passive model of citizenship inherited from the *Herrenvolk* era. Neither, then, provides a means to understand race or to expand democratic participation in the era of globalization.

I conclude in chapter 5 by sketching an outline of the "abolition-democracy," a politics that would abolish the white citizen in order to expand democratic participation as well as eliminate the racial order. I suggest the possibilities of Black radical political thought as a means to reimagine democracy and to leaven the suffocating pragmatism of contemporary democratic theory. Through a brief overview of the work of the original abolitionists, I set out the essential elements of a contemporary abolitionist-democratic politics, emphasizing in particular its radical nature and its emphasis on political action. In undermining the wages of whiteness, the abolition-democracy seeks to redefine citizenship from a passive identity concerned with status to a participatory activity. A democratic politics, I conclude, must be an abolitionist politics.

Throughout the book I take a historical approach toward understanding the relationship between race and American citizenship. In so doing, I take inspiration from Judith Shklar, who writes:

> I want to remind political theorists that citizenship is not a notion that can be discussed intelligibly in a static and empty social space. Whatever the ideological gratifications that the mnemonic evocation of an original

and pure citizenry may have, it is unconvincing and ultimately an uninteresting flight from politics if it disregards the history and present
actualities of our institutions. . . . [P]olitical theorists who ignore the best
current history and political science cannot expect to have anything very
significant to contribute to our political self-understanding. They stand
in acute danger of theorizing about nothing at all except their own un-
easiness in a society they have made very little effort to comprehend.[29]

Unlike Shklar, however, I take an approach also guided by historical materialism, for I am particularly interested in the way in which
white citizenship relates to class relations and the accumulation of capital. I assume that the development of productive forces explains the
general course of a society and that the function of the racial order is
generally related to the development of such forces. As I argue in chapter 2, race is a modern concept; it did not exist prior to the conquest of
the New World and the first stages of capitalist accumulation. Its present meaning and importance, therefore, cannot be separated from the
development of capitalism or from the moral and political thought of
modernity. Thus, I follow Stanley Greenberg when he writes, "Racial
domination . . . is essentially a class phenomenon. . . . Racial domination is not an amorphous, all-encompassing relationship between groups
distinguished by physical characteristics but, for the most part, a series
of specific class relations that vary by place and over time and that
change as a consequence of changing material conditions."[30]

This contrasts with approaches that define race as an ideology.
Matthew Pratt Guterl's *The Color of Race in America*, for example, examines the rise of a biracial order from 1900 to 1940 through an analysis
of the social and political thought of figures such as Du Bois, Madison
Grant, Lathrop Stoddard, and Jean Toomer. Guterl's interpretations of
each are acute and historically sensitive, yet his book too much assumes
that the racial order is shaped by what people write and say about race
rather than how it is reproduced in economic and social structures.[31]
Madison Grant's obsession with the supremacy of the "Nordic" white
race and his fear of the corrupting influence of the lower "Alpine" and

"Mediterranean" races, for example, says much about Grant and other WASP intellectuals' anxieties at the turn of the twentieth century regarding the consolidation of legal segregation and the resultant expansion of the white race to include Southern and Eastern European immigrants, but we should not presume that his ideas illuminate how race actually functioned then. Jim Crow never recognized differences between Nordics and Mediterraneans. Guterl is correct that there is an important ideological component to the reproduction of race, but the history of ideas on race must be placed in a historical-structural context. As Michael Dawson notes, white supremacy is best understood not as an ideology, but as "a system of power relations that structure society."[32]

Nevertheless, given materialism's unfashionable standing these days, I feel obligated to point out that a materialist approach does not require me to reduce all social relations to class or to argue that social and political relationships, including racial ones, are secondary in importance to class relations. While some materialists have taken these positions, doing so generally results in the "uninteresting flight from politics" of which Shklar rightfully warns. Capitalism is not just an economic system that produces commodities. It is also the ensemble of relationships involved in such production. As Michel Foucault writes, the accumulation of capital requires an "accumulation of men."[33] In other words, humans in capitalist societies are "accumulated," or organized and arranged, through forms of power that make them more politically docile and economically efficient. It is my contention that racialized citizenship has been central in constructing the relations of docility-utility necessary for the accumulation of capital in the United States.

While some will question my materialist approach, I suspect that others will criticize my account of white democracy for granting too much agency to whites, particularly white workers, in their complicity with capitalist domination. To these critics my argument may seem to lack an appreciation of the more subtle and impersonal means by which power is exercised. I wholeheartedly agree that power acts through social structures in diffuse and complex ways that lie outside the bounds of rational agency, yet I insist that whites have made choices that have ensured their privileged standing throughout American history and that these choices were crucial in shaping American democracy. White workers had a voice in the Democratic Party, the unions, and the local political machines, and all too often they opted for whiteness rather than class solidarity. Dixiecrats continually obstructed any legislation that whiffed of racial equality. White bosses deliberately established two-tiered wage systems. White parents consistently opposed efforts to desegregate their children's schools. White liberals constantly castigated Black civil rights leaders for "moving too fast." I do not intend for my argument to be too voluntaristic, but white citizenship must be posed as a choice (even if it is not just a choice) in order to suggest political alternatives. Historically white citizens have made the wrong choice about their democratic alternatives, but the beautiful thing about the ability to make a decision is that one can always change one's mind.

CHAPTER 1

A Political Theory of Race

Two truisms dominate contemporary discussions about race in the United States. The first is that the nation has gone "beyond Black and white." While it was never strictly biracial, increased immigration and rising intermarriage rates have made the country definitively multiracial. The second is that race is "socially constructed." It is not a product of physiological characteristics, genetics, ancestry, or behavior, but of social relations and historical contexts that reflect existing distributions of power. The latter truism is embraced more by the academy than the general population, but its effects are spreading beyond the university, such as in the Office of Management and Budget's decision to allow Americans to check off more than one race in the 2000 Census. This suggests that today's academic trend could become tomorrow's common sense. It is rarely noticed, however, that the truisms of multiracialism and social construction exist in tension with each other. The latter insists that race is not about biology or ancestry, while the former implicitly assumes it is. For example, in a widely cited book, journalist Dale Maharidge argues that whites will be a minority in the United States by 2050 because of sweeping demographic changes fueled by immigration.[1] His argument assumes that geographic origins (North America, Latin America, Europe, Africa, and Asia) are the basis of race: the immigration of peoples from different continents will reduce people of European descent to a plurality, rendering a multiracial nation. Yet this scenario presumes that race is determined by ascribed characteristics rather than social relations.

There is no necessary tension between social construction and multiracialism, of course. It is quite possible to say, for example, that Asian Americans constitute a race because they have forged a collective identity in response to discriminatory treatment based on a perceived common ancestry. But this is not the argument made by most commentators today, who instead suppose that the United States is multiracial due to demographics rather than power.

The tension between multiracialism and social construction contributes to a lack of analytical rigor in studying race. In particular, race is frequently conflated with ethnicity, culture, and class. This leads to numerous problems: Does discrimination against poor immigrant workers rest on class or race or both? How do we distinguish them? Is there a bond between, say, Cuban Americans in Miami, fifth-generation Hispanics in New Mexico, Chicanos in Los Angeles, and Mexican immigrants working in Iowa, and if so, is it a racial, ethnic, or cultural bond? Fifty years from now, will lumping Japanese, Korean, Pakistani, and Chinese ethnics into an "Asian" race seem as ridiculous as early-twentieth-century talk of "Nordic," "Mediterranean," and "Alpine" white races does to us now? What distinguishes race from ethnic groups? The only apparent distinction between the Census Bureau's definition of race (which includes "racial and national-origin groups" that "are socio-political constructs and should not be interpreted as being scientific or anthropological in nature") and Hispanic ethnicity (which derives from a person's "heritage, nationality group, lineage, or country of birth") is the specific country to which a person traces her lineage. According to the census, an immigrant from Mexico is ethnically Hispanic but could be of any race, while an immigrant from Ghana is racially Black and ethnically "Not Hispanic."[2] These confusing and inconsistent criteria reflect the tension between the two truisms of American race.

The purpose of this chapter is to use the work of W. E. B. Du Bois to go beyond these truisms to construct a political theory of race. In his mature works of the 1930s and 1940s in particular, Du Bois acutely examines the relationship between democratic politics and the racial order, showing how race is intimately connected to majority rule, individual rights, and conceptions of equality, liberty, and citizenship. This connection is forged by a peculiar collusion between the capitalist class and one section of the working class. These erstwhile enemies are bound together through explicit and implicit agreements, which pay "public and psychological wages" for the workers. In exchange, these workers ensure the stability and order required for the steady accumulation of capital, largely through the terrorization and subordination of the rest of the working class. In Du Bois's language, members of said alliance form the "white world," while everyone else is relegated to the black or "dark world." This *cross-class alliance* produces racial hierarchy within a democratic political order. For Du Bois, race is not biology or geography so much as it is the existence of two worlds cut by the color line. Emphasizing this aspect of his work invites a reinterpretation of his famous concept of "double consciousness," which I argue represents not only a special anxiety of the Black psyche (am I Black or am I American?) but also a form of racial alienation produced by the conflict between the two worlds.

What Race Is Not

The term "race" is used to describe so much in terms of biology, behavior, culture, and social structure that it often seems useless in its ubiquity. Explaining what race is *not* before delving into a political definition of race reduces the confusion surrounding these multiple and conflicting usages. It also reveals how most usages tend to depoliticize our understanding of race.

Race Is Not Biology

From genetics to evolutionary biology to physical anthropology, scientists are in essential agreement that there is no such thing as biological race.[3] Distinguishing humans into coherent, mutually exclusive biological "races" is a taxonomic enterprise that is dependent upon inherently subjective cultural and political criteria. Thus, "the classification into races," geneticist Luigi Luca Cavalli-Sforza asserts, "has proved to be a futile exercise for reasons that were already clear to Darwin."[4]

This conclusion is embraced by most scholars in the social sciences and humanities, who now emphasize the socially constructed nature of race. Nevertheless, the implications of this revelation are often not fully appreciated. Tzvetan Todorov's *On Human Diversity*, for example, describes racism as an ideology that does not reflect scientific reality. However, he still defines races as "human groupings whose physical differences are apparent to the naked eye."[5] While physical differences may serve as a kind of badge that identifies one's membership in a particular race (though not always, as in the case of Jews in Nazi Europe or Catholics in Northern Ireland), in themselves they do not form races. In fact, the attempt to define races according to physical features can lead to confusion rather than clarity. In colonial Mexico, for example, attempts to distinguish races according to skin tone, facial features, hair color and texture, and eye color led Spaniards to identify over twelve races—in addition to white and Black. Such a classification system was too complex to enable a rigid color line like in the American South.[6] The creation of racial hierarchies, in other words, requires a willful ignorance of physical differences as much as it does an acknowledgment of them. Todorov's definition does not define race biologically, but it still treats it prepolitically. That is, it still assumes that races are identities that mark people *before* they enter the public sphere rather than something constructed in the public realm itself.

Race Is Not a Neutral Category

A corollary of the argument that race reflects physical differences is the belief that race is an objective, politically neutral part of a person's identity, while racial prejudice is a negative attitude toward a race based on an unfavorable comparison with one's own race.[7] This conception tends to define racial discrimination as a product of deliberate intentions and actions. As a result, it cannot explain the mountain of statistics that continue to document the mundane but systematic ways in which racial inequality persists, with or without the help of malicious-minded individuals. Further, it implies that racial discrimination, while deeply troubling, largely exists at the margins of society, perpetrated by the ignorant behavior of "extremists," such as the Ku Klux Klan, Nazi skinheads, and even the Nation of Islam, who cling to leftovers of past hatreds. The schizophrenic conclusion is that racism is widespread yet perpetuated by an ignorant few. This usage depoliticizes race by drawing attention to prejudicial intentions and away from the processes of racial formation, which divide humans into discrete groups of hierarchically ordered races according to a sense of "group position" or an orientation one has about how relations between groups "ought to be."[8] An adequate theory of race must account for the persistence of racial hierarchy independent of prejudice and in a world in which open racists are few.

Race Is Not Ethnicity

The ethnicity paradigm, once the most common way in which race was understood in the social sciences, still holds considerable influence today. This paradigm, which posits that race is one determinant (along with culture and ancestry) of a group's ethnic makeup, is based on the European immigrant experience in North America. Its principal question is whether assimilation or cultural pluralism is the best way to accommodate the mingling of various ethnicities in the United States. (Today this debate takes the form of color blindness versus multiculturalism, which I address in chapter 4.) This quandary, however, fails to recognize that the processes of racial formation are different from the processes of ethnic assimilation. An example of the confusion that results from conflating them is Jeff Spinner's *The Boundaries of Citizenship*. Liberal citizenship, Spinner argues, works to break down racial, ethnic, and national boundaries. This is good in that it overcomes differences, discourages discrimination, and encourages inclusion, but bad in that it can, in time, eradicate a group's culture through total assimilation. Despite taking care to distinguish between race and ethnicity in the beginning of the book, however, Spinner's argument is wholly dependent on the ethnicity paradigm. As he acknowledges in a footnote:

"My arguments . . . about different cultural practices in the liberal state will often apply to both Blacks and ethnics. When I discuss the cultural practices of ethnics, I mean members of racial and ethnic groups with practices that differ from those of mainstream culture."[9] Liberal citizenship may break down ethnic differences but it does not necessarily undermine racial distinctions. Indeed, as I argue in the next chapter, ethnic assimilation and democratic citizenship were possible in the United States *because of* racial stratification. Conflating race and ethnicity obscures the deep connection between citizenship and race.

Race Is Not Just Identity

As Cheryl Harris argues, race possesses a "dual and contradictory character" as both an identity and a marker of privilege or subordination.[10] This dual character, unfortunately, is not always acknowledged when race is defined as identity. For example, the change in the 2000 Census allowing persons to check one or more boxes regarding their racial status is unquestionably a victory for those who feel their racial identity is not adequately represented by the four racial groups and two ethnic categories of the previous census.[11] Yet this new classification system does little to illuminate race as a system of power. If anything, it encourages a politics reminiscent of interest group pluralism, in which racial identity becomes simply one "interest" among others competing for influence in a politically neutral marketplace of ideas and policies. The problem with limiting our understanding of race to personal identity is not that it leads to a politics of resentment, victimization, or balkanization, as many critics of identity politics argue, but that it leads to very little politics at all.[12]

Race Is Not a Universal Phenomenon

We have not always had race. The ancient world, for example, had no conception of it. Ancient Greeks divided humanity into the civilized and the barbarian, but this distinction turned on whether a people had established a polis and were appropriately "political," not on the putatively innate characteristics of barbarian or citizen. Similarly, faith and heresy cleaved medieval Europe, but the split was determined by whether or not a person worshipped the appropriate faith. The dark heathen barbarian for whom no amount of civilization could save was not born until the Enlightenment.[13]

Further, racial orders have varied significantly within modernity. Race in the United States differs from race in Europe because the origins of each system are different, as are the uses toward which race is put. This is true even though both systems are based on white dominance and Black subordination. The European concept of race grew out of colonialism. As Hannah Arendt notes, European racism has served as a bridge connecting nationalism and imperialism, two ideologies that are otherwise internally contradictory. By justifying imperial expansion throughout the globe, it calms the grumbling of the domestic poor with spoils won through imperialist enterprises and assurances of racial superiority over the colonized.[14] Race in the United States, however, is rooted in the institution of chattel slavery. As a result, except for the partial exception of the reservation system for Native Americans, American race has distinguished between equals and unequals *within* the polity rather than between nation and colony.

The way in which slavery was enforced is also a crucial factor distinguishing systems of race. In the United States, as I will show in chapter 2, slavery was enforced primarily by working-class members of the dominant race. In Latin America and the Caribbean, on the other hand, slavery was enforced by a third social category between Black and white, the "mulatto."[15] The modicum of power, influence, and social mobility enjoyed by mulattoes (almost all of whom would have been defined as Black in the United States) led them to generally distance themselves from slaves. This is in marked contrast to free African Americans, whose subordinate social status despite their legal liberty generally led them to identify with the slaves. This tripartite color scheme also allows for a degree of social mobility among people of color. With enough money and education in slave Cuba, for example, "The mulatto, even if *obscuro*, or very dark, would be ranked in the white category, and the corresponding Negro would be classified as mulatto, for in Cuba as in the rest of Latin America, 'money whitened.'"[16] As a result, the racial system of Latin America and the Caribbean has tended to reflect class divisions as much as physical features or ancestry. The dominant race is white and the most degraded race is Black, but who belongs to which group is determined by money, education, and appearance, not color caste.

Racial orders vary according to material conditions. For this reason, no universal definition of race is possible. The tendency to treat race or racial discrimination as a universal phenomenon is understandable given the nearly universal presence of prejudice and given that the European, Latin American, and North American racial systems all place white over Black. Yet beyond these generalities, the differences among racial orders are crucial. Ignoring them dehistoricizes race, placing it beyond the political realm rather than within it.

Race Is Not a Fiction

One reaction to the realization that race has no biological basis is to proclaim that we should all give up this harmful superstition immediately. The American Anthropological Association, for example, declared in 1997 that the government should eliminate the term "race," replace it with "ethnicity," and let people define their own ethnicity.[17] The problem, of course, is that eliminating the term is hardly the same as eliminating the power relations that underlie it. A Marxist variant of this approach is to define race as superstructural. In two important articles, the historian Barbara Fields argues that race is an ideology, rooted in colonial America, that reconciled the belief in inalienable human liberty with the practice of chattel slavery, enabling slavery as a mode of production to prosper.[18] Slavery, as a mode of production, is objective, but race, as an ideology, is not. "[C]lass is a concept that we can locate both at the level of objective reality and at the level of social appearances. Race is a concept that we can locate at the level of appearances only."[19] Fields's basic insight—that a political theory of race must reveal the relation between it and class structures—is important. However, her analytical distinction between the "level of appearances" and "objective reality" is neither adequate to understand race nor demanded by a materialist approach. Race is more than an apparition summoned by elites to per-petuate their rule and channeled through the false consciousness of the working class. It is built from real institutions and patterns of social life. It is biological fiction but social fact. Race may lack the concreteness of a class-in-itself, but it is as real as a class-for-itself, for it creates cohesive, conscious, and organized groups of persons who share common interests and a vision of the good life.

To summarize: race is a product of modernity. It is a constructed but socially significant category, distinct from ethnicity, whose meaning and function vary across time and nation. The American racial system is distinguished from other racial systems through its basis in slavery and the means by which it was enforced, which tended to produce a bipolar racial order. But how are the two categories of this bipolarity defined? Most scholars have tried to answer this question by seeking to define "Black." According to F. James Davis, there have been two main criteria for defining Blackness. The "rule of recognition" presumes that anyone with any visible physical features considered African is Black, while the "one-drop rule" states that any person with any known trace of African ancestry—even if it is only "one drop" of blood—is Black.[20] These rules are inadequate because neither explains the power relations involved in racial classification. The rule of recognition at best provides a rough-and-ready way to racially identify people on the streets—the police officer stopping a suspect, the teacher meeting new students, the hip-hop artist sizing up an audience. The one-drop rule seems increasingly absurd and is now unconstitutional. By appealing to physical appearance, ancestry, and geography, both rules obscure rather than reveal the political ramifications of racial classification.

The Cross-Class Alliance

The definitions of race as biological essence, ethnicity, or identity described above assume that race exists prior to the political realm. But race is not static, universal, or derivative of some other more fundamental category. It is dynamic, historical, and relatively autonomous from other social structures. It is a form of power that shapes the public sphere and is in turn shaped by it. It is therefore necessary to set these pre-political notions of race aside and look at how race is reproduced within the political realm. It is especially useful to examine episodes in history in which the racial order is destabilized, for such disruptions heighten contradictions and clarify social relations, illuminating the operation of power. These "moments of madness" can also provide glimpses of new democratic possibilities.[21]

Reconstruction was one such moment in American history, and its master theorist is Du Bois. In a highly original argument, Du Bois posits in his magnificent *Black Reconstruction* that Reconstruction was done and undone by class conflict and class alliances. After the war Northern industrialists, represented by the Republican Party, sought to integrate the largely agricultural Southern economy into the growing industrial economy of the North. But Southern reactionaries, organized in the Democratic Party, were determined to resist the pull toward wage labor and industrialism. Southern states doggedly refused to enfranchise the ex-slaves, enacted Black Codes, carried out white terror, enforced coercive labor contracts, and otherwise made it clear that Southern elites intended to preserve slave labor in all but name. Further, the defeated South still threatened the Republicans' control of the federal government. The full ex-slave population rather than three-fifths would now count in census totals, increasing the South's representation in Congress even as the freedmen remained disenfranchised—and therefore unable to vote for the party of Lincoln. With a wave of ex-Confederates elected into Congress immediately after the war, it seemed possible that a solid Democratic South, armed with greater representation and united with Northern Democrats, could force the Republicans out of power and overturn economic policies, such as tariffs and trade protection, that favored industry over agriculture. Ironically, the South seemed poised to win politically even in the wake of military defeat.

To prevent this, Northern capitalists sought an unlikely partnership with the ex-slaves. By enfranchising the freedmen, the Republicans could gain a foothold in the South and continue to control the national government. The result was Radical Reconstruction: the dramatic, rapid, and unprecedented transformation of the mass of slaves into free human beings, Americans, voters—citizens. Universal male suffrage, Du Bois writes, was a "desperate venture" forced on Northern elites because Southern reactionaries "had refused to grant complete physical freedom to black workers; it refused them education and access to the land and insisted on dominant political power based on the number of these same serfs. Under these circumstances the experiment had to be made. For to surrender now was to have sacrificed blood and billions of dollars in vain."[22]

Du Bois interprets these events through a materialist lens. Despite its bonded labor and the aristocratic pretensions of the planters, he considers slavery part of the American capitalist system because the essential function of the antebellum Southern economy was accumulation. (It was Southern cotton, after all, that fed England's hungry factories and made the industrial revolution possible.) Like other bourgeois societies, then, the South consisted of capitalists (the masters) and workers (the slaves).[23] In fact, Du Bois maintains, slaves were the epitome of the proletariat, the "ultimate exploited." They performed the most difficult and menial forms of labor, they had no way to escape their class position, and they had no one beneath them to lord over. Slaves were the embodiment of Marx's universal class.[24] The significance of Reconstruction is that for a brief moment, an "eternal second," the interests of capitalists and proletarians converged. Northern capitalists' intention was to hold power through the Republican Party. But the unintended consequences of their association with Southern labor, Du Bois argues, were nothing short of revolutionary. Immediately the Republican Party became a proletarian party in the South. The Republican government enfranchised millions of Black and white workers, defended their civil rights, encouraged the freedmen to accumulate savings through the Freedman's Bank, drafted and enforced fair labor contracts through the Freedman's Bureau, and educated a largely illiterate people. Most significantly, it put the working class in power. In the South Carolina constitutional convention of 1868, for example, Du Bois estimates that over sixty percent of the delegates were Black. Three-quarters of these were former slaves, meaning nearly half the convention were freedmen, many of whom were illiterate.[25] Was there ever, Du Bois asks, a more proletarian government?

> Thus by singular coincidence and for a moment, for the few years of an eternal second in a cycle of a thousand years, the orbits of two widely and utterly dissimilar economic systems coincided and the result was a revolution so vast and portentous that few minds ever fully conceived it; for the systems were these: first, that of a democracy which should by universal suffrage establish a dictatorship of the proletariat ending in industrial democracy; and the other, a system by which a little knot of masterful men would so organize capitalism as to bring under their control the natural resources, wealth, and industry of a vast and rich country and through that, of the world. For a second, for a pulse of time, these orbits crossed and coincided, but their central suns were a thousand light-years apart, even though the blind and ignorant fury of the South and the complacent Philistinism of the North saw them as one.[26]

But the moment would soon pass. Eventually, Du Bois notes, Northern capital would recognize the contradictions inherent in the coalition and seek a rapprochement with Southern elites, who themselves would come to accept that the nation's economy was to be defined by industry and wage labor. This is indeed what took place after the presidential election of 1876, in which the Democrats conceded victory to Republican candidate Rutherford Hayes, even though he lost the popular vote, in exchange for the Republicans' agreement to remove the Union troops from the South. This they did, effectively ending Reconstruction. This did not, however, imply an inevitable backslide into segregation, disfranchisement, lynching, and capitalist dominance. Labor's power was formidable and the Black working class could have emerged from Reconstruction victorious had its obvious ally, the white worker, come to its side. Taken for granted by both sides during the war, the white working class was the swing constituency of Reconstruction, Du Bois maintains. If the white proletariat would join the Black proletariat and defend the gains of Reconstruction, the power of this united class would be unstoppable and "we should be living today in a different world."[27] Yet this did not happen. Black workers were refused entrance in the House of Labor. Blocking them were not the capitalists but their fellow laborers, the white working class. Instead of siding with its fellow workers against a common exploiter, white labor chose to curse, condemn, exclude, and mob Black workers. Their choice doomed Reconstruction and working-class struggles for years to come. "When white laborers were convinced that the degradation of Negro labor was more fundamental than the uplift of white labor, the end was in sight."[28]

The key to explaining why white workers sided with the elites on the basis of racial interests rather than with Black workers on the basis of class interests, Du Bois suggests, lies not so much in the particular events of Reconstruction but in a set of privileges white workers had enjoyed even before the Civil War. Du Bois argues that white workers actively oppressed their fellow workers in exchange for the "wages of whiteness."

> It must be remembered that the white group of laborers, while they received a low wage, were compensated in part by a sort of public and psychological wage. They were given public deference and titles of courtesy because they were white. They were admitted freely with all classes of white people to public functions, public parks, and the best schools. The police were drawn from their ranks, and the courts, dependent upon their votes, treated them with such leniency as to encourage lawlessness. Their vote selected public officials, and while this had small effect upon the economic situation, it had great effect upon their personal treatment and the deference shown them.[29]

The wages of whiteness literally pay off in terms of higher wages, two-tiered wage scales, exclusive access to certain jobs, and informal unemployment insurance (first hired, last fired). They also ensure access to land, capital, and markets to those who can afford them, giving white workers-cum-entrepreneurs the chance to become capitalists. But they also grant whites an elevated social status, which in many ways is as significant as the tangible benefits. The public and psychological wages of whiteness grant the white worker the same political rights and privileges accorded elites: legal equality with all other whites, the right to elect leaders, join political parties, assemble and speak freely, bear arms. They provide the white citizen with an air of both equality and superiority: equal to all white people—even the rich—yet superior to all Black people—even the rich. The wages of whiteness ensure that no matter how poor, mean, or low a white citizen may be and in spite of gender or other social identities, he or she still has, in many ways, a social status higher than the most intelligent, well-off Black person. "The most educated and deserving black man," Du Bois solemnly notes, "was compelled in many public places to occupy a place beneath the lowest and least deserving of the whites."[30] The flip side of white wages was Black subordination. The Black man "was subject to public insult; was afraid of mobs; was liable to the jibes of children and the unreasoning fears of white women; and was compelled almost continuously to submit to various badges of inferiority."[31] Black women additionally faced the threat of sexual assault without any expectation of legal or social protection. The wages of whiteness drove a wedge between Black and white workers such that, although they shared a language, dialect, religion, music, food, and (often enough) condition of squalor, they seemed to have almost nothing in common.

Du Bois insists that the white workers' actions cannot be explained away as false consciousness. Devious capitalists plot to divide and conquer the working class by fomenting racial divisions. Some white workers may be irrationally prejudiced against African Americans. Nevertheless, "The bulk of American white labor is neither ignorant nor fanatical. It knows exactly what it is doing and it means to do it. [White labor leaders] have no excuse of illiteracy or religion to veil their deliberate intention to keep Negroes and Mexicans and other elements of common labor, in a lower proletariat as subservient to their interests as theirs are to the interests of capital."[32] White workers, Du Bois emphasizes, repress the Black community because they see it in their (short-term) interests to do so. The tragedy is that in exchange for such wages poor whites maintain a system that exploits them, too. For even as these wages specifically benefited white workers, Du Bois maintains, they were absolutely necessary for the continued power of the capitalist class. In all class systems, laborers must be disciplined if they are to work efficiently.[33] American slavery was no different in this respect. What was unique about the policing of enslaved Southern workers and later free Black workers was that it was done not by a middle group standing between worker and owner (such as a managerial class or a mulatto race/class) but by fellow workers. In this peculiar system of discipline, there were more police than the policed because the entire white population of the "solid South" was conscripted into the struggle to secure the political obedience and economic productivity of the Black worker.[34] But since planters made up only a small percentage of the whites, workers effectively policed workers. Northern white labor also policed the slaves by enforcing the fugitive slave law, sharing the same political party with Southern elites, acquiescing to Southern dominance of the national government, and degrading free Black Northerners. Slavery and later Jim Crow segregation, Du Bois concludes, "was held stable and intact by the poor white."[35] In this way a unique system of "docility-utility" was achieved that maximized the political obedience and economic usefulness of all workers.

This system is reproduced by more than conscious intent and tacit consent. In a sense, race functions like a discipline. Disciplines, Michel Foucault argues, are "techniques for assuring the ordering of human multiplicities." They are specific institutions like armies, workshops, hospitals, and prisons, but they are also "general formulas of domination" in the modern era.[36] This domination is productive as much as it is repressive. That is, disciplines produce subjects who are economically useful and politically docile through norms, techniques, routines, and other rote means of minutely organizing time and space. The wages of whiteness serve precisely this function of organizing, directing, shaping, producing, and repressing individuals in order to create relations of docility-utility.[37] More than a means of dividing and conquering the working class, white privilege is a central form of power in the accumulation of humans that, Foucault notes, always accompanies the accumulation of capital.

Black Reconstruction is one of the most powerful indictments of the promise and failure of Reconstruction. It is also a stinging critique of the American labor movement. But the book's argument goes beyond the events of Reconstruction to provide the basis for a political theory of race. Du Bois shows that racial oppression is a form of social control that perpetuates class relations. The white working class serves as a buffer control stratum between capitalists and the rest of the working class, facilitating social stability by holding down Black workers.[38] But Du Bois shows that race does more than exclude, divide, degrade, and repress. It is also a productive form of power that accumulates humans into particular groups in order to produce relations of docility-utility. It does this through a peculiar arrangement of class relations, which are secured through various privileges granted to members of the dominant race. This *cross-class alliance* between the capitalist class and a section of the working class is the genesis of the American racial order.[39] Members of the alliance are defined as "white" while those excluded from it are relegated to a "not-white" status. Historically, the cross-class alliance has ensured the social stability of American democracy by reconciling political equality with economic exploitation through a system of racial privilege and subordination that deflects attention from class, gender, and other grievances. Whiteness is a privileged position of standing in a democratic society. "The white race," write Noel Ignatiev and John Garvey, "consists of those who partake of the privileges of the white skin in this society. Its most wretched members share, in certain respects, a status higher than that of the most exalted persons excluded from it, in return for which they give their support to the system that degrades them."[40]

The cross-class alliance is the class foundation of the white democracy. Through it, white identity functions something like an exclusive club, in which eligibility requirements are set by the present membership. As Andrew Hacker proposes, rather than asking "Who is Black?" or even "Who is white?" "It might be more appropriate to ask, 'Who *may* be considered white?' since this suggests that something akin to permission is needed."[41] Immigrants from Europe in the nineteenth century, for example, were not automatically admitted into the white race; they had to prove their worthiness—largely by setting themselves apart from African Americans.[42] Physical appearance and ancestry do not define whiteness but are at best badges or markers of membership, a "skin-uniform," as Lerone Bennett puts it.[43] White identity is determined by those who are already part of the white club. To adapt a line from Alain Locke, a white person is a person called white by other whites. The antithesis of "white" is "not-white," a category of subordination that has been occupied by various peoples and social identities throughout American history. Historically, African Americans have been the paradigm of not-whiteness but American Indians, Chinese immigrants, and Mexican workers, among others, have all fallen into "not-white" status at various points in American history.[44]

The cross-class alliance does not make all whites members of one class and all not-whites members of another. Race is not "really" class with a tint of color. The origins of white domination lie in a cross-class *alliance*, not class itself. Class divisions continue to exist in both categories, but "Color overshadows and weakens class and class consciousness."[45] Class consciousness is blunted within the dominant race because social prestige and civil and political rights are granted to all members regardless of wealth, giving poor whites the right to identify with the upper class. It is minimized within the not-white group because the racial structure refuses to recognize social distinctions among not-whites, pressing all members into a single degraded status. As a consequence, the advancement of even the most educated and prosperous members of the group depends on the advancement of all members.

Written and published at the height of the Depression, Du Bois's *Black Reconstruction* was written in part to challenge the racism of the dominant historiography on Reconstruction at the time.[46] But it was also written as the scholastic accompaniment to Du Bois's political break with racial liberalism (he quit the NAACP in 1934) and to distinguish his recent embrace of Marxism from Communist Party orthodoxy. Drafted during Du Bois's bitter rift with the CPUSA over its handling of the Scottsboro Boys case, the analysis of the white working class was intended by Du Bois to criticize the present as well as the past.[47] Elaborating on his long-standing critique of anti-Black attitudes among white labor and of the CPUSA's shortsighted analysis of the "Negro Problem," *Black Reconstruction* and contemporaneously written articles such as "The Negro and Communism" (1931), "Marxism and the Negro Problem" (1933), and "The Negro and Social Reconstruction" (1936) provided an alternative explanation for the Depression and segregation, as well as the failures of traditional liberal and Marxist solutions to them. The strategies of the NAACP and the Communist Party are bound to crash against the rocks of white working-class chauvinism, Du Bois warns, yet neither group understands this. Du Bois meant for *Black Reconstruction* to provide historiographic justification for his third path between liberal integration and color-blind communism: the voluntary "self-segregation" of Black communities into consumer cooperatives and other Black-controlled institutions until the white working class recognizes its historic role in the struggle for socialism and unites with the Black proletariat to achieve it. By building a self-sufficient "Negro nation within a nation," Black people can wait out white chauvinism and prove to white labor "that it is a disastrous error to leave [African Americans] out of the foundation of the new industrial State."[48]

Thus, Du Bois saw Reconstruction and its aftermath as a paradigm for the modern history of race in the United States.[49] The main argument of *Black Reconstruction* concludes with Du Bois writing:

> [T]he chief and only obstacle to the coming of that kingdom of economic equality which is the only logical end of work is the determination of the white world to keep the black world poor and themselves rich. A clear vision of a world without inordinate individual wealth, of capital without profit and of income based on work alone, is the path out, not only for America but for all men. Across this path stands the South with flaming sword.[50]

As the South goes, so goes the nation. Du Bois clearly intended his analysis of the cross-class alliance and the wages of whiteness to be generalized beyond Reconstruction. His critique of the white world, its wages, and the alliance culminate his lifelong critique of racial discrimination begun with "The Conservation of Races" in 1897 and most famously addressed in the 1903 *Souls of Black Folk*.

Double Consciousness and the Two Worlds

Unfortunately, Du Bois is rarely given credit for his groundbreaking work toward a political theory of race. This is no doubt partly due to the nature of scholarship on Du Bois, which tends toward intellectual biography or close textual interpretation rather than normative theorizing, and partly due to normative political theory itself, which almost completely ignores Du Bois and is only just beginning to investigate race.[51] Another reason, however, lies in the way in which Du Bois has been interpreted, particularly his famous conception of double consciousness. In his most acclaimed work, *The Souls of Black Folk*, Du Bois argues that double consciousness is the paradoxical sensation that results from being Black and American in a society that makes these identities contradictory rather than complementary. African Americans desire the freedom, equality, and opportunity American society promises, yet these gifts of citizenship are denied them simply because they are Black. Du Bois summarizes this antinomy in a justly famous quote:

> After the Egyptian and Indian, the Greek and Roman, the Teuton and Mongolian, the Negro is a sort of seventh son, born with a veil, and gifted with second-sight in this American world,—a world which yields him no true self-consciousness, but only lets him see himself through the revelation of the other world. It is a peculiar sensation, this double-consciousness, this sense of always looking at one's self through the eyes of others, of measuring one's soul by the tape of a world that looks on in amused contempt and pity. One ever feels his twoness,—an American, a Negro; two souls, two thoughts, two unreconciled strivings; two warring ideals in one dark body, whose dogged strength alone keeps it from being torn asunder.[52]

The history of Black people in America, Du Bois maintains, is this contradictory experience of being both Black and American and striving "to merge [one's] double self into a better and truer self."[53]

Numerous scholars have embraced double consciousness as the defining experience of Black life in the United States, but Adolph Reed counters that double consciousness is actually an elitist sensation that hardly expresses the consciousness of all Black folk. At the time of *Souls*'s publication, the term was commonly used by Victorian middle-class intellectuals (Black and white) to describe their particular feelings of angst amid a rapidly changing society. Double consciousness, he contends, has little to do with a universal Black experience and more to do with the specific psychic drama of the Black middle class during Jim Crow, a class that considered itself superior to the working class but was prevented by segregation from separating from it. Furthermore, Reed argues, double consciousness was actually never very important to Du Bois's thought. Its significance has been inflated by certain prominent Black intellectuals who find in it an analysis of American social life that fits well with their genteel middle-class liberalism. The claim that double consciousness describes a universal Black condition enables a middle-class consciousness to stand in and speak for Black people as a whole. "Double consciousness," Reed insists, "is the neurasthenia of the black professional-managerial class at the end of the twentieth century."[54]

Reed's critique raises important questions about the class content of double consciousness and its use by later scholars. Nevertheless, it cannot be considered the last word on the matter, for the "twoness" of double consciousness describes more than a psychic rending of the Black soul.[55] It also represents a form of alienation that results from the partitioning of the nation into two "worlds" of race. This is clear from Du Bois's concept of the veil. In *Souls* Du Bois writes of a great veil that hangs down in the midst of the United States. He became conscious of the presence of the veil, a metaphor for segregation, in childhood. After a racial slight at school one day, "it dawned upon me with a certain suddenness that I was different from the others; or like, mayhap, in heart and life and longing, but shut out from their world by a vast veil."[56] The veil is a strange divider. It separates but not like a wall. It is neither opaque nor translucent—one can see through it, albeit obscurely. Nor is it like an ocean dividing the continents, for what happens on one side of the veil inevitably passes through and affects the other. It is a wispy, almost immaterial barrier, yet it divides the nation with the presence of a mountain range. "Surely [the veil] is a thought-thing, tenuous, intangible," he writes in another work. "Yet just as surely is it true and terrible and not in our little day may you and I lift it."[57] He notes in *Souls* that a visitor to the South, where the veil is most explicit, at first might not recognize the "sombre veil of color" that divides the land, for it is rarely discussed. Yet slowly the visitor is awakened to the veil's existence and influence until he "realizes at last that silently, resistlessly, the world about flows by him in two great streams: they ripple on in the same sunshine, they approach and mingle their waters in seeming carelessness,—then they divide and flow wide apart."[58] The veil, in sum, represents the color line that Du Bois so accurately predicted as the problem of the twentieth century.

The veil hangs between two "worlds." These worlds are not Black and American, as is sometimes assumed.[59] As Du Bois explains in *Dusk of Dawn*, humans live in three environments or worlds: (1) the physical environment, (2) the social environment of one's group, and (3) the socio-physical environment of other groups. In the United States these translate into American, Black (or dark), and white worlds.[60] The veil cuts between the Black and white worlds, both of which together form the American world.[61] Double consciousness describes two related but distinct conflicts among these worlds. It refers to the conflict between the Black and American worlds experienced by African Americans—am I Black or am I American?—from which most analyses of double consciousness emerge. But it also refers to the conflict between the dark and white worlds.

> Much as I knew of this class structure of the world, I should never have realized it vividly and fully if I had not been born into its modern counterpart, racial segregation; first into a world composed of people with

colored skins who remembered slavery and endured discrimination; and who had to a degree their own habits, customs, and ideals; but in addition to this I lived in an environment which I came to call the white world. I was not an American; I was not a man; I was by long education and continual compulsion and daily reminder, a colored man in a white world; and that white world often existed primarily, so far as I was concerned, to see with sleepless vigilance that I was kept within bounds.[62]

For Du Bois, racial oppression is a political problem of dark and white worlds arrayed against each other, with the white world determined to subordinate the dark one in order to ensure its control of the larger shared environment.

The white world is less a physical presence than a set of ideas and activities. "In all things in general," Du Bois writes in *Dusk of Dawn*, "white people were just the same as I." He acknowledges some differences in skin color, but they are "vastly overemphasized and intrinsically trivial." And yet, he continues, "This fact of racial distinction based on color was the greatest thing in my life and absolutely determined it, because this surrounding group [American whites], in alliance and agreement with the white European world, was settled and determined upon the fact that I was and must be a thing apart."[63] That "thing apart" is plainly defined for Du Bois. A Black person, he declares, "is a person who must ride 'Jim Crow' in Georgia."[64] Accordingly, one's race is determined by one's status, not the other way around. The cause is the consequence. You are not Jim Crowed because you are Black; you are Black because you are Jim Crowed. (Or as Richard Wright puts it, "Negroes are Negroes because they are treated as Negroes.")[65] If a Black person is one who must ride Jim Crow, the corollary is that a white person is one who need not: It is not that enjoy privilege because you are white; you are white because you enjoy privilege. Du Bois's definition of Black is an implicit critique of not only racial discrimination but race itself. Jim Crow does not just oppress Black people. It creates the dark world, and the white world as well.[66] Races are political categories. They are produced by power; they do not exist prior to it.

Double consciousness, then, represents in part the estrangement the Black world experiences as a result of being cast on the oppressed side of the veil. As Thomas Holt argues, Du Bois considers Black folk as "not so much aliens as alienated."[67] Double consciousness expresses the alienation of a person from any standing in the community and her consequent subjection to that community. Denied all claims to membership in a polity, the dark world is "institutionally marginalized" by the dominant white world. To borrow another phrase from Orlando Patterson, the dark world is "socially dead."[68] This death is not final, however, for double consciousness is dialectical. It produces a "second sight" among African Americans that gives them an epistemic advantage in the struggle against the veil. The goal of this struggle is to merge the double self into a "better and truer self" that recognizes no contradiction between Black and American identities and no distinction between citizens and outcasts. In Hegelian-Marxian fashion, double consciousness implies a struggle between antagonists in which freedom requires the negation of the negation, or the destruction of the white world's power over the dark world.

Despite their disagreement over the significance of double consciousness, Reed and his interlocutors share a common—and limited— understanding of the concept. In so doing they have unnecessarily restricted its interpretation. When double consciousness is understood as a form of alienation produced by the struggle between white and dark worlds, Reed's criticism loses force. For instance, Du Bois acknowledges the middle-class nature of the "Am I Black or American?" side of double consciousness. In the chapter "Of the Coming of John" in *Souls*, Du Bois tells the story of John, a poor Black boy who went away to college. As a child John never felt split or "double," for all he knew was the Black world. He only began to feel a sense of double consciousness when he went away to school and learned something of the larger world—its culture, its luxuries, its freedoms. His education isolated him from his impoverished community, but at the same time the white world denied him the things his education had taught him to appreciate and expect as a person of letters. Only after John advanced in his education and social position did he find himself ostracized from the Black world yet thrown back into it. Ultimately, his sense of double consciousness and his "second sight" drives him to murder and suicide. A similar theme appears in *Dusk of Dawn*, where Du Bois, speaking of "the Negro's double environment," explains that middle-class African Americans feel they have more in common culturally and intellectually with the white world but the white world will not accept them, so they remain in a limbo between their Blackness and their aspirations to assimilate.[69] Their estrangement is the product of a system of racial subordination that refuses to recognize social distinctions among Black people despite the best efforts of the middle class to distinguish themselves by wealth, education, and/or upbringing.

Further, Reed is only partially correct that the concept of double consciousness disappears from Du Bois's works after *Souls*. It is true that he never again used the actual phrase, yet its spirit is woven into many of his later texts. In *Darkwater*, published seventeen years after *Souls*, Du Bois paraphrases his famous paragraph on double consciousness and its second sight: "I have been in the world, but not of it. I have seen the human drama from a veiled corner, where all the outer tragedy and comedy have reproduced themselves in microcosm within. From this inner torment of souls the human scene without has interpreted itself to me in unusual and even illuminating ways."[70] In *Dusk of Dawn*, published in 1940, he redescribes the two worlds, using an allegory in which Black people view the larger environment from a dark cave in the side of a mountain. The cave allegory is a pessimistic revisiting of the veil, which has solidified from a hazy curtain to a thick plate of soundproof glass. The white world peers through the glass in amused indifference or patronizing sympathy, while the Black world, once it realizes the invisible barrier that prevents the outside world from hearing its courteous pleas, abandons all decorum and twists in hysterical frustration and hatred toward the white world.[71] As an expression of the Victorian middle class's soullessness in the face of their prosperity, perhaps double consciousness did die with *Souls*. Reed may also be correct to state that it fails as an expression of the Black experience. Yet when understood in terms of the veil, the "double environment" it creates, and the aliena-tion it produces, it is clear that double consciousness never left Du Bois's thought.

Black and White and Bipolar

The theory of race I have derived from Du Bois is dualistic. It argues that there are two principal racial categories, white and not-white (or the white world and the dark world), both of which are filled by a dynamic and varying selection of ethnic and social groups throughout history. This Du Boisian theory of race as a dialectical conflict between two worlds that produce alienated subjects is a theoretical elaboration of a common theme that runs through African American thought from David Walker to Marcus Garvey to Malcolm X to James Baldwin to Toni Morrison. It is expressed in myth (Elijah Muhammad's tale of the evil scientist Yacub), in literature (Ralph Ellison's *Invisible Man*), and in political program (Black nationalism). Even the great assimiliationist Frederick Douglass adopted a conflict-driven model to explain his con-sciousness as a slave. Of his former master Douglass writes, "What he most dreaded, that I most desired. What he most loved, that I most hated. That which to him was a great evil, to be carefully shunned, was to me a great good, to be diligently sought."[72]

Dualisms are increasingly out of fashion in political theory. They are often regarded as simplistic and insufficient, especially by those who prefer models of difference, pluralism, and/or hybridity.[73] But there is nothing inherently vulgar about dualisms. In fact, theory cannot do without them. Whatever their limitations, dichotomies such as public/private, rich/poor, feminine/masculine, and radical/reformist make use-ful distinctions that pinpoint the locus of political tensions. In explaining how one category defines the other, dualisms emphasize social relations and the role of power and conflict in them. This emphasis is not always found in models of difference or pluralism, given their tendency toward tolerance of different positions. Rather than obliterating diversity, as often charged, historically sensitive bipolar frameworks synthesize it by providing an account of the relations of power that have come to produce differentiation.[74] The key, as Linda Nicholson points out, is to avoid ahistorical uses of dualisms, not dualisms per se.[75] Du Bois's "two worlds" framework remains useful because its two principal categories are not Black and white (which would indeed be insufficient) but the white world and the dark world, both of which may include other social-ethnic-geographic groups besides European and African Americans. As such, it goes "beyond Black and white" while still placing conflict, power, and alienation at the heart of the racial order.

The value of a white/not-white bipolar analysis is evident in that the operations of power it describes are at work even in those analyses that explicitly seek to go beyond racial dualism. One example is Neil Foley's excellent book *The White Scourge*, which describes how white workers in east Texas from the Civil War to World War II tried to force Mexican workers into a racially subordinate status. Mexicans resisted these efforts by fighting against racial discrimination but also by trying to prove themselves white, which they did largely by distinguishing themselves from African Americans. Mexican workers ultimately failed to become white, Foley argues, but they were never fully identified with Black Texans because of their success in distinguishing themselves from African Americans. As a result, Mexican workers fell in between Black and white, revealing the inadequacy of the bipolar model.

> Over time Mexicans came to locate themselves in the ethnoracial middle ground between Anglo Americans and African Americans, not white enough to claim equality with Anglos and yet, in many cases, white enough to escape the worst features of the Jim Crow South. Although Mexicans and Anglos lived in a segregated society that strongly discouraged social interaction, the line of separation was not as rigidly maintained between the two groups as it was between whites and blacks.[76]

Foley's powerful account of race and class in Texas cotton country, however, actually demonstrates the value of the bipolar model rather than its irrelevance. The problem faced by Mexicans in central Texas, as Foley recognizes, was not that they failed to fit into the white or Black worlds by virtue of their brown skin or Mexican heritage. The problem was that, given the bipolar nature of the racial order, they were forced to prove they deserved membership in the white world or face a subordinate status. Caught between the compactor walls of privilege and subordination, Mexican workers both resisted discrimination and tried to prove themselves white, the latter of which involved such sundry tactics as denying their African and indigenous roots and protesting their exclusion from lynch mobs.[77] The tragic predicament of these Mexican workers and their only partial success in resolving it confirm the power and presence of the bipolar model rather than refute it.

Similarly, Claire Jean Kim argues that Asian Americans today are both valorized as a model minority and ostracized from the body politic as inassimilable, thus placing them in a "triangulated" position in relation to African Americans and whites. Race is not a simple binary, Kim holds, but at minimum a triangular relationship of white superiors, Black inferiors, and Asian inassimilables. Kim's triangulation thesis is smart and original, yet as with Foley's work it reveals the underlying presence of a bipolar racial order and its attendant pressures rather than refuting it. On the West Coast in the nineteenth and early twentieth centuries, Chinese, Japanese, and Korean immigrants were clearly racially subordinated as not-white.[78] But when, as Kim reports, Chinese Americans in the Mississippi Delta under Jim Crow did everything within their power to distinguish themselves from African Americans, including giving their children "white names" and joining white churches "in a deliberate bid to become white," this suggests that the Mississippi Chinese attempted to become American citizens by pursuing the classic immigrant route of assimilating by whitening. As Kim herself writes, "If the Black struggle for advancement has historically rested upon appeals to racial equality, the Asian American struggle has at times rested upon appeals to be considered white (and to be granted the myriad privileges bundled with whiteness)."[79] The triangulation that Kim describes, then, is a product of racial bipolarity. The tragic choice forced on Asians and Mexicans has been to either prove themselves white (as Irish, Italian, Greek, and other immigrants before them did) or endure the degradations of not-white status, a status reserved particularly but not exclusively for African Americans.

The changes in American society since the civil rights movement should certainly invite a reevaluation of its racial categories as well as its means of racial formation. Yet a growing Latino and Asian American population does not automatically create a nation that has surpassed racial bipolarity. Races are produced through politics, not demographics. Distilling diverse peoples into white and not-white categories historically has been the modus operandi of the American racial order. Indeed, while white supremacy is usually defined as a form of exclusion, it is just as much a kind of inclusion—into the white "club" for those who can successfully claim membership. Before declaring a multiracial era, one must show that the racial order no longer operates in a bipolar manner.[80] Multiracial formation, in other words, must be demonstrated through an analysis of the social and political order. Simply assuming that an ancestry that is not stereotypically African or European must be of a different race reproduces the tension between multiracialism and social construction and reflects a superficiality with which multiracial theories ironically charge bipolar models. Until proven otherwise, the bipolar model will continue to remain central to American society, as Lawrie Balfour comments, *despite* the wide variety of racial and ethnic identities.[81] Uncritically assuming that contemporary race relations are a "mosaic," a "hybrid," "kaleidoscopic," or that "we are all minorities now" obscures the dualism at the heart of white democracy and adds little to a theoretical understanding of race in the post–civil rights era.

A bipolar analysis also challenges the assertion that there are different "degrees" of whiteness, in which some people are "more white" than others. Several scholars have recently argued that bipolarity does not pay enough attention to the differences, tensions, and instabilities within racial categories as well as between them. John Hartigan Jr., for example, argues that too many analyses of race in the United States unfairly homogenize whites' experiences. He acknowledges that whiteness does have a homogenizing tendency, but there are still "varied forms of racial significance in the disparate circumstances of whites in

North America." Most of this heterogeneity among whites, he holds, is due to class differences. Similarly, Howard Winant argues that white privilege is meted out differently among whites (e.g., less for Jews, Arabs, gays, and lesbians) and that a monolithic understanding of whiteness leaves no room for the role of ideology and conviction in structuring white advantage. Annalee Newitz and Matthew Wray argue that class divisions among whites have disintegrated much of whatever white unity existed under slavery and segregation. Contemporary scholarship, they insist, must treat whiteness as a "complex," "messy," and "ambivalent" social force that takes into account how some poor whites are both "inside and outside whiteness," still white yet somehow less white than others.[82]

The problem with the "degrees of whiteness" argument is that it misunderstands the nature of white identity. Whiteness is not a guarantee of equality among whites but, as I argue in the next chapter, a form of racial standing. Culturally, economically, or anthropologically speaking, there is much differentiation among whites. But as a form of status, whiteness is an absolute: you have it or you don't. White standing does not mean that all whites are treated the same, only that in certain instances their myriad differences are subordinated in the interest of white solidarity.[83] The result, as a European aristocrat visiting the United States in 1809 noted, is that even a poor white may claim equality to a rich white with the challenge, "Do you believe that you are any whiter than I am?"[84] It is important to acknowledge the myriad differences among whites, but it makes little sense to discuss degrees of whiteness, for as Richard Wright once exhorted, "Whose hands ran the business enterprise? White hands. Whose hands meted out the law? White hands. Whose hands regulated the money? White hands. Whose hands erected the churches? White hands. Thus, when the white world is viewed from inside the colored world, that world is a block-world with little or no divisions."[85] Wright's point is that as a "block-world" whiteness is a force *against* social complexity and diversity rather than a reflection of it. It does not make all whites absolute equals, but that was never the intent of white citizenship.[86] It just ensures that no white ever need find himself or herself at the absolute bottom of the social and political barrel, because that position is already taken.

Du Bois's work provides the basis for a political theory of race. His bipolar analysis elaborates a theory of racial formation, conflict, and alienation. His account of the "splendid failure" of Reconstruction reveals the cross-class alliance as the foundation of the two worlds system, in which the white world consists of those who are part of the alliance and enjoy its wages while the dark world consists of those who, denied membership into the white world, must ride Jim Crow. Membership in both worlds is fluid, depending on the prevailing needs, fears, and opportunities of the dominant world. The outcome is a racial order divided into those who are white and those who are not. And although this system has historically worked to the benefit of capitalists, the tragic fact is that it is ultimately perpetuated by the white working class. Du Bois's analysis shows that race is a not a prepolitical entity that exists prior to the public sphere. It is constructed in the political realm itself. For as Charles Mills argues, "Whiteness is not really a color at all, but a set of power relations."[87]

A bipolar analysis, nevertheless, is not a comprehensive picture of race. Race is, as Du Bois notes, a product of "inner cohesion" as well as "outer pressure," or the efforts of the dark world to forge a culture and community in the face of discrimination.[88] A political conception of race is decidedly more concerned with the outer pressure aspect. As such, it does not encompass the cultural and psychological connotations of race, particularly among people of color. Nor can it always make sense of relations among ethnic or cultural groups within the not-white category (between, say, African Americans and Puerto Ricans in New York City). These are significant limitations, and yet limitations of some sort seem inevitable given that, as Linda Gordon points out, race is like language, structured by its irregularities and exceptions as well as its rules, and never fully adequate to explain the world.[89] Despite these shortcomings, this theory of race provides a gateway through which to explore how American democracy has been shaped by the racial order and, in turn, shapes that order. This is the task of the next two chapters.

CHAPTER 2

The Problem of the White Citizen

Two public acts characterized the democratic will of antebellum America: the vote and the riot. The age that heralded the rise of the first mass democracy in the world was also one of the most violent, turbulent times in American history. Riots, lynch mobs, insurrections, and other disturbances swept the urban landscape like a panic. In 1835 alone, seventy-one people died in 147 riots across the country. Between 1830 and 1865 over seventy percent of all cities with a population of 20,000 or more experienced some kind of major civil disorder.[1] Jacksonian mobs rioted for many reasons but the greatest number were in defense of slavery and Black subordination. Mobs attacked Black people, abolitionists, "amalgamators"—anyone whose actions or mere existence raised the specter of social equality. But the riots were not the spontaneous actions of a few drunk mechanics gone mad. Hardly. The majority were organized, disciplined, and under the leadership of the city's most prominent gentlemen. Mayors, congressmen, attorneys general, physicians, lawyers, and newspaper editors directed the mobs' activities at night and defended them in the morning, often citing them as expressions of the "will of the majority." The riots, participants argued, were necessary to preserve American democracy from attempts to undermine it by abolitionists, Negroes, and Tory agents.[2]

How could such violence be done in the name of democracy and slavery alike? How could men, esteemed and lowly, invoke the heroes of the Revolutionary War as they burned Black tenements? How could citizens of a democratic republic perpetuate such tyranny and terror? These questions go to the heart of the problem of race in American democracy. Their answer, I argue, lies in an analysis of the relationship between race and democracy that was established in the antebellum era. In particular, it lies in the relationship between what it meant to be a citizen and what it meant to be white.

A common apology for the white mobs is that they represented a sad aberration of democracy. The universal democratic ideals of the Declaration of Independence and the Constitution had not yet been fully implemented in the body politic due to significant exclusions based on race, gender, and class. Racist mobs were tragic proof that the United States had a ways to go before it would fully live up to its own ideals. Underlying this explanation is the assumption that the mobs were anti-democratic. But this is certainly not how the rioters understood their actions. They took themselves to be protectors of republican institutions. Mob leaders presented themselves as patriots—several claimed to have ancestors who came over on the Mayflower—while mobs christened themselves with names like the Sons of Liberty and the Minutemen. The mobs saw anti-Black riots as absolutely democratic, whether they involved tarring Black people or smashing abolitionist presses. The question, then, is not whether the white rioters were democratic but what kind of democracy they believed in, practiced, and fought for.

Riots and other acts of racial oppression served to protect the color line. But this line was much more than a bar that excluded certain people from membership in the republic or that undermined democratic ideals. It constructed democratic citizenship itself. And in turn, citizenship served to construct and defend the color line. The result was the white citizen. To say that the antebellum American citizen was white is not an empirical observation. Rather, it is an acknowledgment of a successful political struggle in which certain persons won the right to proclaim themselves white and therefore citizens or potential citizens, largely by distinguishing themselves from slaves and free Black persons.

The origins of this struggle lie in seventeenth-century colonial Virginia. Not just racism but the American racial order itself was invented on the plantations of the colonial South, largely by extending social and political rights as well as economic opportunities to one section of the poor while withholding them from another. The story then moves to the Jacksonian period, in which the rise of mass democracy is interdependent with the development of a racialized class consciousness. Using Judith Shklar's conception of citizenship as standing, I argue that white chauvinism did not contradict citizenship but was constitutive of it. As American workers fought to define themselves as producers and citizens, many of them also fought to define themselves as white. I then turn to Tocqueville's *Democracy in America* to show that democracy and white tyranny were not contradictory tendencies in the age of Jackson. The twin "inevitabilities" Tocqueville observes—the "gradual progress of equality" and the intractability of racial prejudice—coexisted because equal citizenship *depended* on a system of formal and informal controls that maintained racial hierarchy. This hierarchy was enforced by white women as well as white men, for although white women were the legal and social dependents of white men in the nineteenth century, they nevertheless enjoyed racial standing. Black women and men, on the other hand, were not citizens at all but the antithesis against whom citizenship was defined. I argue that the distinction between dependent citizenship and anticitizenship helps explain the relationship between gender and race in the United States. Finally, I return to Du Bois's critique of the white working class to show how, in defending their racial prerogatives, white women and men closed off opportunities to imagine freedom and equality in more radical ways. In so doing, they disfigured democratic movement in the United States.

Slavery and the Origins of the White Race

Race as we now know it did not exist when the first colonists landed on the shores of the New World. (Native Americans may have been "uncivilized" in manner and "tawny" in color to the first settlers, but their humanity was not in question.) The first inkling of a new way to organize human beings accompanied the arrival of the first Africans to James-town, Virginia, in 1619. The exact social status of these immigrants from the West Indies and Africa is unclear, but most scholars agree that while some arrived already enslaved, others arrived as or became servants; still others were or became free. Regardless, all of the first African immi-grants, slave, servant, or free, possessed most of the same rights and duties as other Virginians. They could buy and sell cattle, sue and be sued, earn money, do penance in the church, and if enslaved sometimes purchase their children's freedom, or even their own. The first African Americans held minor political offices, voted, and owned property—including slaves and servants.[3] But by 1660, lines were being drawn to separate Africans from all other settlers. By 1700, they were definitively distinguished socially, economically, and politically from other colonists. Just how the status of Africans, initially tenuous yet generally divided along the same class distinctions that differentiated English colonists, declined to slavery and debasement while the lot of the English poor appreciably improved tells the story of how not just racial discrimina-tion but race itself was invented in North America.[4]

According to Edmund Morgan, there were two ingredients that formed the foundation of the American system of race. The first was hatred of Indians. Initially, the English saw Indians as savages but potentially assimilable into English civilization. This was an ethnocen-tric vision, certainly, but not a racist one. After an attack on Jamestown in 1622 by a confederation of Indian tribes reacting to English expan-sion in the region, however, the English gave up any plans to "civilize" the first peoples. Indians became an implacable enemy, and the new wisdom was enslavement or extermination.[5] The second ingredient was indentured servitude. Servitude was a condition shared by most poor colonists, including many Africans. It was often as harsh and degrading as slavery. Servants could be bought or sold by any master so long as they were still under contract. A master could unilaterally extend a term of service as punishment for trifling or invented offenses. Given the mortality rate in the early part of the seventeenth century (Morgan esti-mates it was as high as fifty percent until the 1650s), many servants died before fulfilling their terms. Their chances of freedom and survival slim, servants were in a position similar to slaves and perhaps worse, for the limited terms often encouraged masters to work servants as hard as they could before their term expired.[6]

The degradations of servitude and the constant threat of Indian attack combined with hardening class distinctions to produce a volatile social order in Virginia by the 1660s. In addition, most of the land was already claimed by established tobacco growers, leaving only the dangerous frontier available to freed servants. Further, the colony had an acute shortage of potential spouses. Even by the turn of the century, just one-third of all colonists were women. The result was a class of young, landless, largely single, and increasingly rowdy freemen. Yet even as the colony's restless free English population grew, the tobacco plantations continued to require a cheap, exploitable, and stable labor source. From the planter's perspective, something had to be done.

The Virginia elite's solution to its labor problem was slavery. Mortality rates in the colony began to level off by the 1660s, making slaves a better bargain than indentured servants because slaves could now be expected to live and toil longer than the five or seven years of a servant's contract. And anyway, the number of servants arriving in the colonies was not keeping up with the demand for labor. On the other hand, imported African or West Indian slaves were plentiful, cheap, and politically powerless. They had no "rights of Englishmen" to appeal to or representatives to defend their interests. The planter's option for slavery as the principal form of plantation labor was therefore chosen based on rational economic calculations and the existence of a ready supply of a politically weak labor source.[7] It was not made based on some notion that Africans were an inferior race biologically predisposed to hard labor. That came later.

African slavery solved the labor problem, but it could not guarantee social peace. If anything, it contributed to a climate of rebellion, for might not slaves make common cause with disgruntled freeman and collectively resist their poverty and degradation? A frightening omen of this was Bacon's Rebellion of 1676, in which an anti-Indian crusade by poor Europeans and Africans turned mutinous as men led by Nathaniel Bacon trained their arms on the rich as well as the Indians, sending the Virginia leadership scurrying to offshore English ships for protection.[8] Though short-lived and producing no lasting results, Bacon's rebellion proved the insurgent dispositions of the poor freemen and their willingness to unite with rebellious slaves. (For example, the last group of Bacon's men captured was a band of eighty Africans and twenty Englishmen.) Poor Africans and Europeans were already living, working, fighting, and suffering together. Some slept together.[9] Obviously, poor Englishmen and -women of the first fifty or so years of Virginia's history did not share in the virulent racial prejudice that would rule the land by the eighteenth century. Whatever prejudice did exist at the time—and undoubtedly there was some—was apparently weaker than nascent class loyalties.

Morgan argues that in order to prevent class unity and another rebellion, Virginia's elite deliberately attempted to divide the dangerous freemen from the dangerous slaves with a "screen of racial contempt." Slavery was affixed exclusively to Africans by law and, through a series of legislative measures, the African and English populations were divided and set against each other. While there had been earlier laws fastening lifetime slave status to already enslaved Africans and their offspring, six years after Bacon's rebellion only non-Africans and non-Indians were excluded from the possibility of enslavement. Through a series of acts from 1670 to 1705, the Virginia assembly made laws distinguishing Africans and Indians from the English. They forbade Africans and Indians to own Christian servants, in which the legal definition of "Christian" now excluded baptized African and Native Americans. They forbade Africans from striking any Christian servant, allowing servants to bully slaves without fear of reprisal, an act that Morgan says placed servants "psychologically on par with masters." The government seized all property slaves had been allowed to accrue and distributed it to "the poor," that is, to English servants. Only Christians could now own property. The law forbade sexual relations between "Christians and negroes." It punished Englishwomen severely for having children by an African father. It defined a child's social status according to the status of the mother, meaning that all children of English male–African female relationships would be cast into the degraded group. Africans and Indians were denied the right to vote, testify in court, serve on juries, or possess arms. Racial domination—at the time inchoate, novel, and a mere prototype of what it later became—was a deliberate policy of the Virginia ruling elite. "If Negro slavery came to Virginia without anyone having to decide upon it as a matter of public policy, the same is not true of racism," Morgan writes. "By a series of acts, the [Virginia colonial] assembly deliberately did what it could to foster the contempt of whites for blacks and Indians."[10]

The systematic exclusion of Black people—free or slave—through such legislation is a primary fact of American history. It is tragic enough, but to interpret colonial law as a form of power that excluded, repressed, divided, and dominated would only tell the most obvious part of the story, for it was also a *productive* form of power. It produced new types of social relationships, new forms of knowledge, and a particular form of government. As Michel Foucault admonishes, "We must cease once and for all to describe the effects of power in negative terms: it 'excludes,' it 'represses,' it 'censors,' it 'abstracts,' it 'masks,' it 'conceals.' In fact, power produces; it produces reality; it produces domains of objects and rituals of truth. The individual and the knowledge that may be gained of him belong to this production."[11] We can see the productive nature of power at work in colonial Virginia, for the early legislators did much more than legalize discrimination against African and Native Americans; in drawing discriminatory lines, they created race itself. Slavery was the most profitable form of labor in colonial Virginia, but *racial* slavery was the solution to the threat of servile insurrection and the problem of how to efficiently and peacefully get the workers—slave and free—to work. Such a system was not the product of inevitable prejudices against Africans on the part of the English but of political decisions made to address immediate, particular problems of social control.[12] Not just racial oppression but race itself was a product of these political choices. Race was not something that was already there, ready to be picked up by colonial elites and used to divide the masses against themselves.[13] In Theodore Allen's words, the white race literally had to be invented.

Further, the races were produced and hierarchically ordered through the powers and prerogatives of citizenship. Through various legislative measures and social pressures, Virginia elites simultaneously fastened Africans to a lifetime, hereditary, degraded status and created a new group of relatively privileged people heretofore unknown in human history. Remarkably, these measures amassed rich and poor, planter and servant, esteemed and lowly into a single group unified less by ancestry than by the right to own property (including human property), the right to share in the public business, and a pledge to ensure the degraded position of all those defined as Black. As all those of discernible African descent—servant, slave, free, unfree, propertied, propertyless—were thrown down into a single subordinate group, all those who could prove themselves unenslaveable were raised up to a superior group. As their right to possess property was recognized, as their poll tax was reduced, and as their opportunities for land and citizenship increased inversely with the degradation of African Americans, poor English colonists came to identity themselves as "white." They shared this new identity with the planters, further elevating their status and self-esteem. As the benefits of this new social arrangement accrued to poor Englishmen-cum-whites, they came to have a stake in slavery and its racial basis. In this way, the construction of race in the colonial era was achieved through the elaboration of the rights and privileges of the citizen.

Race emerged from the needs of the Virginia upper class to craft a docile and productive labor force. But as the benefits of whiteness became apparent to English laborers, they came to embrace the system by which privileges were conferred in exchange for policing slaves. As the slaveholder T. R. R. Cobb described the arrangement,

> The mass of laborers [i.e., slaves] not being recognized among citizens, every citizen feels that he belongs to an elevated class. It matters not that

he is no slaveholder; he is not of the inferior race; he is a freeborn citizen; he engages in no menial occupation. The poorest meets the richest as an equal; sits at his table with him; salutes him as a neighbor; meets him in every public assembly; and stands on the same social platform.[14]

In allying themselves with the large planters, poor whites traded class solidarity for whiteness and its accompanying privileges. Racial oppression, then, was reproduced from below as well as from above. The consequences would be fateful in the development of the American democratic creed. Starting in colonial Virginia, Americans and immigrants came to connect freedom with race. The civil rights of the colonist not only served as the basis for American citizenship; they were simultaneously privileges reserved for the white race.[15]

Citizens and Slaves of the White Republic

Race was produced through colonial law, but it was not yet connected to democracy. This occurred in the first half of the nineteenth century. By 1820 the Founding era had passed, and economic developments had already made anachronistic Jefferson's vision of a country of virtuous yeoman farmers. The North in particular was transforming itself into an urban, industrializing nation. In 1820, sixty-three percent of the labor force in New England worked in agriculture; by 1850, only thirty-nine percent did.[16] Overall, the number of people working in manufacturing jumped 127 percent between 1820 and 1840 and the percentage of people living in towns of eight thousand or more nearly doubled. By 1860 half of all white men worked for wages.[17] The first waves of European immigration began in earnest in the 1830s, with over 600,000 people depositing themselves in American cities in that decade alone, looking for work and freedom. That number climbed to 2.6 million between 1851 and 1860, to the point where by 1860 nearly twenty percent of the population of the northeast was foreign born.[18] The emergence of an industrial working class was accompanied by the rise of mass democracy as property requirements for suffrage were swept away, giving the ordinary man the vote for the first time in Western history. It is this era of rapid industrialization, immigration, and democratization, gener-ally referred to as the Jacksonian era, in which the relationship between whiteness and republican citizenship was cemented.

As the young republic reconciled itself to an industrial future and as workers clamored for political power, Northern labor republicans of "the Democracy" (as the Democratic Party was known then) adopted a new political identity to replace Jefferson's yeoman farmer as the bulwark of democratic-republican ideals: the producer.[19] The producer ethic held that society should be run by those who produce for it: small farmers, mechanics, laborers, and Southern planters. Bankers, specula-tors, and other representatives of America's quasi-aristocratic class were not producers but parasites who lived off the labor of others. This busi-ness class, with its banks and corporations and its control of the press and institutions of education, wanted to do more than simply subject workers to long hours at low pay. It wanted to press workers down into slavery. Lacking conscience or mercy, nonproducers were a hated lot in Jacksonian ideology, for they threatened cherished republican freedom. As an adage of the time went, "Corporations have neither bodies to be kicked, nor souls to be damned."[20] Labor republicans feared that the republic's existence—and their place in it—was fragile and uncertain. The decline of republican institutions and the corruption of civic virtue are typical fears of classical republicanism, but they were given new life in the era of the "tumultuous republic" in which nothing—the perma-nence of the Union, employment, social status, masculinity, or race—could be taken for granted. The producer ethic was forged out of wage labor and the fear of economic and political dependency. Dependence was slavery, and workers did not have to look far to see what that looked like in practice.

As Judith Shklar agues, American citizenship was a product of this combination of working-class political power and the fear of fall-ing into slavery. In its standard liberal conception, citizenship is defined as equality in the political sphere, equal opportunity in the economic realm, and the right to participate in public affairs. Shklar acknowledges these elements, but she maintains that in the United States the primary significance of citizenship is that it provides persons with social status, or standing. The importance of American citizenship does not derive from the political power it imparts; on an individual level such power is practically insignificant. Nor does it derive from equality of rights, for it is the *distinction* between citizen and noncitizen that matters. The value of American citizenship, Shklar argues, is that it confers dignity and standing upon members of the polity over and against noncitizens. The struggle for American citizenship, then, is the struggle for standing, understood as inclusion in the public sphere.[21]

The quintessential noncitizens of the nineteenth-century American polity were white women and slaves. The exclusion of white women from the vote was essential to reconstructing a masculine identity damaged by the degrading demands of industrial labor. Proletarianized men could not depend on their position as wage laborers to provide a foundation for their household authority like a yeoman farmer could. To compensate, the notion of the father as the family "breadwinner," whose wages support the family, became the basis of male authority. In defense of this new male, labor republicans took up the struggle for a "family wage" that would enable the male worker to earn enough to provide for himself and his family.[22] This new working-class manhood, while securing the male's place at the head of the household in the private realm, presupposed women's exclusion from the public realm. Thus efforts by women to participate in public affairs were ridiculed by the official public.[23]

But it was slavery that particularly distinguished citizens from noncitizens and that has had the greatest impact on American citizenship.[24] Shklar argues that American citizenship has been forged as a "virtuous middle" between the lazy lord and the servile slave. The nation had a notable lack of aristocrats but an abundance of slaves. Further, slavery in the States was quite literally the opposite of liberty in a way European republicans could only imagine. "In Europe the slave was a metaphor drawn from the annals of classical antiquity. In America slavery referred to a living presence."[25] To white workers facing a life of wage labor or "wage slavery," the possibility that they could become actual slaves was acutely felt. To distinguish themselves from slaves they had to make themselves citizens. As Shklar writes, "Black chattel slavery stood at the opposite social pole from full citizenship and so defined it. The importance of what I call citizenship as standing emerges out of this basic fact of our political history. The value of citizenship was derived primarily from its denial to slaves, to some white men, and to all women."[26]

The hatred of slavery passed easily into hatred of the slaves. As white workers came to fear the slave, they came to fear Black people and to measure white liberty against Black subjugation. "Working Americans," David Roediger notes, "expressed soaring desires to be rid of the age-old inequalities of Europe and of any hint of slavery. They also expressed the rather more pedestrian goal of simply not being mistaken for slaves, or 'negers' or 'negurs.' And they saw not nearly so great a separation between these goals as we do."[27]

The votes of Jackson Democrats, combined with their fear and hatred of Black people, produced what the sociologist Pierre van den Berghe calls a *Herrenvolk* democracy, a regime that is "democratic for the master race but tyrannical for subordinate groups."[28] Under this regime, which persisted until the civil rights movement, all whites are political equals while all not-white persons are relegated to an inferior status. The result is a curious mix of democratic government and egalitarian values along with state repression, mob violence, and an ideology, justified by religion and science, of the eternal inequality of humanity. This mix is epitomized in Vice President of the Confederacy Alexander H. Stephens's famous "Cornerstone Speech" of 1861:

> Many governments have been founded on the principles of subordination and serfdom of certain classes of the same race; such were, and are in violation of the laws of nature. Our system commits no such violation of nature's law. With us, all the white race, however high or low, rich or poor, are equal in the eyes of the law. Not so with the Negro. Subordination is his place. He, by nature or by the curse against Canaan, is fitted for that condition which he occupies in our system.[29]

Shklar shows that citizenship in a *Herrenvolk* democracy has a twofold nature. It is a mark of equality in that all citizens possess the same rights and responsibilities, but it is also a mark of distinction between those who are citizens and those who are not. A standing conception of citizenship provides citizens with a glass floor below which they can see but cannot fall. Success is not guaranteed by the glass floor, but citizenship assures that one cannot be degraded below it and that one can always see those beneath it and feel superior to them. This twofold nature of American citizenship generates conflict, for it simultaneously enshrines political equality (among citizens) and produces inequality by excluding some people from full citizenship. This conflict, Shklar argues, "has marked every stage of the history of American democracy."[30]

Shklar's argument about citizenship as standing goes a long way toward explaining the relationship between slavery, race, and citizenship. She explains the powerful negative relationship between citizenship and slavery: one is a citizen because one is not a slave. She also points out that slavery and Blackness are inextricably connected in the American mind. However, Shklar does not complete the thread. Citizenship was defined against slavery. Blackness and slavery were associated. Black and white were diametrically opposed. All that is left is to complete the square: to be a citizen was also to be white. This is not an empirical observation of who had the vote at the time. Whiteness was not a biological status but a *political* color that distinguished the free from the unfree, the equal from the inferior, the citizen from the slave. Citizenship was not just standing, as Shklar argues, but *racialized* standing.

As the antithesis of the white citizen, then, Black people in the Jacksonian era were not simply noncitizens but *anticitizens*.[31] They were not merely excluded from the social compact, they were the Other that simultaneously threatened and consolidated it. This was graphically illustrated in who won—and lost—the vote in the 1820s and 1830s. As the Democracy ascended, suffrage was extended to all white males as it was stripped from Black men. New York in 1821 and Pennsylvania in 1838, for example, eliminated their property requirements for voting and proscribed Black male suffrage in the same stroke. From 1819 to the Civil War, every state admitted to the union limited the franchise to white males in their constitutions. By 1860, only six percent of the Northern Black population lived in states in which they could vote (Massachusetts, New Hampshire, Vermont, Rhode Island, and Maine), and only half of eligible voters in these states did vote due to white terror at the polls. The white republic was also defended in state referendums. In the North between 1840 and 1870, equality with Black people was overwhelmingly rejected by white voters in seventeen of nineteen referendums.[32] In addition, Black Northerners were excluded from schools, militias, juries, seats in public transportation, participation in social activities, and the possession of firearms. In some places they were even prohibited from walking on sidewalks.[33]

The changes in citizenship rights effected in the Jacksonian era did more than merely include some and exclude others. These laws and social norms produced the white citizen.[34] Equality and liberty went from abstract principles to lived experiences for the masses of ordinary men (and women to a lesser degree), but they became concrete not as universally held rights but as privileges reserved for members of the white club. White citizenship represents the democratization of social status, extending it from the upper class to the masses by transforming it from a perk of wealth to a perk of race. What Shklar implies but fails to elaborate, then, is that citizenship as standing links democracy to race. Standing not only reconciles equality and freedom with slavery; it builds white domination into democracy.[35] Thus, the democratic problem is not simply the legacy of slavery and racial exclusion or the failure of American democratic practices to live up to American democratic ideals. The democratic problem lies in the white citizen itself.

Because of its political significance, whiteness was not something that could be taken for granted in the antebellum era. It was a badge of status that indicated full membership in the community and rights to all the accompanying perquisites: the right to vote, to earn, to prosper, to educate one's children, to own a firearm, even to riot. Recently arrived immigrants quickly learned that, like citizenship, membership in the white race could not be assumed but had to be earned. One did not receive the rights of American citizenship because one was white but rather the reverse: one was white because one possessed such rights.[36] Thus, the process of immigrant assimilation—as citizens, Democrats, Americans—was also a process of assimilation into whiteness.[37]

The most striking example of this process was the Irish, not because their immigration experience was unusual but because they were escaping a land from which they had suffered something akin to racial oppression. One of the most discriminated-against ethnic groups in antebellum America, Irish immigrants were not guaranteed admission into the white club.[38] As historian Noel Ignatiev argues, the Irish sought to assimilate by allying themselves en masse with the Democratic Party, by forming the bulk of the modern police force, and by fighting to join labor organizations. But the prerequisite of entrance into these institutions was proof of whiteness, which implied a commitment to the degradation of African Americans.[39] Thus, the Irish took up anti-Black discrimination with zeal. They were at the forefront of the many anti-Black riots that convulsed the North. They also led efforts to exclude Black labor from work sites, to contain and repress Black neighborhoods through policing, and to keep Black people away from the polls in places where they were allowed to vote. Many Irish workers openly supported slavery despite the antislavery efforts of respected Irish independence activists such as Daniel O'Connell. These actions were the on-the-street supplement to the legal disfranchisement of Black persons; their intent was to show white citizens that the Irish deserved racial standing. The Irish struggle for white citizenship was an eminently political battle, the outcome of which, Ignatiev argues, "was not the inevitable consequence of blind historic forces, still less of biology, but the result of choices made, by the Irish and others, from among available alternatives. To enter the white race was a strategy to secure an advantage in a competitive society."[40] It was so important to become a citizen in the Jacksonian era in part because it was so important to become white. Once conjoined, the two identities were practically interchangeable.

Like any social system, the white-citizen/Black-slave quadrangle could not fit all persons into its prefabricated containers. So that free Black persons would not form an exception to the rule, they were deliberately degraded by law and custom below all those defined as white and pushed down toward slavery. Though nominally free, Black men and women remained potentially enslaveable, since the fugitive slave law put the burden on them to prove they did not belong to any master who might claim them. The infamous Dred Scott case of 1857, in which the Supreme Court ruled that the Black person has no rights that a white person is bound to respect, settled any question of free African Americans' status, placing all Black people firmly below the status of any white.[41]

None of this meant that membership in the white club was without its costs. As Roediger points out, for Northern workers in the early 1800s, "to be white was both an urgent necessity and a lifeless burden." It guaranteed standing but it was a cultural straitjacket that cut white workers off from their preindustrial past, from connections to Black workers and American Indians, and ultimately from their very humanity.[42] It must also be said that whiteness was no guarantee of prosperity. White standing, as Ignatiev notes, meant that members of an immigrant ethnic group could enter the labor market as free laborers rather than indentured servants, that they could compete for all jobs instead of being confined to certain ones, and that their entrepreneurs could operate outside of a segregated market. It meant they had the right to vote and be elected, to hold positions in the Democratic Party political machine, to be tried by a jury, to live wherever they could afford, and to spend their money as they pleased. These are not signs of prosperity, only its prerequisites. The price the Irish and other immigrant groups had to pay to earn them underlines the exploitation they endured in this country. Nevertheless, they quickly determined that becoming white— not so much by looking white as by proving themselves sufficiently anti-Black—was the best way to escape their miserable conditions and become American citizens.

Black people's participation in the political and social order, then, was not simply a matter of inclusion and exclusion. The white-citizen/ Black-slave relation stood at the center of American democracy like a village square. In order for whites to be "independent citizen-earners" (to use Shklar's phrase), all Black persons had to be thrown down as a mass below all whites, irrespective of class, gender, or other social distinctions. African Americans held up the glass floor, giving whites (especially poor whites who had little else) something to fear, despise, and look down at. This sense of superiority confirmed their standing as citizens in a democratic republic.[43]

Tocqueville and the Two Inevitabilities

White citizenship, then, reconciles racially oppressive practices with democratic ideals. This is reflected in Alexis de Tocqueville's classic account of antebellum democracy, *Democracy in America*. Rogers Smith contends that the book is the quintessential example of a text that brackets racist traditions from democracy.[44] But in fact it does no such thing. Rather, in Tocqueville's *Democracy* as in Jackson's democracy, slavery and racial prejudice are tangents to the greater story of expanding equality not because Tocqueville brackets them but because he recognizes that white domination makes equality possible. Tocqueville saw little contradiction between the spread of egalitarian ideals and the practices of slavery and racial oppression because white citizenship reconciles them. Indeed, there would be no contradiction until slaves and abolitionists made one.

Based on Tocqueville's travels to the United States and Canada during Jackson's presidency, *Democracy* is a tale of societies (European no less than American) transforming themselves into democracies. Equality, not distinction, is the watchword of these new republics. Throughout both volumes of the book, Tocqueville grapples with an emerging new world whose template is America. As a young aristocrat, he approaches this world with anticipation and trepidation. At times he has great faith in the future; at other times it seems the world has gone mad.

> Where are we, then? Men of religion fight against freedom, and lovers of liberty attack religions; noble and generous spirits praise slavery, while low, servile minds preach independence; honest and enlightened citizens are the enemies of all progress, while men without patriotism or morals make themselves the apostles of civilization and enlightenment! Have

all ages been like ours? And have men always dwelt in a world in which nothing is connected?[45]

Regardless of his mixed feelings about this transformation, he regards it as inevitable. "[T]he gradual progress of equality is something fated. The main features of this progress are the following: it is universal and permanent, it is daily passing beyond human control, and every event and every man help it along."[46] Nevertheless, there is one place where "the gradual progress of equality" is completely halted: race relations. He discusses this in the longest chapter of either volume, "Some Considerations Concerning the Present State and Probable Future of the Three Races that Inhabit the Territory of the United States."

Tocqueville counts three "naturally distinct, one might almost say hostile" races in America: whites (also referred to as Anglo-Americans), Negroes, and Indians.[47] The majority of the chapter is devoted to the degraded condition of the African and Native races.[48] Tocqueville generally treats American Indians as part of nature and as distinct from civilization. *Democracy* begins, for example, with a description of North America's first inhabitants and its geography, essentially regarding Indians as a part of the physical landscape. He doubts whether the advanced elements of Natives' culture could have come from them alone; a more sophisticated civilization must have preceded them and passed its religion and language along to them. Their destruction by an advanced civilization was fated.

> The Indians occupied but did not possess the land. It is by agriculture that man wins the soil, and the first inhabitants of North America lived by hunting. Their unconquerable prejudices, their indomitable passions, their vices, and perhaps still more their savage virtues delivered them to inevitable destruction. The ruin of these people began as soon as the Europeans landed on their shores; it has continued ever since and is coming to completion in our own day. Providence, when it placed them amid the riches of the New World, seems to have granted them a short lease only; they were there, in some sense, only waiting.[49]

Tocqueville, however, is far from seeing Indians as entirely depraved. He certainly sees nothing to justify their wholesale slaughter by white settlers. He criticizes the state's role in their expulsion and extermination, particularly the role of state governments. Furthermore, while he sees Indians as the counterpoint to civilization in certain ways, he does not doubt that they could join and fully participate in Anglo-American culture if they wanted to. Unfortunately, Indians are too free and too proud to accept the kinds of dependence that civilized society requires of its members, and so they choose to suffer rather than assimilate. Indians refuse to adapt to modern society, so they will be destroyed by it.[50]

Tocqueville is less charitable toward African Americans. Unlike Indians, who face doom because of their stubborn independent spirit, Africans' future on the continent is threatened because they are servile and dependent. Tocqueville condemns slavery as a great evil and considers it to be the primary cause of Black people's degradation rather than their "nature." Nevertheless, slavery has so degraded Africans' intelligence and soul that they no longer know how to be free.[51] At the same time, because slavery brings white and Black people into close daily contact (whereas Western expansion drives whites and Indians apart), the fate of Black and white Americans is uniquely intertwined. "The Indians die as they have lived, in isolation; but the fate of the Negroes is in a sense linked with that of the Europeans. The two races are bound one to the other without mingling; it is equally difficult for them to separate completely or to unite."[52]

Tocqueville resisted the rising trend of scientific racism in the 1830s led by his friend, the Count Joseph-Arthur de Gobineau. While Gobineau believed that a person's character derived from unchangeable racial characteristics and that such characteristics organized people into hierarchically ordered races, Tocqueville continued to insist that the environment was the predominating influence on a person's character and behavior.[53] Tocqueville's rejection of scientific racism, however, did not prevent him from judging other cultures inferior to European civilization. It is also clear that he somewhat fears Native and African Americans, particularly slaves. As George Fredrickson has persuasively argued, Tocqueville's views on Black people were strongly influenced by advocates of colonization, and he absorbed that movement's negrophobia.[54] Yet in spite of this, Tocqueville was one of a shrinking number of whites and Europeans of his day who recognized the humanity of Native and African Americans.

Tocqueville's ambiguities on race are well documented in the secondary literature. He is a contested figure because of them—and because he is one of the few theorists of the political theory canon to write extensively on American race relations.[55] He is both hailed as an early critic of America's racist betrayal of the principles of the Declaration of Independence and criticized for holding to an ideal of a homogeneous republic in which there is no place for Native or African Americans. He is held to be both antiracist and negrophobic, an agitator against slavery and an advocate of forced labor, one who sympathized with the slaves while doubting they could ever become whites' equals.[56] The debate is anachronistic, however, for Tocqueville held all of these positions. His firm belief in the impossibility of *racial* equality never disrupts his faith in the inevitable spread of equality. These positions appear contradictory to post-*Herrenvolk* eyes but not to Tocqueville or his white contemporaries. Taking white citizenship for granted, they saw no necessary tension between equality and white domination, for as a Jackson Democratic slogan read, "Negro's Elevation Means Your Degradation."[57]

Tocqueville argues that there are two possibilities regarding the fate of whites and African Americans, who "face each other like two foreign peoples on the same soil." Either they "mingle completely" or "they must part." Tocqueville does not believe the first option is a real possibility. Ironically, the only thing that could possibly get Black and white people to "mingle" in democratic America is a despot. As long as America remains a democracy, no one, he insists, would dare attempt to bring about social equality. Indeed, "the freer the whites in America are, the more they will seek to isolate themselves" from Black and Native peoples.[58] It is not just that race is the one terrain where the march of equality will not tramp, he implies; it is that equality and white supremacy are symbiotic. As the fervor for equality deepens, so does racial conflict. In essence, Tocqueville makes the startling claim that while equality is an inevitable trend in the United States, *racial* equality is incompatible with its democracy, since only a despotic regime can bring the races together. America will have democracy or racial equality, but it will not have both. The implication of Tocqueville's argument is that the United States is democratic and white supremacist simultaneously, and that there is no necessary contradiction between the two.[59]

Tocqueville's famous critique of the tyranny of the majority further explains how equal citizenship and racial oppression went together in the Jacksonian era. One of *Democracy*'s principal themes is the middling tendency of democracy. Democracy eliminates the highs and lows of aristocratic society. There is no nobility but there is no valor; there is no monopoly of control of art but there is no great art; there is free speech but there is no original thought. In the sweep of the equality of conditions it becomes nearly impossible to distinguish oneself from the mass. Hence the danger that mass opinion could overwhelm the public sphere is very real. But as Tocqueville recognizes, one form of majority tyranny was already realized in the Jacksonian era: white tyranny. In the chapter "The Omnipotence of the Majority in the United States and Its Effects," he asks a Pennsylvanian why free Negroes cannot vote in a state founded by Quakers and known for its tolerance. The person retorts that there is no such law preventing Negroes from voting; they have that right. Why don't they show up at the polls, then, Tocqueville asks. The gentleman answers that Negroes do not vote because they are intimidated from doing so by the white majority, which is prejudiced against them. Tocqueville blurts, "What! The majority, privileged to make the law, wishes also to have the privilege of disobeying the law?"[60] As the anecdote shows, white citizenship is built into majority rule. *Herrenvolk* democracy functions through a combination of democratic decision-making by white majorities and extralegal practices of terror, such as those involved in preventing Black men from voting. The white majority not only makes the law but decides whether, how, and on whom it will be enforced. White tyranny does not contradict the democratic will but is an expression of it.

Tocqueville, then, was not contradicting himself in recognizing two "inevitabilities" in American democracy. The inevitable progression of equality occurred simultaneously with the inevitable increase of racial prejudice because the elaboration of equality and liberty depended on racial oppression. *Democracy in America* reflects the fact that the white citizen in the age of Jackson contained both inevitabilities within his or her breast. Tocqueville writes, "The southern American has two active passions which will always lead him to isolate himself: he is afraid of resembling the Negro, once his slave, and he is afraid of falling below the level of his white neighbor."[61] In the North, he observes, "[the] white man no longer clearly sees the barrier that separates him from the degraded race, and he keeps the Negro at a distance all the more carefully because he fears lest one day they be confounded together."[62] White citizenship alleviates this fear of hitting bottom. It ensures that whites cannot fall to the level of Black people, free or slave, and that no matter how poor or mean a white person may be, she or he is, in certain respects, equal to any other white. (In his notebooks Tocqueville records an interview with a lawyer who tells him that in New Orleans, "There is not a white beggar but has the right to bully the wretch he finds in his way and throw him in the dirt, crying out: 'Get off, mulatto!'")[63] Equality and racial privilege became antinomies only with the arguments of abolitionists, the appeals of free Black persons, and the mutinous plans of slaves. "It was the Negro himself who forced the consideration of this incongruity," Du Bois writes, "who made emancipation inevitable and made the modern world at least consider if not wholly accept the idea of a democracy including men of all races and colors."[64] Slavery was always deplored by some as a violation of the Rights of Man, but it took the publication of David Walker's *Appeal*, the speeches of Frederick Douglass, the underground railroad led by Harriet Tubman, and the revolt of Nat Turner to raise to the level of public consciousness the notion that white domination might violate equality. But by then such domination had come to constitute equality itself.

It is to Tocqueville's credit that his argument recognizes this, at least implicitly. It is true that in his writing and in his work in the

French government he opposed social equality among white and Black people. (For example, he advocated the enforced labor of ex-slaves in the French colonies to prevent them from leaving the plantations upon emancipation.)[65] This is a consequence of his inability to recognize the centrality of Black agency in determining Black people's own destiny. But his negrophobia does not undermine his acute analysis of the relationship between democracy and race in the United States. Such an analysis gives many of his famous predictions their staying power. It enables him, for example, to forecast that racial conflict will long outlast slavery, since the problem does not lie merely between master and slave but also between Black and white. Well after slavery is abolished, Tocqueville foresees, Americans will still have to "eradicate three much more intangible and tenacious prejudices: the prejudice of the master, the prejudice of race, and the prejudice of the white."[66] Tocqueville is also among the first to point out that racial prejudice is buried deep in social mores and practices. "I plainly see that in some parts of the country the legal barrier between the two races is tending to come down, but not that of mores; I see that slavery is in retreat, but the prejudice from which it arose is immovable."[67] Even when legally free, Tocqueville observes, the Black race is indelibly linked to slavery and a degraded status in the minds of white Americans. "Memories of slavery disgrace the race, and race perpetuates memories of slavery."[68] Tocqueville's elitism and negrophobia demand criticism, but his insight that in the *Herrenvolk* era, white tyranny sustains democracy rather than contradicts it is profound.

Gender and the White Citizen

The coexistence of racial standing and equality was not the only paradox of citizenship in the *Herrenvolk* era, of course. Women as a class were also denied full citizenship. Indeed, they did not win the vote until 1920, fifty years after the Fifteenth Amendment granted it to Black men. Clearly, gender also has been an organizing principle of American citizenship.[69] Denial of full citizenship due to gender shares important similarities with its denial due to race, particularly the exclusion of a category of people based on ascribed characteristics. In many ways, male domination is rooted more deeply in the social structure than white supremacy, pervading the most intimate of human relations. Yet gender and race also function in significantly different ways in regards to citizenship. As the legal and social dependents of men throughout much of the *Herrenvolk*, white women enjoyed only a dependent citizenship, yet a form of citizenship nonetheless. Black people (male and female), on the other hand, were not citizens at all. They were anticitizens against whom civil society was defined. Dependent citizenship in the *Herrenvolk* era produced a tension between women's desire for full citizenship and the felt need to restrict citizenship to those with racial standing. As a result, it tended to yield a call for gender equality that was compromised by the imperative to preserve the racial standing of white women and men alike.

As Carole Pateman argues, male domination functions through a sort of "fraternal contract" among men. Modern patriarchy is not so much the rule of the father as it is the rule of the brothers, in which men expressly or tacitly agree among themselves to guarantee each other's rights, including the right to dominate women. Excluded from the fraternal contract, women are incorporated into civil society indirectly via the marriage contract, which admits them as semipolitical beings whose rights are dependent on the full citizenship of their husbands. The marriage contract incorporates women into civil society, but as dependent citizens relegated to the private sphere.[70]

Two pillars of dependent citizenship in the antebellum era were coverture and antimiscegenation law. Coverture is a legal practice, imported from English common law, that at marriage transfers a woman's civic identity to her husband. A woman is "covered" by her husband's citizenship. Under coverture, women cannot independently hold property, enter contracts, make wills, testify in court, retain earnings, or exercise legal authority over their children. The husband, in effect, becomes a surrogate for the state in the legal life of the woman.[71] Antimiscegenation laws regulate marriage between people of different "races" in order to prevent "race-mixing." They reverse patriarchal tradition by defining the social-racial status of a child according to the race of the mother rather than the father. Regardless of the father's race, only a white mother can have white children while a Black mother can only have Black children. Antimiscegenation law guaranteed the white father that his "official" children (i.e., those borne by his white wife) were white while any offspring due to sexual liaisons with Black women would belong to the subordinate group, keeping the dominant race "pure."[72]

Coverture and antimiscegenation laws subordinated female citizenship to male citizenship. As a result, white women were not full citizens in the *Herrenvolk* democracy. Nevertheless, they were still citizens. As Linda Kerber points out, white women were issued passports, could be naturalized, could claim the protection of the courts, and were obliged to pay taxes. Although the dependents of white men, "White women have been citizens of the United States as long as the republic has existed."[73] On the other hand, Black persons, whether female or male, free or slave, were anticitizens. Marked by slavery, they were the antithesis of freedom and as such stood outside of citizenship rather than being incorporated into it, even in a dependent or derivative fashion.[74] White women's status in the *Herrenvolk* was defined by the public/private split, in which society is divided into the political and social sphere on the one hand and the household on the other and in which women are confined to the latter. White women in the nineteenth century endured a form of "civil death" in which they legally disappeared into the private realm while "covered" by the husband or other male surrogate in the public. Slavery, however, was a form of "social death" in which the person disappears as a social being from the community altogether.[75] As Cheryl Harris argues, "'Slaves' and 'women' were constituted as subordinated categories; however, they were unequal to white men for different, although related, reasons. The disability of race differed from the disability of gender: slaves were not free individuals, but a class completely outside the social compact, while women were within the polity but not the public sphere."[76] White women stood outside the public sphere, but slaves and free Black persons stood outside civil society altogether.

Harris describes this arrangement as a racial patriarchy, a "social, political, economic, legal, and conceptual system that entrenched the ideology of white supremacy and white male control over women's reproduction and sexuality." Such a system functioned "by subordinating all Black people along lines that were articulated within and through gender, and all women along lines that were articulated within and through race."[77] White women were "protected" from the "burden" of owning property by coverture laws, giving them only a derivative right to property. Black women, however, could not own property at all because they were property or (for free Black women) potentially property. Antimiscegenation laws granted white women a form of standing by default, too. Citizenship and property rights were passed down through the father's line but a child's status as free or slave (and thus white or Black) was determined by the mother's status. Accordingly, for a father's children to be indisputably free (and white), their mother by definition had to be, too. The perverse nature of racial patriarchy granted white women racial standing even as it oppressed them as women.

White women could count on dependent citizenship to provide a variety of direct and indirect racial privileges. They enjoyed favored access to certain occupations such as teaching, nursing, and clerical work. They enjoyed access to better housing, schools, and child care as well as easier access to plumbing, heating, electricity, and time-saving household appliances. They might look forward to the right to be treated like a "lady." White women who had to work (always a smaller proportion than women of color) could look forward to higher wages and occupational segregation. Their children could not be sold. These advantages were among the fruits of favored standing in the *Herrenvolk* era.[78] They were clearly incomplete compared to the full menu of wages enjoyed by white men, but as Dana Frank points out, "Such women nonetheless enjoyed a sense of superiority and pride in being white."[79] By sharing in the proceeds of white citizenship, white women came to have a stake in its perpetuation, even as they were barred from full citizenship themselves.

Racial standing compromised struggles against gender subordination because it often pit the struggle for women's liberation against the concern to preserve one's racial prerogatives. Many white women in the suffrage movement, for example, demanded equal citizenship on the grounds that granting the vote to Black men but not to "civilized" white women was an insult. They further suggested that white female suffrage would double the white vote and thereby help protect the nation against "the rising tide of color" that many whites feared in the early twentieth century.[80] Indeed, as Aileen Kraditor notes, "This in time became the single most important argument [for women's suffrage] used in the South."[81] The result was that when women's suffrage was finally won, it turned out to be "the biggest non-event in electoral history," as Shklar notes, because "women had adopted the dominant attitudes of their time and place . . . completely."[82] Similarly, Paula Baker argues that (white) women fragmented politically after they won the vote in 1920 due to the lack of a distinct women's politics or culture. Unable to form a political bloc, they could not appreciably increase their power in the political system.[83] The imperative of securing white unity across gender lines blunted the radical potential of women's political participation.

The second wave of the feminist movement continued to trip on the white problem, even among those who explicitly criticized white privilege. Marilyn Frye, for example, recognizes whiteness as "a social or political construct of some sort" and concludes that as a white feminist she must "set [herself] against whiteness" and "give [herself] the injunction to stop being white."[84] Frye's argument is valuable as an early call for the abolition of white identity, yet she associates racial privilege entirely with white men. "Those who fashion this construct of whiteness, who elaborate on these conceptions, are primarily a certain group of males. It is *their* construct."[85] White women (particularly feminists and lesbians) play an insignificant role in perpetuating whiteness, according to her, because they have few associations with white men. Frye ignores the ways in which white women perpetuate white citizenship even in a patriarchal society.

The differences between dependent citizenship and anticitizen-ship make it "dangerous and historically inaccurate," as Harris writes, "to suggest that the position of Black women and white women, even white women who were not economically privileged, were functionally equivalent."[86] Scholars and activists are increasingly calling for analyses that illuminate the intersections of race, class, and gender.[87] It is indeed vital to understand how these forms of power interact. Yet as Harris indicates, the attempt to demonstrate the interconnections of multiple forms of power sometimes obscures these relations rather than illumi-nates them. In emphasizing the similarities in how gender, race, and class function, the distinct character of each form is often downplayed. When this occurs, Patricia Hill Collins argues, intersectionality can per-petuate a "new myth of equivalent oppressions" by tending to treat race, gender, and class as identical experiences. In the United States, she points out, race has been more salient than gender or even class in the lives of Black women. Treating gender and race as functional equivalents, therefore, discounts a primary experience of Black women. "Although this approach [intersectionality] is valid as a heuristic device," she argues, "treating race, class, and gender as if their intersection produces equiv-alent results for all oppressed groups obscures differences in how race, class, and gender are hierarchically organized, as well as the differential effects of intersecting systems of power on diverse groups of people."[88]

Given this, a critique of the white citizen is preferable to a cri-tique of the white *male* citizen in the context of this book's argument because the former distinguishes between dependent citizenship and anticitizenship and therefore better captures the hierarchical manner in which race, gender, class, and citizenship intersect.[89] As Evelyn Brooks Higginbotham argues, race in the United States is a "metalanguage" that "resounds over and above a plethora of conflicting voices."[90] As a consequence, dependent citizenship and anticitizenship intersect, but the former has been refracted through the prism of the latter. "Despite the predominance of patriarchal rule in American society," bell hooks stresses, "Racism took precedence over sexual alliances in both the white world's interaction with Native Americans and African Americans, just as racism overshadowed any bonding between black women and white women on the basis of sex."[91] Although white women were not full citizens, they were white citizens. White citizenship is gendered, but it is not exclusive to one gender.

This is not to say that white women's oppression was insignificant. Racial patriarchy in the *Herrenvolk* placed unique burdens on white women. Punishments for miscegenation were much harsher for them than for any other group, since they bore the burden of racial purity. The Naturalization Act of 1907, for example, actually stripped a white woman of her citizenship if she married an "alien ineligible for citizenship," such as a Chinese immigrant.[92] The effect of antimiscegenation law was to restrict access to white women's bodies to the husband alone while it generalized access to Black women's bodies to include the white owner and possibly other males. The sexual abuse of Black women was essentially decriminalized, while the sexuality of white women was rigorously policed. The result was different types of subjugation—white women were the private property of their husband or father while Black women were the public property of men—but subjugation nonetheless. Just as white men's complicity in the racial order provided privileges that ultimately undermined their ability to challenge class domination, white women enjoyed racial standing at the cost of weakening their position from which to confront gendered and class forms of power. The tragic price was paid for in political defeats, compromised victories, and a stunted political imagination.

The Limits of the White Imagination

The *Herrenvolk* democracy's pernicious effect on the white imagination was noted by Tocqueville. Slavery makes white men lazy, wasteful, hedonistic, and aggressive. It "enervates the powers of the mind and numbs human activity." It makes white men scorn labor, because labor is something slaves do, and it makes masters aristocratic in their temperament.[93] As others have noted, the white political imagination compels whites to try to evade exploitation rather than confront it, to scoff at manual labor as being beneath them, and to seek pleasure outside of their labor rather than through it.[94] It generates scorn among slaveholding women, who must remain "pure" (and silent) as their mates rape their slaves. The racial order, in other words, shapes the way whites see the world. In particular, it affects what Sheldon Wolin calls political vision. Political vision or imagination serves three functions. First, through exaggeration and extravagance it allows us to see things that might not otherwise be apparent. The state of nature, for example, allows Hobbes to show his readers the basic presuppositions on which a political order rests, even though he acknowledges such a condition never really existed. Second, political vision provides a view of society in its "corrected fullness" that renders complex political phenomena comprehensible. Marx could not know or explain every detail and subtlety of capitalism, but he abstracts important phenomena to draw a picture that generally explains how capitalism works and its effects on humanity. Finally, political vision is the means by which we criticize the values of society and transcend them by imagining a new society and better values.[95] It is this third function that has been so deformed by white citizenship.

The distortion of white citizens' political imagination is one of the central lessons of Du Bois's *Black Reconstruction*. Du Bois contends that slavery and anti-Black discrimination were defended by the white worker because "it fed his vanity because it associated him with the masters."[96] By tying their beliefs, actions, and aspirations to the planters, poor whites were able to look down on slaves and later the freedmen. But the cost, Du Bois argues, was the inability to see Black people as fellow workers exploited by the same system and abolition and Reconstruction as labor struggles that had profound implications for whites' freedom as well. Du Bois calls this tragedy of history the "American Blindspot." The labor movement, which logically should have been a force for greater democracy, refused to recognize that slavery and racial discrimination compromise the political power of the entire working class. It was determined to see Black labor as an enemy and so refused to include Black workers—free or slave—in its ranks. The consequence was that the American Blindspot drove a wedge between black and white labor such that "there probably are not today in the world [Du Bois is referring to the 1930s] two groups of workers with practically identi-cal interests who hate and fear each other so deeply and persistently and who are kept so far apart that neither sees anything of common interest."[97] This is not to say that class conflict between white workers and capitalists was nonexistent or that white workers did not engage in democratic struggles. Du Bois recognizes that poor whites had ambiva-lent feelings toward slavery and many even opposed it. Nevertheless, when they engaged in class struggles, it was often to defend or build upon their standing. Poor whites struggled against planters and indus-trialists, but the hard-won gains they extracted too often took the form of racial privileges.

The "American Assumption" (Du Bois's term for the American Dream) accompanies the Blindspot. The Assumption that any ordinary person can become wealthy through hard work and thrift, Du Bois asserts, gave birth to a shallow definition of freedom limited to economic opportunity, the absence of government interference in private ven-tures, and the right to elect public officials.[98] The Assumption presumes that the community is an obstacle to individual freedom rather than its conduit. So, for example, public assistance that does not appear to be "earned" by the individual becomes a "handout" indicating dependence rather than independence.[99] By downplaying the structural aspects of economic failure, it resists any form of wealth redistribution, whether it is forty acres and a mule, a welfare check, or the redistribution of oppor-tunities through affirmative action. By embracing the Assumption and its negative conception of freedom, Du Bois argues, the labor move-ment encouraged poor whites to strive to become capitalists rather than challenge capitalist exploitation. In turn, "capitalists not only accepted universal suffrage but early discovered that high wages in America made even higher profits possible; and that this high standard of living was itself a protection for capital in that it made the more intelligent and best paid of workers allies of capital and left its ultimate dictatorship undisturbed."[100]

The white citizen's political imagination tends toward a limited notion of equality as well as freedom. In the *Herrenvolk* democracy, rich and poor whites alike were hostile to the notion of "social equality" because it implied both radical economic transformation and equality with Black people. By definition, the *Herrenvolk* could not consider social equality as racial equality, but it also could not consider social equality as economic democracy because the redistribution of wealth would require breaking up the cross-class alliance between white labor and capital that guaranteed both accumulation and whites' privileges. Condemnation of one form of equality led to condemnation of the other, as white citizens saw "in every advance of Negroes a threat to their . . . prerogatives."[101] Thus, a fervent desire to prevent social equality, no less weak in the North than in the South, stamped the polity, driving whites into a collective madness. White parents in the antebellum North pulled their children out of school and swore they would rather their children grow up in ignorance than have them sit next to a Black pupil. Devout Christians denied themselves religious instruction rather than share a pew with a Black parishioner. Southern towns in the 1960s drained their community pools rather than integrate them. Postal workers crossed out the "Mr." and "Mrs." and other titles of respect on envelopes addressed to African Americans. White women refused to relieve themselves in factories lacking segregated washrooms. Labor radicals demanded "stomach equality," which would equalize wealth but leave white supremacy intact. In the antebellum era, many such actions and proclamations were rounded out with a public condemnation of the abolitionists for promoting social equality or "amalgamation." A mob sometimes ensued. It is no wonder civil rights workers were frequently called "communists" by segregationists. As symbols of social equality, both civil rights and communism stood as threats to the *Herrenvolk* democracy; both had to be purged from American citizenship.

The burden of racial standing undermines the very vision of the white citizenry, disfiguring its notions of democracy, freedom, equality, and what to expect from politics. If James Baldwin is correct that a more democratic society requires "the most radical and far-reaching changes in the American political and social structure," then he is surely correct that the white citizen is an obstacle to such changes, for "white

Americans are not simply unwilling to effect these changes; they are . . . unable even to envision them."[102] Whiteness, then, does not simply exclude some persons from enjoying democratic rights. It does much more: it produces a particular conception of democracy that not only denies active participation and social equality but cannot even imagine them.[103]

The tragic aspect of the white political imagination is not simply its refusal to consider the possibility of a society where all races can live together in peace and equality. As the dominant group, the white race is by definition aggressive and inegalitarian. (As Marx puts it, slavery made whites "filibusters by profession.") Further, the white political imagination is not able to recognize that the advancement of "whites" depends on the advancement of those who are not white and that so long as the dark world is degraded whites will be, too. The democratic problem is not the refusal to envision a society free of all exclusions based on race or other social distinctions. The tragic limitation of the white imagination is that a people imagined itself white at all.

CHAPTER 3

The Peculiar Dilemma of Whiteness

In 1860, an Alabama fire-eater named William L. Yancey proclaimed to a Northern audience, "Your fathers and my fathers built this government on two ideas: the first is that the white race is the citizen, and the master race, and the white man is the equal of every other white man. The second idea is that the Negro is the inferior race."[1] In 1962, Alabama governor George Wallace proclaimed at his inaugural address, "Segregation now! Segregation tomorrow! Segregation forever!" William Yancey presumably died with his politics intact. But thirty years after his famous speech, Wallace would say that segregation was "Wrong, wrong, wrong" and earnestly claim, "I'm not a racist at all."[2]

What happened to Wallace but not Yancey? Both believed that being white and being a citizen were indissolubly linked. Yet one eventually renounced the defense of white citizenship that his fellow Southerner took to his grave. What roiled the racial seas such that segregationists like Wallace would repudiate three hundred years of white supremacist ideology within a single generation? Is the miraculous transformation of George Wallace the gravestone of the white democracy?

Perhaps. Yet even as Governor Wallace repented for past sins, the average white family's income in Alabama was nearly double that of the average Black family's. A white Alabaman twenty-five years of age or older is twice as likely to possess a bachelor's degree as is a Black Alabaman. Black people made up twenty-six percent of the population of

Alabama in 1996 but received just four percent of the doctoral degrees awarded by the state's universities.[3] Yancey's posterity apparently still enjoys the wages of whiteness.

This chapter explores how whiteness has changed since the end of *Herrenvolk* democracy yet how it continues to pose a dilemma for democracy and democratic theory. With the passage of the Civil Rights Act of 1964 and the Voting Rights Act of 1965, whiteness lost its state sanction. Government policy today aims to ensure a "color-blind" society in which race has no negative bearing on the social, economic, or political status of individuals. Nevertheless, choose any indicator— infant mortality rates, prison sentences, traffic stops, college graduation rates, wealth accumulation, life expectancy, SAT scores, unemployment rates—and the result is the same: the persistence of white advantage and Black, Latino, and Native American disadvantage. Although no longer an officially recognized form of standing, whiteness, or the condition of racial privilege in a democratic polity, persists at every level of American society as a norm that sediments accrued white advantages onto the ordinary operations of modern society, making them seem like the "natural" result of individual effort.

Thus, the white democracy remains. The status value of white citizenship has been weakened since the days of Wallace's last stand at the schoolhouse door, yet the expectation and/or enjoyment of racial privilege persist. Unfortunately, democratic theory generally has not confronted the enduring problem of whiteness. This is because, I argue, much of it has relied too heavily on a politics of inclusion to resolve problems of race and difference. Such a politics understands racial discrimination as a form of exclusion from the public sphere to which the solution is inclusion. Whiteness is certainly an exclusionary power, but it is also a form of privilege. Lacking an analysis of racial privilege, the politics of inclusion cannot grasp the full scope of whiteness, which is not so much a problem of difference or exclusion as it is a problem of *alliance*. Furthermore, a politics of inclusion offers little in terms of increased participation in politics. In fact, I argue, the quest for inclusion often precludes greater participation, since the goal of that quest is to attain standing rather than empower. But expanded participation in itself cannot solve the whiteness problem either. In the hands of a white majority, a call for "community control of schools," for example, can easily become a tool to enforce segregation and perpetuate white domination.

The result is a peculiar dilemma. In a white-controlled polity, a strategy of inclusion may undermine explicit racial discrimination but does little to undermine whiteness as a norm. Nor does it increase participation. Yet simply expanding participation is also insufficient because in a racial polity, the quest for greater participation may actually serve to strengthen the tyranny of the dominant race. The key to resolving this dilemma between participation and inclusion, I argue, is through the *dissolution of whiteness* as a significant social-political category. Dissolving or abolishing whiteness not only includes the excluded, it undermines the tyranny of the white majority and expands democratic participation.

I hasten to add that abolishing whiteness is not the same as abolishing race itself. Although dissolving the category "white" implies dissolving its antithesis "not-white" as well, it does not require abolishing Black, Chicano/a, Indian, or other such identities, since they have a cultural and social content independent of their membership in a subordinate not-white category. But since the white category has little content independent of its position of privilege, it could conceivably disappear as a viable identity.

My argument begins by using recent work in the field of critical race theory to explain how whiteness has shifted from a form of standing to a norm after the civil rights movement. I then examine the politics of inclusion through an analysis of theories of difference. I argue that William Connolly's "ethos of pluralization" has the potential to dissolve whiteness but his own application of it ends up sustaining white identity, in part because it remains tethered to the politics of inclusion. I then turn to Iris Marion Young's *Justice and the Politics of Difference*. Young overcomes the limits of inclusion by smartly redefining inclusion from an end in itself to a means toward a participatory politics. The missing ingredient to her analysis is a critique of privilege that could connect her argument for participation to the problem of whiteness. This connection is made by Lani Guinier in her work on the tyranny of the majority. Guinier shows that the problem with white tyranny in the electoral process is not so much that it excludes African Americans as it prevents their participation. Her work is significant because it links the dissolution of whiteness to the expansion of participation in the public sphere. In so doing, it overcomes the participation-inclusion dilemma and suggests that attempts to abolish whiteness not only fight racial discrimination, they potentially flow over the containers of liberal democracy.

The Death of *Herrenvolk* Democracy

As Anthony Marx shows, states do or do not pursue policies of racial oppression depending on whether such policies efficiently diminish conflict between classes and within the dominant class. The United States, he argues, opted for policies that produced the white citizen because the cross-class alliance created stability. "To hold together the nation-state, preserving stability needed for growth, whites were unified across class by race. . . . Economic interests were subordinated to white racial unity, with this class compromise made explicit and enforced by state policy varying in response to ongoing class tensions."[4]

White citizenship persisted through the Civil War. It was briefly threatened by Reconstruction but quickly resumed with new strength, guaranteed by segregation laws in the South and extralegal means of exclusion, intimidation, and terror throughout the nation, all tacitly sanctioned by the federal government. Segregation reestablished familiar patterns of white–Black relations while the South slowly industrialized, urbanized, and transitioned from slave labor to sharecropping to wage labor. In the Southwest, segregation imposed white domination on a region in which the racial order was typically more fluid than in the South and North and in which Mexican Americans were technically full citizens according to federal law before the Civil War.[5] In this period, commercial farmers and businessmen in primary industries like mining insisted on tight control over the subordinate population and a strong state role in guaranteeing a dependable supply of productive yet docile labor. On the other hand, white workers, particularly unskilled or semiskilled ones, demanded that the state reserve certain areas of employment for them. These demands sometimes conflicted with each other, but they provided a basis for cross-class unity as well. As Stanley Greenberg argues, despite conflicts over the details of racial domination under segregation, "Each [class sector] calls on the state to take control of the subordinate worker, to draw racial lines somewhere in the society and economy."[6] For its part, the state enjoys a fair degree of autonomy as it balances the competing interests within and between classes. Under segregation no less than during slavery, citizenship as standing was the glue that held the complex alliance between the state, white workers, and various sectors of capital together. As John Cell notes, segregation was not a throwback to another era nor did it pander to the meanest elements of the South. It was the child of economic development and modern politicking.

> Mystifying, rationalizing, and legitimizing a particular configuration of caste and class, [segregation] enabled white supremacy to survive in an increasingly threatening, hostile world. . . . Far from being the crude, irrational prejudice of ignorant "rednecks," segregation must be recognized as one of the most successful political ideologies of the past century. It was, indeed, the highest stage of white supremacy.[7]

Nevertheless, segregation was a vulgar system on the ground. It meant that the poorest, lowest, meanest white person was held in higher esteem than even the most sophisticated, prestigious, and wealthy Black person. "The Jim Crow laws put the authority of the state or city in the voice of the street-car conductor, the railway brakeman, the bus driver, the theater usher, and also into the voice of the hoodlum of the public parks and playgrounds," writes C. Vann Woodward. "They gave free rein and the majesty of the law to mass aggressions that might otherwise have been curbed, blunted, or deflected."[8]

Ironically, the very success of Jim Crow paved the way for its collapse, as the same impulse for stability that led the state to enforce racial oppression led it to give in to the demands of the civil rights movement. Segregation reduced intrawhite conflict, which enabled the industrialization and urbanization of the South and Southwest. The mechanization of agriculture, the proletarianization of the countryside, resistance among commercial farmers and businessmen to two-tiered wage scales, and the diminishing role of organized labor relaxed demands for a tightly controlled, bound labor force. These developments lessened the importance of a bipolar racial order in securing social stability. Further, the New Deal and World War II deepened the federal government's presence in the South. Once entrenched, it was in a position to intervene on behalf of the civil rights movement.

But it did not intervene at the behest of capital. Contrary to the conceit of economic liberalism, racial hierarchy does not automatically dissolve in the magic elixir of markets. Abstract economic principles state that social distinctions should be irrelevant in the marketplace. All that matters is buying low and selling high. Practicing "pure" market logic prior to the civil rights era, however, would have been economic suicide for many a merchant. White diners would not patronize a restaurant that served Black people; unions would strike a business that hired or promoted Black labor; white home buyers would not purchase homes in neighborhoods where Black families lived. Any daring entrepreneur who followed the abstract logic of the green rather than the *Herrenvolk* world of white and not-white would be out of business very shortly. This is because capitalism is not inherently antagonistic to white supremacy. As long as the state ensures the social stability necessary for accumulation, capitalists tend to accommodate themselves to the existing political regime, whether it be constitutional monarchical, welfare liberal, social democratic, dictatorial, fascist, or *Herrenvolk*. As Greenberg writes, "The racial order makes demands on industry no more unpalatable or burdensome than the impositions of socialist and fascist governments—indeed, probably less. Businessmen can live with separate toilets and promotion lines, as they learned to live with pension programs and price regulations."[9] It is disorder from below, not buying and selling from above, that undermines a racial order. Only when Southern businesses faced increasing pressure from civil rights protesters, such as during the Birmingham campaign of 1963, did businessmen urge local governments to end segregation.[10] Clearly, desegregation was a *political* development; it did not flow from the logic of economics. Jim Crow reached a point at which it was unable to ensure social stability at a reasonable cost. When the *Herrenvolk* democracy produced disorder rather than order, business and political elites suddenly had a dream.

The essential principle of *Herrenvolk* democracy—democracy for whites, tyranny for everyone else—was finally overthrown by the civil rights movement. With the passage of civil and voting rights legislation in 1964 and 1965, the standing of the white citizen was officially abolished and the state became committed to protecting the rights of all rather than the privileges of the majority.[11] No longer does the state ensure that the lowest white is socially superior to the most esteemed not-white. Instead, the essential principle of the new color-blind democracy is the formal political equality of all citizens, achieved through the removal of official racial barriers.[12]

The color-blind democracy represents a victory by the civil rights movement over the *Herrenvolk* regime, but it did not abolish the cross-class alliance. Instead, whiteness has metamorphosed into less visible but no less real forms. White privilege can be overt and explicit, as in the days of "whites only" facilities, or it may consist of covert and tacit advantages that whites enjoy with or without conscious acknowledgment, such as redlined neighborhoods or exemption from criminal profiling. This latter form dominates the post–civil rights era. Contemporary white privilege is like an "invisible weightless knapsack" of unearned advantages that whites draw on in their daily lives to improve or maintain their social position, even as they hold to the ideals of political equality and equal opportunity.[13] The simultaneous sense of equality and privilege that marks whiteness persists as one of today's most formidable challenges to a more democratic society. The civil rights movement, then, stands not as a bookend of white privilege but as a watershed between the two eras of the white democracy, *Herrenvolk* and color-blind, or the eras of standing and normalization.[14]

From Standing to Normalization

Whiteness persists because the color-blind democracy presupposes racial distinctions rather than overcomes them. It does so in a fashion similar to the way in which private property is presupposed by the state even after it is "emancipated" from it. As Karl Marx argues, when property is abolished in the public sphere by eliminating the property require-ment for suffrage, private property itself is not abolished. Instead, it thrives as the ruling principle of the private realm. When the state abolishes distinctions of property, birth, education, and occupation by granting all adult males equal political rights, it frees private interests to act unfettered. Social distinctions of property, education, and occupa-tion continue to exist but they are now "private" matters that lie outside the jurisdiction of the political realm, immune from public accounta-bility. "Far from abolishing these real distinctions, the state only exists on the presupposition of their existence; it feels itself to be a political state and asserts its universality only in opposition to these elements of its being."[15]

The relationship between race and the state is similar. Once "emancipated" from the state, race is cast into the private realm. But as with private property, it does not disappear. Instead, the color-blind democracy redefines race from a relationship of superiority and inferi-ority to a politically neutral category. An individual's race now appears as a "natural" attribute that should have no bearing on one's political or economic life. Rather than eliminating race, the color-blind state makes it *prepolitical*: it understands races as formed prior to the public sphere through essentially "private" or natural means such as biology, ancestry, culture, or even personal choice. The political emancipation of race is, of course, a big step forward. Nevertheless, transforming race into a prepolitical category does not abolish its political influence. Just as the emancipation of property withdraws inequalities of wealth from public deliberation, the emancipation of race removes the cross-class alliance from public scrutiny.

The prepoliticization of race has three important consequences. First, race remains publicly significant even as it becomes a private matter, for the test of a successful color-blind democracy is how well racial diversity is accommodated. The peaceful coexistence of various racial identities is a sign of a stable social order, while the absence of diversity indicates the potential for instability. Obligations of diversity justify extensive state regulation. Decisions that were once the ultimate prerogative of the private individual—whom to hire, whom to allow to dine in your restaurant, to whom to sell your home, whom to allow in your social club—are now publicly regulated. Numerous relationships— student and teacher, school and neighborhood, neighbor and neighbor, owner and customer, employer and employee, cop and suspect, real estate agent and buyer and seller—are subjected to increased state scrutiny, albeit for color-blind purposes. Just as Foucault maintains that sex was not repressed in nineteenth-century Europe but proliferated through various techniques and deployments, race is reproduced through the various practices of the color-blind democracy.[16] Second, a prepolitical conception of race redefines racial domination from white supremacy to abstract discrimination. Ignoring the history of the *Herrenvolk*, the state assumes that all prejudice and discrimination are equally noxious. Antiwhite attitudes are as significant as anti-Black prejudice. "Racist" no longer describes a social structure but an individual's character. The problem is no longer segregation but "hate," not systematic inequality but "intolerance," not privilege but "extremism." Racism, as Lewis Gordon writes, becomes an "equal-opportunity affair."[17] Finally, in regulating nondiscrimination and diversity, the color-blind state redefines whiteness from a privileged identity to a politically neutral racial category. The white race becomes simply one race among others and the historical effects of three hundred years of systematic white privilege are rendered politically invisible.

Thus, the transformation of race into a prepolitical category does not eliminate the significance of whiteness so much as it *normalizes* it.

Rather than a form of public standing, whiteness in the color-blind state functions as a norm in which racial privilege is sedimented into the background of social life as the "natural outcome" of ordinary practices and individual choices, making it difficult to discern any systematic explanation for the advantages whites continue to enjoy after the civil rights movement. The state's official position of color blindness and its interest in regulating diversity mask the fact that the "normal individual" is still the white individual and that the freedom of the white individual remains the standard against which social progress is judged.[18]

Whiteness as norm functions in at least two ways. As Cheryl Harris argues, it is a property interest that forms the background against which legal disputes, rights claims, and equal opportunities are framed, defined, and adjudicated.[19] It is a form of property because it shares the same premise as property: the right to exclude. In the *Herrenvolk* era, whiteness was literally a property interest that stood for the expectation of favored status, the protection of legal claims on Native or Mexican land, and the prospect of owning another human being. "Whiteness was the characteristic, the attribute, the property of free human beings."[20] The color-blind state changed the form of whiteness, Harris acknowledges, but kept its exclusive character intact. While courts no longer protect explicit forms of discrimination, they still refuse to eliminate inequalities of resources that whites have built up over time, such as the $29,000 in median assets possessed by white families in 1994 compared to the $2,000 in median assets for Black families.[21] The color-blind democracy thus provides for formal political equality but not substantive equality or the redistribution of resources to rectify white advantage. "Whiteness as property has taken on more subtle forms" since the civil rights movement, "But [it] retains its core characteristic—the legal legitimation of expectations of power and control that enshrine the status quo as a neutral baseline, while masking the maintenance of white privilege and domination."[22]

Whiteness also acts as a filter that provides whites an edge in an "equal opportunity" society.[23] In the *Herrenvolk* era, standing was akin to aristocratic privilege. Once achieved, it was inheritable, stable, and enduring. But as white standing was swept away by the civil rights move-ment, "the possibility of aristocratization" that white privilege offered disappeared as social advancement became subject to the competitive rules of the market rather than inhering partially in racial privilege. In the absence of racial standing, access to status shifts to institutions of merit such as the university and the job market. Yet as Immanuel Wallerstein argues, in a world with too many qualified people seeking too few status-holding positions, "merit," "desert," and "qualified" become political terms. With the talent pool too large and too deep, it has to be skimmed somehow, essentially through means that seem arbi-trary and unfair to its victims. In such a context, whiteness operates as a filter that reduces the possibility that whites or their children will fall victim to the "arbitrary triage" that pares the pool of status seekers that merit can trim by only so much. Rational whites act to secure what-ever advantages they can by opposing those policies that undermine white advantage, such as affirmative action and school desegregation, although such struggles are usually carried out on the grounds of "in-dividual rights" or "community control" rather than explicit appeals to white supremacy.

Whiteness is reproduced through these processes of normalization even as the color-blind democracy outlaws racial discrimination. White advantage is deposited into the social structure through means as osten-sibly race neutral as the generational transfer of wealth, criminal profil-ing, college entrance exams, and tracking in schools. Whiteness is both an *interest in* and an *expectation of* favored treatment within a color-blind society. This is the cognate of the dual sense of equality and supremacy that characterized white identity in the *Herrenvolk* era. The result is a racial order in which, as Lawrie Balfour writes, "the persistence of hier-archy is simultaneously condemned and taken for granted."[24]

For those who are not white, the normalization of white privilege often feels like the same emperor in new clothes, as whites continue to enjoy advantages in nearly every aspect of social life. Meanwhile, persons of color continue to suffer *Herrenvolk*-era humiliations like racial profiling as well as persistent fits of white terror inflicted by racial "extremists." For whites, on the other hand, normalization is standing's poor cousin. In the *Herrenvolk* democracy, standing was an individualizing form of power. Its functioning required that every individual white person enjoy standing over every not-white person. Just a few exceptions threatened the entire system. By granting standing to whites collectively, the *Herrenvolk* granted status to each white individually. The color-blind democracy, however, by definition requires that some not-whites enjoy greater status than some whites, otherwise the "color-blind" state would still be a *Herrenvolk* system. Whiteness thus tends to shift from an individualizing to an aggregate form of power. Guaranteed standing is replaced by statistical advantages. Poverty, violence, inferior schooling, poor health, high incarceration and unemployment rates, lack of assets, and substandard housing continue to disproportionately affect those who are not-white, while whites continue to disproportionately escape them. But because they are probabilities, not guarantees, the aggregated advantages of normalized whiteness hardly seem like privileges. It means almost nothing to a particular white man to know that, on average, white males live almost ten years longer than Black males. The statistical likelihood that a white teenager will score two hundred points higher on her SAT than a Black teen is no guarantee that the white teen will actually perform at that level, much less get into the school of her choice. Such statistics, however telling they are of the continuing wages of whiteness, are small comfort to a world used to more.

In this way, normalization contains within it the seeds of future instability. The result could be a reactionary effort to reestablish *Herrenvolk* forms of white privilege; evidence of this possibility is easily perceptible today.[25] Yet instability also presents an opportunity to expand democracy if whites can be convinced that short-term racial privileges are not worth their long-term costs. Overcoming the material, public, and psychological wages of whiteness, then, is not only crucial to eliminating the racial order; it is a vital component of efforts to expand democratic participation. Attempts by theorists to connect the struggle against racial hierarchy to a radical democratic politics, however, have been thwarted by a peculiar dilemma.

The Participation-Inclusion Dilemma

To consider the challenge whiteness poses for democratic theory, we must return to the work of Judith Shklar. *American Citizenship* stands as one of the strongest challenges to political theories that argue, in one way or another, for more participation by ordinary people in those affairs that affect their daily life.[26] Shklar argues that the primary value of American citizenship is the social status it confers, not the political power it bestows. Theories of democratic participation seek an ideal form of political activity that emulates the ancient Greek polis, but the disenfranchised in American history have not struggled for participation but standing.

> The concept of the Aristotelian citizen as ruler has not really had much bearing on Americans. . . . [Disenfranchised Americans] have asked for something quite different, that citizenship be equally distributed, so that their standing might also be recognized and their interests be defended and promoted. The call for a classical participatory democracy may, therefore, be far from democratic, because it does not correspond to the aspirations of most Americans now and has never done so in the past.[27]

Theorists and activists of democratic participation often have to learn this lesson the hard way, when they discover that the people for whom they are fighting to empower often do not seem interested in greater participation.

The exclusive character of citizenship, rooted in the antithetical relationship between the citizen and the slave, represents the basic challenge of American democracy for Shklar. The democratic task is not to implement far-flung models of strong democracy but to achieve the full inclusion of excluded groups in order to grant all Americans equal standing as independent citizen-earners. The minimum requirements for standing, she argues, are the right to vote and the right to a job. What one does with the vote—or even whether one uses it—is relatively unimportant; what counts is the status that comes from possessing it.

Likewise, one's job need not be fulfilling or enjoyable, only recognized as essential to a sense of belonging.[28]

Shklar's argument poses a dilemma between inclusion and participation. A politics of inclusion holds that the central problem of modern democracy is the numerous systems of exclusion that accompany it and that the principal means toward a more democratic society is the full inclusion of excluded populations into the polity. The "quest for inclusion," Shklar argues, is to grant equal standing to all. Yet the problem with inclusion, as she readily confesses, is that it tends to produce a passive form of citizenship that is disinclined toward expanded participation because its objective is the *possession* of status rather than the *exercise* of one's power in public affairs. On the other hand, a politics of participation assumes that substantive citizen participation in deliberation and decision making is the benchmark of a democratic society. According to Shklar, arguments for participation do not speak to the real political desires of Americans, who seek standing. But the problem runs deeper than that. Theories of democratic participation rarely confront the problem of racial standing. In a racial polity, expanding participation strengthens the grip of the white majority, since whites set the agenda and determine who participates and how. The most participatory institution of the *Herrenvolk* democracy, after all, was the white riot. By ignoring the problem of whiteness, a strategy for participation may contribute to the tyranny of the white majority.

Of course, inclusion and participation are not necessarily contradictory. Inclusion is a prerequisite for democratic participation—one cannot be active in a club unless one has been let into it—and the purpose of inclusion is often to empower the formerly excluded to act in the public sphere. The dilemma between them is a historical consequence of racialized citizenship in the United States, not an inherent contradiction. Nevertheless, the dilemma is impressive. The quest for inclusion expands the membership of the polity but discourages greater participation in it because it reproduces citizenship as standing. The quest for participation promises more democracy yet it does not confront the problem of racial standing; thus, it may end up tightening the tyrannical grip of the white majority. As presently constructed, neither holds out much hope for a more democratic society. How, in a polity in which whiteness and democracy have been inextricably connected, can greater participation be achieved without inviting a lynch mob?

This dilemma is usually posed as a tension between political participation and individual rights: Can a participatory democracy protect an individual's rights against a majority tyranny?[29] This version, however, incorrectly assumes that rights are an effective deterrent against white tyranny. Yet the Bill of Rights existed alongside slavery and lynch law, so this is not the best way to understand the dilemma. This is most evident when inclusion and participation are each understood as individual strategies for a more democratic society. A strategy of inclusion seeks the full admission of all persons into the polity, while a strategy of participation aims to expand participation within the polity. The former tends to emphasize the need to guarantee political equality and equal opportunity in the face of discrimination, while the latter tends to emphasize the need to expand deliberation and decision making by ordinary persons. These strategies should be complementary, but the history of white supremacy in the United States places them at cross-purposes.

The strategy of inclusion fails to resolve the dilemma for two reasons. First, it may eliminate white standing but it does not abolish whiteness as norm. For example, Shklar recognizes that racial inequality persists even after the Civil Rights and Voting Rights Acts, but her solution for it—a state-guaranteed job for everyone—does not necessarily abolish white privilege. Such a guarantee would no doubt aid many people of color, perhaps a disproportionate number of them compared to whites, but the right to a job or even a living wage does not necessarily undermine whites' privileged access to the best jobs, the highest salaries, and the most lucrative contracts. Nor do such measures necessarily undermine "first hired, last fired" policies, glass floors, or wealth imbalances that favor whites. The second problem is that inclusion is not a strategy for greater participation. The absence of substantive participation by ordinary citizens in the affairs that affect them is not a problem for Shklar's "dystopic liberalism," but it is for any theory that seeks to stretch the limits of liberal democracy.[30]

A strategy to *dissolve* or *abolish* the cross-class alliance that constitutes whiteness addresses both of these problems. Whiteness is the dominant category in the racial order. Abolishing the category eliminates the social significance of white identity and hence "abolishes" the identity itself. Practically speaking, an abolitionist strategy has two prongs. It seeks to eliminate overt and normalized systems of white privilege, such as redlining, racial profiling, and tracking in schools, and supports any policy or program, such as affirmative action and reparations, that undermines white advantage. It calls attention to and seeks to redress any outcome (such as racially skewed mortgage rejection, unemployment, and life expectancy rates) in which racial privilege is evident yet is explained away as the "natural outcome" of markets or the aggregation of individual choices. The second prong opposes any attempt to reconstitute whiteness in the post–civil rights era. Efforts to resuscitate a "progressive" or "antiracist" white identity have gained currency in the education field and elsewhere, but as I argue in the next chapter, this noble cause faces historical forces too stiff to overcome. White identity in the United States has always reflected an interest in and an expectation of favored treatment. This burden of historical privilege presents an almost insuperable obstacle to transforming "white" into a radically democratic identity. In the absence of a usable past, efforts to reinvent whiteness tempt to raise demons that should be exorcised instead.

An abolitionist strategy seeks to break up the cross-class alliance in order to eliminate explicit and sedimented forms of white privilege. Yet it is also a strategy for greater democracy. Abolishing the cross-class alliance creates opportunities to forge new social relations with radical democratic potential. Replacing white unity with class unity, for example, would go a long way toward challenging inequalities of wealth that democratic theorists have long recognized as a significant obstacle to a more democratic society. Abolition also opens up opportunities to expand democratic participation. Whiteness inhibits attempts to expand democracy because the coexistence of racial privilege and democracy gives whites an interest in preserving the former at the expense of the latter. Dissolving whiteness eliminates this conflict of interest and thus holds potential to expand participation.

Of course, a just distribution of wealth and greater democratic participation do not follow automatically from the dissolution of whiteness; they are only possibilities. Further, I readily acknowledge that the notion of abolishing white identity is difficult to imagine. Nevertheless, it is not without historical and philosophical precedent. The abolition of feudalism abolished lord and serf. The abolition of slavery abolished master and slave. The abolition of capitalism promises to do away with bourgeois and proletarian. In much the same way, the dissolution of whiteness suggests the abolition of the categories "white" and "not-white" themselves. As the dissolution of the aristocracy paved the way for representative government and the abolition of slavery inaugurated Radical Reconstruction, the dissolution of whiteness could potentially expand the boundaries of contemporary democracy.

Abolishing whiteness is not the same as abolishing race. "White" and "not-white" are antithetical categories; abolishing one implies the abolition of the other. Identities such as Black or indigenous, however, refer to a cultural identity as well as a subordinate (not-white) status in the present racial hierarchy. Eliminating the subordination of these identities does not necessarily imply eliminating their cultural content. But whiteness, as I argue in the next chapter, possesses little cultural content independent of its position of privilege, meaning it could potentially disappear as a socially significant identity even if other racial identities persist.

The politics of inclusion dominates democratic theory's approach to race despite its inability to eliminate normalized whiteness or to expand democratic participation. Meanwhile, the historical dilemma between inclusion and participation is rarely considered. Some consider racism to be symptomatic of broader problems.[31] Others scarcely mention it.[32] Still others assume that inclusion and participation are symbiotic:

the politics of inclusion are slowly, if unevenly, removing discrimination from American society, which in turn encourages participation, which further reduces discrimination.[33] An increasingly common response is to define racial discrimination as a problem of difference. According to this perspective, the plurality of identities—ethnic, national, racial, cultural, gendered, religious—is both the central problem and grand opportunity of contemporary politics. Modern society is plural and diverse, yet it rests on a series of exclusions. The philosophical-political challenge of theories of difference is to construct a politics that understands difference as an asset to democracy rather than a threat.[34] Theories of difference are potentially useful in cutting through the participation-inclusion dilemma because they tend to be more attuned to the limits of inclusion. Nevertheless, they can still be tripped up by the problem of whiteness and the dilemma it creates. An example of this lies in one of the most important texts on the politics of difference, William Connolly's *The Ethos of Pluralization*.

Difference and the Politics of Inclusion

The Ethos of Pluralization begins as a conversation with pluralism. Connolly acknowledges that conventional pluralism has its strengths: it is premised on the irreducible diversity of the social sphere and often encourages the development of difference, especially in situations where cultural consensus is impossible. Nevertheless, conventional pluralism assumes that diverse identities, interests, and cultures orbit around a "universal" ideal, like reason, civic identity, or rational self-interest, and it tends to assume that individuals' identities are coherent and fully formed prior to their entrance into the public sphere rather than constructed in the public sphere itself. As such, conventional pluralism treats identities as largely static and unchanging. The assumption of stable identity gives rise to the construction of a "normal individual" against which "abnormal" identities are measured. This is the "unconscious conservatism" at the center of the conventional pluralist imagination: new additions to the public sphere must conform to the norm, else they are considered a potential threat to social stability.[35]

Connolly characterizes conventional pluralism as "arboreal." Arboreal pluralism assumes a treelike conception of difference: multiple and diverse branches jut out everywhere but are connected to a common trunk of values. Arboreal pluralism's fear is that diversity can be taken too far: the overproliferation of identities can fragment the public sphere like too many heavy branches, burdening the trunk to the point where it splits. This fear is unnecessary, Connolly argues. It reflects the limits of the arboreal imagination rather than the amount of diversity a society can actually accommodate. He proposes a "rhizomatic pluralism" to overcome the limits of conventional pluralism. A rhizome is a plant that has no central trunk or stem but instead consists of a network of roots below and shoots above that spread throughout the environment, appearing in a variety of locations and connected only through the network itself. A rhizomatic pluralism rejects the notion that there can be too much diversity. A public sphere will fragment under the stress of difference only if its identities declare themselves normal or truthful and exclude other identities as abnormal, false, or deviant. "To pluralize is not to fragmentize," he writes. "To dogmatize is to fragmentize."[36] A rhizomatic pluralism avoids this sort of fundamentalism by embracing *pluralization*, which not only encourages the proliferation of identities but recognizes that changes in relations among identities alter identities themselves. Pluralization rests upon an "ethos of critical responsiveness" that "opens up cultural space through which new possibilities of being might be enacted" and respects the plural and "multifarious ways of being."[37] The democratic task, Connolly asserts, is to pluralize the political realm by "[striving] to cultivate an ethos of critical responsiveness to political movements that challenge the self-confidence and congealed judgments of dominant constituencies."[38]

The ethos of pluralization is an important revision of pluralism. Connolly convincingly argues that it is fundamentalism, not diversity, that threatens social stability. He points to normalization as a central problem for expanding democracy. Further, while conventional pluralism understands diversity as the presence of multiple but fixed, already-formed identities in the public sphere, pluralization assumes that such identities are "self-revisionary." That is, the emergence of a new identity or changes in an existing one inevitably modify other identities, since they are constructed and reconstructed through relations of difference. For example, a rhizomatic pluralism would not just include oppressed races in the public sphere on an equal footing with whites; it would reconfigure "Angloid nationality" itself by compelling it to shed its presumptions of superiority and normalcy.

> The long term result of such a series of shifts [in the self-recognition of a dominant constituency] in several domains would be the historical transition of America *from a majority nation presiding over numerous minorities in a democratic state to a democratic state of multiple minorities contending and collaborating with a general ethos of forbearance and critical responsiveness.*[39]

The ethos of pluralization would not just welcome other peoples into a polity once reserved exclusively for whites. It would alter white identity. "The politics of enactment . . . presses hegemonic identities, which are always dependent upon the very differences they define, to translate this experience of disturbance into a will to modify *themselves* so that they no longer remain exactly what they were."[40]

The terms Connolly uses to describe changes in dominant identities, such as "modify," "self-revise," "reconfigure," and "transition," are not wholly equivalent to terms such as "abolition" and "dissolution." Nevertheless, his claim that the entrance of new identities in the social sphere creates "new possibilities of being" for existing identities suggests a compatibility between rhizomatic pluralism and a strategy of abolition. "Critical responsiveness to the injuries of Otherness," he writes, "implies a comparative denaturalization and reconfiguration of hegemonic identities whose character depended on these specifications of difference."[41] If a dominant identity possesses little meaning outside of a system of subordination, as in the case of whiteness, its "denaturalization and reconfiguration" could easily be read to imply its dissolution. After all, "white" is not so much a signifier for a pinkish people of predominantly European ancestry as it is for a system of power that constructs relations of subordination and privilege. Dismantling these relations leaves white identity as little more than an empty signifier that is barely useful to describe a skin color. The ethos of pluralization points in the direction of white abolition, since it holds that a politics of racial difference implies the erosion of white dominance—and thus white identity itself.

Notwithstanding this compatibility, however, Connolly's argument arrives at political conclusions that, if followed, would solidify whiteness rather than dissolve it. A rhizomatic pluralism, he maintains, would modify "Angloid identity" and compel it to shed its presumptions of supremacy and normality. Given this, the political task would seem to be to encourage those activities that confront and undermine such presumptions. Yet Connolly rejects a direct approach to confronting whiteness. He argues that the issues addressed by welfare liberals in the post–civil rights era—women's rights, racism, ecology, discrimination—ignore the hardships faced by the white working class, pushing it into the open arms of the right. "The politics of welfare liberalism from the late sixties onward betrayed the white working class, driving a section of it toward a fundamentalism of gender, self, race, and nation."[42] He suggests that the "fundamentalisms" of the white working class could be "renegotiated" by retooling programs currently aimed at white women and people of color, such as affirmative action, so that they incorporate a class or income dimension. This would "go a long way toward easing the sense of insult and discrimination among Reagan Democrats, for their children . . . would no longer be singled out as the only constituency that deserves to be stuck in the crumby jobs now available to it."[43]

This indirect approach of fighting racial discrimination by incorporating a class dimension into race-specific programs is increasingly popular in left-liberal circles. Ruy Teixeira and Joel Rogers, for example, argue that although the white working class comprises about fifty-five percent of the electorate, its needs have long been ignored by the political system. The party that can win over this "forgotten majority" will dominate the political landscape well into the twenty-first century. Doing so will require advocating a stronger government that can improve basic aspects of workers' lives, from health insurance to education to retirement to a healthy balance between work and family life. The Democrats are ideologically better situated to carry out such a program than the Republicans, but to do so Democrats will have to shift their focus from the condition of gays, women, and minorities toward advocating "universal" programs that help all of the working class. Thus, they should replace programs such as affirmative action and busing with class-based affirmative action and "class-based integration" programs.[44]

This argument is ironic because the American welfare state historically did not ignore the white working class but catered to its interests. The Social Security Act excluded farmworkers and domestics (most of whom were Black) from receiving benefits. The Federal Housing Agency promoted residential segregation and channeled money toward white suburbs. The Environmental Protection Agency located garbage dumps and toxic waste sites away from white neighborhoods, while the federal highway system destroyed housing in Black neighborhoods to connect white suburban commuters to their downtown jobs. All of these welfare liberal programs were premised on the consolidation of the "possessive investment in whiteness."[45] Given this, the white working class's alienation from progressive politics is more likely due to its resistance to programs that erode its privileged standing than welfare liberals' supposed overemphasis on oppressed groups. Confronting whites' expectations of favored status is key to expanding democracy. "Inclusive" or class-based programs, however, downplay whites' historical privileges. In so doing, they appease white expectations rather than challenge them.

This is not to say that class-based programs would not help African Americans and other people of color. They likely would, and they might even distribute benefits to people of color disproportionately compared to whites, as Teixeira and Rogers contend. Nevertheless, the success of such programs still depends on how well they comport with what Derrick Bell calls the "white self-interest principle": whites will support social and political programs aimed at African Americans (directly or indirectly) only if whites stand to benefit from them as well. This leaves such programs politically vulnerable should their support wane. This vulnerability signifies the continuing power of whiteness.[46]

An ethos of pluralization is equipped to avoid these pitfalls. It undermines the power of dominant identities by challenging them to not merely recognize new identity claims but to transform themselves in the process. Unfortunately, Connolly does not follow through on the implications of his argument as it relates to white identity.[47] Pursuing class-based programs rather than ones that directly undermine white advantage may appear to be more inclusive and less divisive, but due to the historical dilemma between participation and inclusion in a white-dominated polity, they can unintentionally perpetuate white normalization instead. What is needed is a politics of difference that directly challenges whiteness and links this challenge to a participatory politics. The basis of such a politics lies in the work of Iris Marion Young and Lani Guinier.

Participation and the Politics of Difference

Young's argument for participation emerges out of her critique of what she terms the distributive paradigm of justice, which understands justice as the fair and ethical distribution of a society's benefits, burdens, and resources. Young's main criticism of the paradigm is that its focus on distribution tends to conceive of citizens as passive consumers of goods. This tends to depoliticize social life because the emphasis on distribution takes precedence over the organization of production and decision-making processes.[48]

Young proposes a more active conception of justice, a politics of difference, that improves on the distributive paradigm by including deliberation and decision making as elements of justice as well as distribution. The primary concern of justice, Young argues, should be to confront domination ("the institutional constraint on self-determination") and oppression ("the institutional constraint on self-development").[49] Domination and oppression, she argues, are group conditions. Similar to Connolly's conception of identity, her concept of social groups is as "expressions of social relations."[50] Individuals do not just constitute groups;

groups constitute individuals. Justice, then, is the elimination of the oppression and domination of social groups through self-determination and the ability to develop one's capacities. It is "the institutionalized conditions that make it possible for all to learn and use satisfying skills in socially recognized settings, to participate in decisionmaking, and to express their feelings, experience, and perspective on social life in contexts where others can listen."[51]

The strength of Young's argument is twofold. First, it emphasizes participation as a key democratic ideal in addition to political and social equality. Redistributing wealth is less an end than a prerequisite for the ability to participate democratically in the processes and institutions of collective life.

> Justice equally requires . . . participation in public discussion and processes of democratic decisionmaking. All persons should have the right and opportunity to participate in the deliberation and decisionmaking of the institutions to which their actions contribute or which directly affect their actions. . . . Democracy is both an element and a condition of social justice.[52]

Second, it challenges Shklar's conception of citizenship as standing, not by merely expressing a preference for participation over standing but by connecting the elimination of oppression to the practice of participation. Shklar's remedy for the exclusion of African Americans and others is to include them in the polity. Young's remedy is not just their inclusion but also their participation, which is necessary for a group's self-determination and the development of an individual's capacities.

Young's concept of a social group has been one of the most controversial parts of her argument. Liberals such as Ronald Beiner charge that it promotes the "ghettoization" of identities and undermines the significance of the state. Postmodernists such as Chantal Mouffe criticize it as essentialist and unable to account for the construction of new identities. Critical theorists such as Nancy Fraser argue that the concept is modeled too closely on the ethnic group and as a result gender, class, race, and sexuality do not fit into it well.[53] Young's account of the social group is problematic, particularly for the reasons pointed out by Mouffe and Fraser. The debate as it stands so far, however, overlooks the real limitation of the concept: it does not consider *privilege* as a problem of justice in addition to oppression and domination. As a result, like Connolly, Young does not consider that a politics of difference might imply the dissolution of privileged social groups. A critique of privilege is implied in her analysis, since the oppression of one group is almost always done for the advantage of another. An explicit analysis of privilege, however, would have avoided many of the pitfalls of her concept of a social group, since it would shift the problem from subordinate groups to the antidemocratic nature of dominant groups. It would also redress the central difficulty of her controversial proposal for group representation, which would grant specific representation for oppressed groups. The paradox of this proposal is that it presumes the presence of oppressed groups yet its purpose is to end oppression; hence the proposal initiates its own obsolescence. A political program for the dissolution of the privileged group, however, does not require group representation, for abolition does not bring about equality between groups so much as it transforms the very structure of group relations in the polity.

Nevertheless, Young's emphasis on participation helps to reveal the limits of inclusion in challenging the whiteness of American democracy. Combining her orientation toward participation with a critique of privilege, I suggest, can overcome the participation-inclusion dilemma. The latter element of the synthesis is found in Lani Guinier's critique of majority tyranny.

The Tyranny of the White Majority

In *The Tyranny of the Majority*, Guinier argues that the central danger of majority rule is not that it threatens the rights of individuals or minorities but that it is a winner-take-all system in which fifty percent plus one of the voters win everything while everyone else gets nothing. This turns politics into a zero-sum competition for power rather than a means of including everyone in the processes of governance. This danger is exacerbated in a polity in which the majority is racially prejudiced against the minority to such an extent that the minority is consistently excluded from representation and policy making. When this happens, majority rule perpetuates racial inequality, as the combination of a winner-take-all system and white prejudice turns African Americans into permanent political minorities. Permanent minority status prevents African Americans from participating meaningfully in politics even when their political rights are guaranteed by the Voting Rights Act. Whether in the *Herrenvolk* or color-blind eras, "Racial polarization in the electorate and in the legislative body . . . [transforms] majority rule into majority tyranny."[54]

Guinier proposes a procedural remedy for the problem of (white) majority tyranny. Democratic procedures, she holds, are just as important as substantive values or ideals, since "procedural rules, in a very real sense, shape substantive outcomes."[55] Eliminating permanent majorities requires turning zero-sum electoral outcomes into "positive-sum" outcomes, or results in which everyone wins or at least takes a turn at winning. She proposes replacing fifty percent plus one majorities and the territorial districting of representatives with a cumulative voting system, in which voters receive the same number of votes as there are seats to vote for, but rather than being limited to voting only for representatives within their geographic district, they can vote for any representative. Further, voters can distribute their votes as they please, "plumping" them with one candidate or distributing them among several according to the intensity of their preferences. Such a system, Guinier argues, would not only make it likely that at least one of a voter's candidates will be elected, it also encourages greater political participation. Cumulative voting provides citizens with an incentive to organize alliances that can vote as a single bloc or to form strategic coalitions with other groups to gain mutual benefits, since "any politically cohesive group can vote strategically to win representation."[56] It would encourage people to vote according to their interests rather than where they live (as geographic districts do) or who they are (as race-based districts do). It would eliminate gerrymandering as well as "safe" districts controlled by one party that are largely immune to political competition. Cumulative voting, Guinier argues, would make elections competitive and give citizens an incentive to participate beyond simply voting.

Guinier's argument demonstrates that majority tyranny does not just exclude minorities; it builds white advantage into the electoral process and inhibits participation, even given the protections of the Voting Rights Act. White privilege is normalized through ostensibly race-neutral legislative districting and a winner-take-all system. Guinier makes a qualified defense of race-conscious districting in *Tyranny of the Majority*, arguing that given the current system of territorial districting, racial gerrymandering to create majority-Black or -Latino districts is sometimes necessary to ensure Black and Latino political representation.[57] Ultimately, however, this solution cannot dislodge white advantage because the creation of majority-Black districts only *includes* people of color into representative bodies (and as permanent minorities at that). It does nothing to enhance the extent or quality of their *participation*. A better solution, she argues, would be to scrap group-based representation altogether (geographic as well as racial) and replace it with interest-based representation that employs cumulative voting.

The problem of the white majority, Guinier shows, cannot be resolved through inclusion alone. Inclusion, of course, is preferable to life prior to the Voting Rights Act, yet for Guinier, like Young, the goal is not simply to ensure representation for minority groups but to enhance their participation. "The right to a meaningful voice does not measure participation simply by counting competitive votes; it examines the extent to which a system mobilizes broad-based voter participation, fosters substantive debate from a range of viewpoints, and provides and reinforces opportunities for all voters to exercise meaningful choice throughout the process of decision making and governance."[58] Guinier's proposals are aimed not so much at securing representation for permanent minorities but toward *eliminating permanent majorities*. This requires undermining the power of whiteness through procedures that foster the participation of everyone.

Guinier offers her proposals in the interests of fairness and in the belief that they will fulfill the potential of modern democracy. As such, her argument does not necessarily test the boundaries of liberal democracy. Nevertheless, her critique of majority tyranny does have radical democratic potential because it connects a critique of racial privilege with an orientation toward participation. Guinier's contribution to democratic theory is not her specific proposals, which are overly proceduralist and have been suggested (and even implemented) elsewhere, but her theoretical orientation.[59] She demonstrates that the tyranny of the white majority remains a central problem of American democracy and shows how it is a problem of privilege and participation as well as one of exclusion and inclusion. Her argument suggests that abolishing the white majority would not only include people of color, it would undermine normalized white advantage. In so doing, it could expand participation and foster political conditions that make more radical forms of democracy possible. Guinier does not make this argument explicitly but she hints at the transformative possibilities of her theory when she writes, "The winner-take-some-but-not-all approach contemplates 'strong democracy,' meaning an invigorated electorate that participates (as opposed to spectates) throughout the political process."[60]

The democratic problem of whiteness persists after the *Herrenvolk* era. Its shift from a form of standing to a norm has obscured and weakened the value of whiteness in some ways, but the cross-class alliance continues to function through the normal operations of contemporary democracy. It persists as a problem for democratic theory as well, not only in that it is the engine of racial discrimination but also in that it continues to drive a wedge between inclusion and participation. Strategies to include persons of color into the polity by giving them equal standing with whites do little to expand participation. Yet strategies to expand participation can easily end up bolstering white majority tyranny, as Guinier shows. Neither strategy alone, then, is sufficient for democratic theory. A politics that emphasizes the abolition of whiteness, however, directly confronts racial privilege in a way that includes the excluded and encourages the expansion of democratic participation. It resolves the participation-inclusion dilemma and suggests a critique of liberal democratic institutions as they presently exist.

This is not to say that dissolving whiteness would be easy. It requires not only activities and policies that undermine the wages of whiteness but the creation of a new political ideal. Sketching this alternative "abolitionist-democratic" politics is the task of the final chapter. Such an ideal must go beyond the two existing attempts to address the problem of whiteness, color blindness and multiculturalism, for as I explain in the next chapter, both ultimately fail to eliminate the problem of the white citizen. Creating a new hegemonic ideal is undoubtedly a difficult task. Yet I submit there is little alternative. So long as the white citizen simultaneously insists on his or her privileges and denies they exist, the potential for white reaction remains. So long as the politics of inclusion dominates thinking on race, democratic theory will continue to run into the participation-inclusion dilemma and continue to have difficulty stretching its imagination beyond the boundaries of liberal democracy. A participatory politics must be an abolitionist politics.

CHAPTER 4

The Failure of Multiculturalism
and Color Blindness

On 27–31 July 1997, police officers in Chandler, Arizona, a rapidly growing suburb south of Phoenix, conducted a massive sweep of downtown, searching for illegal aliens. Working with local Immigration and Nationalization Services officials, they stopped people with brown skin at random and greeted them in Spanish. If the person replied in Spanish, they demanded to see papers proving legal residency. In the process of arresting and deporting 432 people, they stopped thousands of people who were playing soccer, hanging out at their apartment complexes, or walking down the street. Sometimes entire families were searched. No white people were stopped and asked to prove their residency. A brown-skinned driver pumping gas at a convenience store had to produce papers proving her legal status while the pale-skinned driver at the next pump was ignored. Latino community leaders quickly filed a $35 million lawsuit against the city, charging that the sweeps were part of a downtown revitalization project by the Chandler city government designed to attract middle-class white consumers away from thriving downtowns in nearby Tempe and Scottsdale.[1]

A year and a half later, the *Arizona Republic* cheerfully reported that Chandler was set to celebrate its fourth annual Multi-Cultural Festival, complete with Middle Eastern belly dancing, Irish step dancers, and Mexican mariachis. All of this was designed as "a celebration of all our various backgrounds," according to festival director Karen Drake.

Chandler Councilwoman Patti Bruno said the diversity of Chandler (whose population is nearly eighty percent white) is "awesome" and something for the city to be proud of.[2]

The Chandler government's two minds about race—police raids and cultural festivals, white dollars and ethnic flavor, green cards and guacamole dip—is an increasingly common phenomenon in American cities. Racial profiling and diversity celebrations go hand in hand in a country that is glad to be done with segregation yet is uncomfortable with all the consequences desegregation implies. Americans celebrate Martin Luther King Jr. as they lock up more Black men than ever before; they praise diversity but agonize over affirmative action; they dance to mariachis after sweeping the streets for brown skin.

The passing of *Herrenvolk* democracy was one of the most significant events in American history. As Chandler's agonies show, however, its death did not signal the end of the white democracy but rather a new phase. The previous chapter explained how the white citizen manages to persist in a state committed to race-neutral policies. I argue in this chapter that whiteness also persists in the two main ideological alternatives to *Herrenvolk* ideology, color blindness and multiculturalism. Each ideal presents itself as the heir of the civil rights legacy. Both promise to do away with the last vestiges of racial discrimination. And each points to the other as a central obstacle to achieving a truly discrimination-free democracy.

The color-blind ideal appeals to that which Americans share beyond the boundaries of race. It asserts that formal political equality and equality of opportunity is all that is necessary to end discrimination. Political efforts that favor one group or culture perpetuate inequality, even if the intent is to eliminate it. The multicultural ideal holds that an individual's particularity and uniqueness, especially in regards to culture, define her at least as much as what she shares in common with others. It therefore calls for policies that preserve the cultural diversity of a society and that root out inequalities between cultures. Advocates of each ideal typically differ over the extent and nature of racial discrimination as well as the proper means to achieve a society in which race no longer holds any political advantage or stigma. Both ideals, however, share a fundamental weakness: neither effectively confronts the problem of the white citizen. The white political imagination persists in the color-blind ideal through a conception of race in general and white in particular as a politically neutral identity that simply refers to a set of physical or social characteristics. It endures in multiculturalism through a definition of race as culture that simply considers whiteness one culture among others. Each blanches power from whiteness, defining away the cross-class alliance rather than confronting it. In this way, both ideals provide a surreptitious means by which white democracy can persevere. The result is the sort of racial schizophrenia that grips Chandler, in which the polity protects white privilege, celebrates diversity, and denies any social significance to race at the same time.

In this chapter I critique the color-blind and multicultural ideals for their insufficient attention to whiteness, or the condition of racial privilege within a democratic polity. Examining Justice John Harlan's dissent in *Plessy v. Ferguson* and Abigail and Stephan Thernstrom's influential *America in Black and White*, I argue that the color-blind ideal perpetuates white citizenship even as it attempts to make race publicly insignificant, since it allows white privilege to continue unabated in the private realm. Examining Charles Taylor's work on the "politics of recognition," the new field of "whiteness studies," and Nancy Fraser's attempt to bridge the gap between the "economic" and "cultural Left," I argue that multiculturalism perpetuates white citizenship by presuming whiteness to be a culture, thereby obscuring its principal function as a form of power. The effort to characterize racial subordination in the United States as a cultural phenomenon is unhelpful because it transposes what are best understood as *political* conflicts regarding race—over rights, freedom, equality, power, and the reach of the state—into *cultural* dilemmas. This shifts the emphasis of scholarship and policy on race from a focus on racial oppression to efforts to achieve mutual respect or "recognition" between cultures. This is unfortunate, for this sort of depoliticization of race thwarts the valuable contribution political theory can make to the study of race in the global era.

The Death of the *Herrenvolk* Ideal

The color-blind and multicultural ideals emerged in the wake of international and domestic contexts that, combined with the civil rights movement, delegitimized the *Herrenvolk* ideal. A world war against Nazism made homespun ideologies of racial supremacy difficult to defend. The ensuing cold war and the decolonization of Africa and Asia made white supremacist rhetoric a burden for U.S. foreign policy rather than a rallying cry for American dominance.[3] By the mid-1960s the majority of Africa's nations had won their independence and one-third of the world lived under regimes calling themselves socialist, meaning that capitalism was not the only viable economic system at the time and liberal democracy was not the only political imaginary with large-scale purchase. In the fight against the Soviet Union for the allegiance of Third World nations, *Herrenvolk* ideology was a competitive disadvantage.[4] In an increasingly global market in which oil, gold, diamonds, metals, spices, and other raw materials were possessed by newly independent nations led by people with dark skin, white notions of racial superiority were no longer a business asset at the bargaining table, to say the least.

Domestically, things had changed as well. As the reign of King Cotton finally ended in the mid-twentieth century and as the Southern economy diversified and industrialized, a captive Black workforce immobilized through segregation and white terror became a fetter to Southern production rather than its foundation. The end of large-scale European immigration to the States precipitated a labor shortage, drawing African Americans to cities in the North during both world wars. In turn, urbanization concentrated Black economic and political resources. Further, the rapid growth and political influence of the American West, whose economy was not as tightly tethered to Black subordination as it was in the South and the North, began to shift the nation's center away from the Mason-Dixon line and the Black-white racial axis. Finally, the slow but steady legal victories against segregation, wrenched one by one by the NAACP, increased Black political power, challenged white liberals' complacency on race, and cleared space for the civil rights movement to operate.[5] Finally, the world that white supremacy built would be transformed.

The victories of the civil rights movement brought important changes to the African American community. In the *Herrenvolk* era, the Black middle class consisted primarily of preachers, teachers, lawyers, small business owners, nurses, doctors, and undertakers, all of whom were confined to a segregated market. By raising the status of all whites above all not-whites, *Herrenvolk* democracy effectively held back the social advancement of the "Black bourgeoisie," preventing them from breaking away from the Black working class. A shared degraded status meant that any improvement in the status of the middle class required an improvement in the lives of all Black people. As a result, racial consciousness among the Black middle and working classes tended to trump class tensions.[6] But in the wake of civil rights victories, new avenues of advancement in the larger economy slowly opened up for the Black middle class, opportunities that were largely unavailable to workers. Various restrictions continue to impede the accumulation of Black capital, and class stratification within the Black community is still not as deep as it is among whites.[7] Nevertheless, the rise of a Black middle class whose fortunes are tied to the larger market rather than the Black community, however tenuous, put another crack in the racial status quo.[8]

As the *Herrenvolk* collapsed, then, so did its ideology. Given an increasingly global economy, a fragile but growing Black middle class, worldwide independence movements, and civil rights and Black power movements at home (not to mention the myriad movements they influenced, from antiwar to feminist to American Indian to Chicano to Puerto Rican to gay and lesbian), a reflexive presumption of whites' inherent superiority could no longer explain the facts on the ground or offer a viable ideal of the good life. New times call for new ideas. The death of the *Herrenvolk* demanded a new way to make sense of race. Yet given white citizens' anger over their loss of racial standing and their resistance to substantive Black freedom, any new hegemonic vision would have to balance a commitment to equal rights and opportunities with the need to mollify white anxieties. It would have to safeguard the material and social advantages whites had accumulated and come to expect as a matter of right under the *Herrenvolk* while condemning the existence of such advantages. The color-blind and multicultural ideals emerged in this context.

The Color-Blind Ideal

The fundamental premise of the color-blind ideal is that one's race should carry no status in the public sphere. People should be judged according to character and merit, not membership in an ascribed group. The just state would grant no recognition to any particular race or ethnic group via public policy, legislation, jurisprudence, or law enforcement, whether for purposes of discrimination (as in the *Herrenvolk*) or for combating it (such as affirmative action). The state's only role regarding race is to prevent discrimination so that all individuals may have an equal opportunity to succeed economically and socially. Thus the state must deliberately ignore or be "blind" to one's race.

The color-blind ideal rests on a distinction between public and private realms. The defining characteristic of relationships in the realm of politics and civil society is equality. All citizens are equal in the eyes of the law; one's race is not to be recognized except possibly as a neutral description for classification purposes.[9] In the private sphere, race may be recognized as the individual sees fit.[10] Given this public/private split, the essence of the color-blind ideal is not so much that races do not exist—some color-blind advocates note that there are no biological races; others assume there are—but that their existence is politically irrelevant, since the state may not take them into account either way. If the essential principle upon which multiculturalism is based is the politics of recognition (as I explain below), the backbone of color blindness is the principle of public *nonrecognition* of racial identity.

The intellectual origins of the color-blind ideal lie in Supreme Court Justice John Marshall Harlan's famous dissent in the 1896 *Plessy v. Ferguson* case. The seven-to-one majority opinion of the Court declared that Louisiana's laws segregating Black passengers on its trains were constitutional on the grounds that providing separate but equal facilities did not deny African Americans their rights guaranteed by the Thirteenth and Fourteenth Amendments. In his dissent, Harlan insists that the segregation of public facilities does in fact violate the civil rights of African Americans. Expanding the definition of "public realm," Harlan argues that the Civil War amendments pertain not only to voting and serving on juries, as the majority opinion states, but also to personal liberty. They therefore explicitly prohibit differential treatment according to race.[11]

Harlan's eloquent rebuttal of the majority opinion as well as his famous "our constitution is color-blind" phrase has made him the founding father of the color-blind ideal. Even though many Black writers and orators made similar arguments well before his famous dissent, the acclaim accorded to Harlan is entirely appropriate, for his dissent foreshadows the limitations of the color-blind ideal as well as its strengths. For example, the full "color-blind" passage reads:

> The white race deems itself to be the dominant race in this country. And so it is, in prestige, in achievements, in education, in wealth, and in power. So, I doubt not, it will continue to be for all time, if it remains true to its great heritage, and holds fast to the principles of constitutional liberty. But in view of the constitution, in the eye of the law, there is in this country no superior, dominant, ruling class of citizens. There is no caste here. Our constitution is color-blind, and neither knows nor tolerates classes among citizens. In respect of civil rights, all citizens are equal before the law. The humblest is the peer of the most powerful. The law regards man as man, and takes no account of his surroundings or of his color when his civil rights as guarantied by the supreme law of the land are involved.[12]

In the same paragraph Harlan defends a color-blind Constitution and sanctions the social superiority of the white race. This is not necessarily hypocritical, as is sometimes suggested: Harlan could be simply soothing whites' egos as he attacks the basis of their power. The real problem with the passage lies in what Harlan protects from political incursion. A color-blind Constitution would guard the political and civil rights of Black people, but it would do nothing about whites' overwhelming control over educational, financial, and political resources. Nor should it, he argues, since these lie outside of the public realm. White domination in these areas is understood as the normal condition of society and reflective of the white race's "great heritage." Harlan shifts the line between public and private from where the majority opinion draws it (voting and jury duty as public, all other activities private) by incorporating civil society into the public sphere, yet he still uses the line to both condemn segregation and insulate whites' material advantages from public intervention. Harlan expands the number and kind of activities toward which the state must be color blind to include the enjoyment of public accommodations, but he still protects certain activities (such as the accumulation of education and wealth) from redress by claiming that inequalities in these areas are natural and therefore immune from public deliberation and decision making. Harlan's "color-blind" defense of civil rights for African Americans, then, sanctions white privilege even as it would bring about formal political equality.[13]

This contradiction is reproduced in one of the most sophisticated and comprehensive arguments for color blindness today, Stephan and Abigail Thernstrom's *America in Black and White*.[14] The Thernstroms gather voluminous data to show that African Americans have made great strides in income, housing, education, politics, and every other social indicator since the *Herrenvolk* era, and that the gap between Black and white is getting smaller every day. Further, these gains have been accompanied by dramatic changes in whites' attitudes toward Black people. Yet contrary to popular wisdom, they claim, neither the civil rights movement nor affirmative action is responsible for this progress. The boom in Black economic empowerment and the shift in white attitudes began in the 1940s and 1950s, before the civil rights protests and without any sort of affirmative action. Black progress was the cumulative result of the migration of African Americans to the North, where jobs were more plentiful and wages higher; the ideological imperatives of World War II, which made racism disgraceful; and the waning prejudices of whites, who began to recognize and reject the gap between American egalitarian ideals and racial discrimination. "The unprecedented progress of the 1940s and 1950s was not, for the most part, the product of deliberate decisions by government officials or by the leaders of organizations seeking to change public policy," they assert. "Immense progress was made by black Americans before the idea of racial preferences was seriously entertained by anyone."[15]

Given this, the Thernstroms conclude that color-blind public policies are the best way to unite Americans across the racial divide. Racial preferences, they argue, are divisive and have done little historically for Black progress or to undermine white prejudice. Having neither need nor business in maintaining such programs, the government should pay heed to Justice Harlan's words and create a color-blind social policy that treats people as individuals rather than members of an ascribed group. This, they hold, is a responsible middle ground between the racist policies of the past and the sky-is-falling racial doomsaying of today's affirmative action liberals. "It is on the grounds of individuality that blacks and whites can come together," they argue, not by clinging to the divisive discourses of race.[16]

The Thernstroms' plea is a noble one. Nevertheless, their argument for color blindness naturalizes white advantage by shifting the blame for persistent racial gaps onto African Americans. The Thernstroms argue that Black poverty is almost exclusively the result of out-of-wedlock births and the decline in Black marriage rates. Their "spatial mismatch" theory explains away high Black unemployment by claiming that Black people simply do not live where the jobs are. Residential segregation is largely due to African Americans' preference to live together. The riots of the 1960s ruined the racial peace, not the oppression that precipitated them. Affirmative action, not whites' resistance to it, is responsible for widening the racial breach. Their chapter on Black poverty concludes by arguing that poor Black people just have to buckle down, refuse to sell drugs, accept minimum wage jobs, and work their way up like immigrants do. Ultimately, they excuse whites from virtually any responsibility for persistent problems within the African American community. "[T]he serious inequality that remains [today] is less a function of white racism than of the racial gap in levels of educational attainment, the structure of the black family, and the rise in black crime."[17] *America in*

Black and White implies that any residual forms of white advantage are merely incidental—or are African Americans' fault.[18]

The color-blind ideal sends the message that the white citizen no longer poses a challenge to American democracy. Paul Sniderman and Edward Carmines, for example, argue that the primary obstacle to a united country is no longer white racism, for public opinion polls show that white Americans have largely overcome their prejudices. Today, they claim, political tensions that are commonly attributed to whites' prejudice are actually debates over the appropriate reach of state power in civil society. "The current clash over race must be interpreted in the context of a deeper debate on the proper role of government," they write. "The contemporary debate over racial policy is driven primarily by conflict over what government should try to do, and only secondarily over what it should try to do *for blacks*."[19] In order to win support for programs that can help the poorest Americans, Sniderman and Carmines conclude that political leaders need to "reach beyond race" and appeal to universal moral principles that all Americans share. Similarly, Jim Sleeper argues that the task of color-blind liberalism is "to nurture some shared American principles and bonds that strengthen national belonging and nourish democratic habits" rather than obsess over that which divides us.[20]

Such arguments can only perpetuate the advantages of white citizenship, regardless of the color-blind dreams from which they originate. The color-blind ideal's plausibility rests on denying the historical connection between white identity and racial oppression or on it being tucked away safely in the past, as the Thernstroms do. This formalistic conception of whiteness perpetuates subordination by denying the existence of all but the most blatant forms of racial privilege and discrimination.[21] By redefining racism from a social system of oppression to a set of individual prejudices, systematic yet nondeliberate patterns of privilege pass beneath the color-blind bar even as they continue to provide vastly different life chances between whites and not-whites. The problem becomes hate rather than systematic racial oppression, prejudice rather than privilege, pathology rather than discrimination. As George

Lipsitz notes, "As long as we define social life as the sum total of conscious and deliberate individual activities, then only *individual* manifestations of personal prejudice and hostility will be seen as racist."[22] By assuming the political neutrality of whiteness, the color-blind ideal does not eliminate white privilege but removes it from public consideration. In so doing, it provides a means for the white citizen's continued survival. Color-blind ideals were useful in challenging *Herrenvolk* democracy, but after Jim Crow they ironically become a means of perpetuating privilege because they define away the power relations inherent in race rather than transform them. Thus, the color-blind ideal offers little to proponents of a more democratic society. Unfortunately, neither does its principal alternative, multiculturalism.

The Multicultural Ideal

Multiculturalism is a term of many uses. In one sense it simply describes a fact of the world. If culture is "the context within which people give meanings to their actions and experiences, and make sense of their lives," then most nation-states are by definition multicultural, for they contain numerous cultures within their borders.[23] In a more normative sense, multiculturalism represents an acknowledgment of the cultures of other peoples and a moral ideal of tolerance toward them. In a third sense, multiculturalism is not just a normative ideal but a political imperative. In this conception, which I term the multicultural ideal, cultural diversity is not only a moral good, it is necessary for democracy because the full inclusion of all citizens into the polity implies public recognition of their cultural identities. Rather than suggesting a color-blind universalism that would subordinate the sources of an individual's identity (such as her culture, race, religion, or gender) to that of "the citizen," the multicultural ideal asserts that a healthy public sphere must provide cultures (particularly minority cultures) the protection they need to survive and flourish. So long as they follow the rules of a common democratic civic culture, multiculturalism is perfectly compatible with a universalism that, as Amy Gutmann puts it, "counts the culture and cultural context valued by individuals as among their basic interests."[24]

As a fact of the world or as a commitment to tolerance, multiculturalism is largely unobjectionable today. There is great disagreement, however, over the multicultural ideal—its desirability, its implementation, and the kind of democratic politics it prefigures. Much of this debate revolves around Charles Taylor's influential essay "The Politics of Recognition."[25] The driving question of the essay originates in Taylor's earlier work on Hegel, in which Taylor argues that Hegel's challenge to modern democracy is to ask how much diversity a society can endure without dissolving. Modern society is fundamentally self-interested; it is thus fractured and alienated. Yet absolute freedom (or participatory democracy) requires homogeneity because the participation of all citizens in political deliberation requires a common foundation of purpose. The question for Taylor, then, is "What kind of differentiation can modern society admit of?"[26] What is needed, he argues, is a "meaningful differentiation" that both knits communities together and distinguishes them from others. "The Politics of Recognition" is his attempt at such a differentiation.

Human life, Taylor asserts, is fundamentally dialogical. That is, individuals construct their own identity, but not by themselves. We only become fully human through interaction with others, particularly those who in some way matter to us. "Thus my discovering my own identity doesn't mean that I work it out in isolation, but that I negotiate it through dialogue, partly overt, partly internal, with others."[27] Taylor argues that in the premodern era, identity was defined according to one's "honor" or status in a system of social stratification. In the modern era, by contrast, individuals must construct their own identity through the concept of dignity. While the underlying premise of honor is that only some may share in it, the premise of dignity is that everyone potentially possesses it. The demand for dignity thus results in "a politics of equal recognition," in which individuals demand the right to be recognized as equal to all others.[28] Recognition, then, is the acknowledgment of one individual's self-conscious identity by another self-conscious being.[29] In Anthony Appiah's words, the politics of recognition "asks us to acknowledge socially and politically the authentic identities of others."[30]

But the politics of recognition has an element of uncertainty built into it. Whether one was a prince, priest, or pauper in the premodern era, the social hierarchy guaranteed a person's identity. Yet in the modern era persons can lose their identity. They can fail to be recognized or they can be "misrecognized" by others. Historically, misrecognition has been the experience not only of individuals, but of entire groups. Misrecognition, then, is a lack of due respect shown for an individual or group by another individual or group. It is not just a rude snub. Because our identities are created dialogically, misrecognition can be internalized, resulting in a damaged sense of identity that can "inflict a grievous wound, saddling its victims with a crippling self-hatred."[31] The problem of misrecognition, Taylor argues, is the fundamental dilemma of the modern era.

The politics of recognition has assumed two forms in response to this dilemma. The politics of universalism insists that the way to achieve dignity and equal worth is to emphasize that which brings us together as members of a common community, in particular the possession of equal rights and entitlements. This is the color-blind ideal. The politics of difference, on the other hand, demands recognition not on the basis of what humans share but on that which makes them unique. All persons are of equal worth but each person possesses a distinct identity, often derived from membership in a cultural group. It is this distinctiveness that defines us and that demands equal recognition. Advocates of the politics of universalism contend that an emphasis on human particularity, particularly cultural differences, separates individuals rather than brings them together. A common political identity, usually citizenship, is necessary to cohere a democratic public. Advocates of difference counter that the politics of universalism has actually been quite particular (i.e., white, male, and propertied). Further, it has often denied the individual the opportunity to fashion her own publicly significant identity. "Universalism," its critics charge, is actually ethnocentric and elitist.

Taylor agrees that the politics of universalism tends to homogenize social life and can easily slide into ethnocentrism—and often has. Still, he is uncomfortable with the politics of difference (which he identifies with poststructuralism) because, he argues, it refuses to evaluate the moral worth of particular cultures, since it claims that all standards of judgment are inherently tainted by power. Taylor thus seeks a third path, not between the politics of difference and the politics of universalism so much as between a homogenizing liberalism that can easily turn ethnocentric and a poststructuralism that has abandoned moral judgment. His goal is a universalism that can respect and protect the demands for recognition by individuals and cultures alike.

Taylor's solution is a "substantive liberalism" that he distinguishes from the "procedural liberalism" of universalism and the "difference" politics of poststructuralism. According to procedural liberalism, a liberal society can adopt no substantive view about what constitutes the good life. The state is restricted to a procedural commitment to protect the rights of individuals so that they are able to pursue their private goals. In contrast, Taylor argues that it is possible for a society to define a common good without violating liberal principles. Quebec, for example, expresses a collective desire to preserve its French language and culture but does not trample on the rights of those Quebecois who disagree with this goal, such as indigenous peoples and Anglophones. Cultural survival is a substantive good: it makes a collective claim as to what the good life should, in part, consist of—such as that Quebec should be a French-speaking territory. This good is worth preserving as a matter of state policy, Taylor argues. A substantive liberalism can be perfectly in keeping with principles of universalism while avoiding the dangers of homogenization so long as it respects the rights of those who do not share in the collective definition of the good.

> A society with strong collective goals can be liberal . . . provided it is also capable of respecting diversity, especially when dealing with those who do not share its common goals; and provided it can offer adequate safeguards for fundamental rights. There will undoubtedly be tensions and difficulties in pursuing these objectives together, but such a pursuit is not impossible, and the problems are not in principle greater than those encountered by any liberal society that has to combine, for example, liberty and equality, or prosperity and justice.[32]

Taylor's theory of recognition is intended to explain the conflict between English- and French-language cultures in Canada, particularly in Quebec. It has attracted a great deal of critical attention in the United States, as numerous theorists have contemplated its value for American multiculturalism.[33] This attention, however, has often failed to question the applicability of Taylor's theory to the American context. Misrecognition may be Canada's fundamental dilemma, but it is not the United States'. A theory of the equal recognition of cultures cannot make sense of the American experience, in which the organizing principle of group formation has been race, not the uneasy coexistence of two language-based cultures.[34] A multiculturalism borrowed from Taylor assumes that social identities are defined culturally. Accordingly, each race must possess a corresponding culture. But this is an assumption that must be proven rather than asserted. An analysis of cultural groups implies equality: I grant your culture recognition because I feel it is potentially as worthy as mine. Racial injustice, however, is premised on relations of *inequality* between dominant and subordinate groups. Multiculturalism is premised on the valuing of difference, but racial oppression, for all the differences it concocts to divide white and dark worlds, also depends on the *suppression* of difference in order to forge disparate cultures and ethnicities into homogeneous races. Lack of recognition and racial subordination, then, are not the same thing. When conflated, the unfortunate tendency is to emphasize the former at the expense of the latter. Applying Taylor's theory of recognition to the United States requires making race equivalent to culture: the problem of the white citizen is redefined as whites' "misrecognition" of persons of color. But race and culture are not synonymous.

The conflation of racial and cultural identity points to a second problem with Taylor's theory of recognition: it lacks an analysis of power. Taylor acknowledges that power may prevent an individual from being recognized as she desires and that the state may need to protect against such misrecognition, but there is little sense in "The Politics of Recognition" that identities themselves are constructed (and not merely repressed) through power relations. As Linda Nicholson puts it, Taylor focuses too much "on the other to be recognized and too little on the practice of recognition itself."[35] Taylor interprets the problem of the modern age as the problem of misrecognition and the psychological damage it inflicts on its victims. The modern era, he argues, brought about the collapse of honor and thus the instability of identity. But honor did not die with feudalism. As I argued in chapter 2, honor or status as a white person has been central to the creation of American citizenship. The "adored trinity" of Southern slave masters consisted of cotton, slaves, and honor, while nonslaveholding whites in the North and the South alike derived honor by associating with the masters and the "master race."[36] Status or "honor" as a white citizen is a modern form of social standing that insulates one from the possibility of misrecognition.

Racial oppression is not a problem of misrecognition but a problem of *power*—the attempt by one group to maintain its standing and privileges over another group.[37] Taylor is loath to raise the question of power because he believes it will throw him in the bog of poststructuralism and its "half-baked neo-Nietzschean theories."[38] Yet the persistence of standing and its traces in the post–civil rights era make it absolutely necessary to address race as a form of power.[39] Unfortunately, by avoiding the question of power, the politics of recognition takes away the single most important contribution political theory can make to the study of race: an analysis of race as a specifically political construct that is intimately connected to issues of democracy, participation, social stability, and power. The politics of recognition tends to lead political theory away from this sort of theorizing and into an unfruitful exploration of "cultural differences." Conservative arguments about the "cultural pathologies" of African Americans are a particularly noxious example of this. Such problems, however, are also evident in progressive race theory, including much of the new "whiteness studies."

Multiculturalism and Whiteness Studies

The dangers of conflating culture with race are apparent, ironically, in the emerging field of "whiteness studies," which aims to study race not through a study of the oppressed but through an inquiry of the privileged.[40] An underlying assumption of much of the work on whiteness in

the disciplines of education and cultural studies is that race is not biology but culture. Thus, whiteness must be a culture as well, and since all
cultures should be equal, the logic goes, white identity deserves a place
at the multicultural table. The problem, of course, is that whiteness
historically has not been an expression of culture so much as a form of
standing reflecting relations of inequality, discrimination, privilege, and
terror. The political and pedagogical challenge as whiteness studies
defines it, then, is to find a usable white history that, once disassociated
from the strange fruit of white supremacy, can provide the basis for a
nonracist white identity that can constructively join the multicultural
tapestry.

And if no such history can be found, it will have to be invented.
Even the strongest advocates of a reconstructed white identity have
found it very difficult to locate a white culture independent of whiteness's
historical function as a form of privileged standing. Henry Giroux, for
example, blames identity politics for the inability of white youth to
develop solidarity with youth of color.[41] Identity politics has alienated
poor white youth and led to a "crisis of self-esteem" by denying them
an ethnicity of their own. White people, especially white youth, need
an identity and a culture to which they can belong. Given American history, he argues, such an identity will inevitably be tied to race. Giroux
complains that conservatives have appropriated whiteness for their own
politics, duping some poor white youth into right-wing politics along
the way. The only thing that can save them from the right-wing reaction, Giroux holds, is a reconstructed, progressive white identity. Thus,
the political and pedagogical task is to locate serviceable elements of
the white experience and use them to form the basis of a new, antiracist
white culture and identity.[42] Giroux strongly resists claims that whiteness is nothing but a racist identity. Even if true, he warns, telling this
to white youth would be psychologically damaging, for these youth
need to find a place for themselves in the multiracial mosaic. "Defining
'whiteness' largely as a form of domination . . . while rightly unmasking
whiteness as a mark of ideology and racial privilege, fails to provide a
nuanced, dialectical, and layered account of whiteness that would allow

white youth and others to appropriate selective elements of white identity and culture as oppositional."[43] Whiteness is more than a form of oppressive power, he asserts; it is also a possibility.[44]

Giroux's effort to create a progressive white culture seems promising, but the reconstruction of white identity is a dangerous undertaking. Some of the perils are evident in Joe Kincheloe and Shirley Steinberg's introduction to the anthology *White Reign*. Kincheloe and Steinberg anxiously warn about "the white identity crisis" and how it "cannot be dismissed simply as the angst of the privileged." In fact, their primary criticism of multiculturalism is that it has yet to produce a "compelling vision of a reconstructed white identity."[45] The task of educators, they assert, is to create "a positive, proud, attractive, antiracist white identity that is empowered to travel in and out of various racial/ethnic circles with confidence and empathy."[46] They even call for a redirecting of pedagogical energy toward the development of a progressive white identity: "Such pedagogical work is anything but easy; progressive Whites will require sophisticated help and support to pull them through the social, political, and psychological dilemmas they all will face."[47] This "sophisticated help" includes funding as well as support groups of people of color to help "progressive whites" cope with unsympathetic white colleagues! With Kincheloe and Steinberg, whiteness studies reaches its logical if absurd endpoint—instead of challenging discrimination, it demands people of color support groups; instead of channeling funds to deprived students of color, they now go to aggrieved whites; rather than undermining white privilege, effort is devoted to reconstructing and sustaining white identity. The desire to create a positive white identity quickly turns a well-meaning antiracism into white narcissism.

Despite their vigorous arguments for an antiracist white identity, white culture advocates have yet to define what "white culture" is apart from white supremacy. Neither Giroux nor Kincheloe and Steinberg attempt to define white culture.[48] Adam Cornford identifies white culture "by its blandness and avoidance of controversy or risk, by its cleanliness-as-absence. . . . One might say, then, that contemporary whiteness is . . .

the 'degree zero' of culture, the suppression of culture as local, specific, traditional, kin- or community-oriented, non-rational, or non-capitalist." David Cochran suggests, "In spite of dramatic ethnic, social, regional, religious, and economic diversity, white Americans do in fact share a common cultural identity. Those with little else in common do share white skin, and this positions them in American life in a way unavailable to black Americans."[49] Both definitions are problematic. Cornford's definition is not inclusive of all whites—rednecks and skinheads hardly fit the bland or avoidance-of-controversy criteria—while Cochran curiously boils white culture down to "white skin." Further, the keywords Cornford and Cochran use to define white culture ("suppression" and "position," respectively) refer more accurately to relations of power.

This suggests that it is more useful to understand whiteness as a form of power rather than as a culture. After all, it is not white culture that unites a Brooklyn cop, a Silicon Valley entrepreneur, a rural West Virginian, a Portland hippie, and a Phoenix metal head; it is white *power*: the expectation and/or enjoyment of preferential treatment. Further, while whites dominate American society, this domination does not constitute American culture as white. As Albert Murray points out, American culture can in no way be defined as white but is "incontestably mulatto," given the pervasive influence of African, American Indian, and other peoples.[50] Equating whiteness with culture and white culture with American culture ignores the central contribution of peoples of color to American society, perpetuating assumptions of whiteness as normative.

This is not to suggest that whiteness is culturally insignificant. Whiteness clearly has cultural effects. Nor is it to say that politics and culture can be neatly distinguished. If, as Cochran writes, whiteness involves "the elevation of norms and practices that embody the experiences of white Americans to the position of neutral and universal standards used to judge everyone," this is clearly a cultural and a political practice.[51] Nevertheless, the attempt to raise one group's way of seeing the world to a hegemonic position is fundamentally an issue of power. If all that whites share *as whites* is an expectation of favored treatment, then whiteness is best understood as a relationship of power, not a cultural identity.

Whiteness studies' failure to understand whiteness as a form of power follows from the politics of recognition's tendency to understand racial conflict in terms of the misrecognition of cultures rather than the persistence of relations of privilege and subordination. If the problem is misrecognition, the challenge becomes to make all races equal, which compels not only a multicultural politics but also, as Giroux and Kincheloe and Steinberg argue, a reconstructed white identity that can helpfully join a multicultural polity. But whiteness cannot be understood apart from the history of white supremacy. The new whiteness studies sets as its task to fit white identity into the multicultural mosaic. But if whiteness cannot be dissociated from unjust power relations, what can such a politics offer the multicultural tapestry besides a rip? If, as Marx says, the formulation of a question is its solution, then the misformulation of a question is its problem. The dilemma of how to construct a progressive white identity evaporates when whiteness is critiqued as a political category rather than a cultural identity.

The Redistribution-Recognition Dilemma

A central flaw of the multicultural ideal, as with color blindness, is its tendency to depoliticize race. Unfortunately, this flaw persists in attempts to go beyond the politics of recognition to address socioeconomic issues in addition to cultural ones. As is evident in the work of Nancy Fraser, combining economics with culture still provides little means to understand race as a political category. As a result, the white citizen slips between the "redistribution-recognition dilemma."

In *Justice Interruptus* Fraser identifies two primary forms of contemporary injustice, socioeconomic and cultural. The former includes exploitation, economic marginalization, and material deprivation, while the latter includes cultural domination, disrespect, and nonrecognition of one's culture. Struggles for redistribution strive to reduce economic inequalities while struggles for recognition seek to elevate the status of formally subordinated identities. Modern justice, Fraser argues, requires both redistribution and recognition. Unfortunately, the two are largely dissociated from one another today, divided between a "social Left" that emphasizes issues of redistribution and a "cultural Left" that emphasizes issues of recognition. The effort to bring them together is complicated by their opposing tendencies. Claims for recognition tend to differentiate people because they call attention to the specificity of a group. Claims for redistribution, on the other hand, tend to undermine the economic arrangements that underpin group specificity and thereby promote group "de-differentiation." The problem posed by the redistribution-recognition dilemma is that one type of politics stresses those aspects of life that distinguish people from each other while the other type tends to stress those aspects that bring people together. The task for political theory, Fraser argues, is to combine recognition and redistribution so that their aims support rather than conflict with each other. Regarding race specifically, she poses the question accordingly:

> Whereas the logic of redistribution is to put "race" out of business as such, the logic of recognition is to valorize group specificity. Here, then, is the antiracist version of the redistribution-recognition dilemma: How can antiracists fight simultaneously to abolish "race" and to valorize the cultural specificity of subordinated racialized groups?[52]

Fraser maintains that there are two types of remedies for injustice. Affirmative remedies of redistribution (such as the welfare state) and recognition (such as mainstream multiculturalism) attempt to address inequities without challenging the present social system. Transformative remedies (such as socialism and deconstruction) aim to achieve justice by restructuring the underlying frameworks that generate inequities. Transformative remedies, she argues, are more apt to "soften" the redistribution-recognition dilemma because they destabilize the structures that reproduce inequalities, while affirmative remedies make only surface adjustments. While Fraser doubts that the redistribution-recognition dilemma will ever be resolved completely, she asserts that transformative remedies represent the best means to achieve justice.

Fraser's analysis is a welcomed attempt to expand the debate over recognition inaugurated by Taylor. But the redistribution-recognition dilemma as she constructs it is not without difficulties of its own. Fraser assumes that struggles for recognition are inherently "dissociated" from struggles for economic justice. However, if the political question of capitalism is how to get workers to work in a system that exploits them, then resistance to the means by which workers are induced to labor—such as the privileges or terrors of white citizenship—could challenge the system of exploitation itself. Thus, struggles that may appear to be primarily over recognition often initiate significant struggles for redistribution. The life of Martin Luther King Jr., whose public career began by fighting for integrated buses and ended by supporting striking garbage workers, is a case in point. Fraser's analysis does not acknowledge this.[53] Further, Fraser assumes that struggles for recognition tend to divide people rather than bring them together. But this is not always the case. In the resistance to white supremacy worldwide, for example, Blackness has typically been an expansive and universalizing identity rather than a restrictive and particular one. Cape Coloreds and Asians identified themselves as Black in apartheid South Africa, Pakistanis identify as Black in England, and African American communities responded to the one-drop rule by welcoming Indians, "mulattoes," "quadroons," and "octoroons" into their ranks. Du Bois meant for his terms "black world" and "dark world" to include all the world's oppressed peoples of color. And to this day one can find those who insist that old John Brown was more of a Black man than a white one. Even when controversies over the purported ethnocentrism of Black Power and Afrocentrism are taken into account, Blackness stands as not only a cultural identity but a potentially universal political color that has historically forged a broad unity of persons dedicated to resisting an unjust social order.[54]

The biggest problem with Fraser's remedy for the redistribution-recognition dilemma, however, is that, like the color-blind and multicultural ideals, it leaves little room for politics. Following Habermas, Fraser makes an analytical distinction between culture and socioeconomics. Some issues belong to the socioeconomic realm while others belong to the "lifeworld" or cultural system. Yet as Lawrence Blum points out, this dichotomy undermines a focus on specifically political issues such as citizenship, participation, and governance, none of which are entirely economic or cultural derivatives.[55] As a result, Fraser's conception of justice tends to underplay politics.[56] By following Taylor's logic even as she expands on it to include economic issues, Fraser is led to theorize race as a set of cultures seeking recognition rather than as a set of norms, power networks, institutions, and alliances. Thus, as with Taylor's defense of recognition, Fraser's dilemma and her resolution of it ultimately lead away from an analysis that could link race to politics, democracy, and citizenship rather than toward it.

The subordination of politics to culture and socioeconomics ends up accommodating white citizenship rather than challenging it. For example, Fraser argues that one of the drawbacks of affirmative remedies is that they appear to benefit only particular groups rather than all persons, since they dole out benefits to underserved populations rather than transform institutional structures. Such remedies are apt to "fan the flames of resentment" and are vulnerable to a backlash by those who feel that the recipients of such benefits are receiving special treatment. Affirmative action, for example, tends to produce conflict among people who might otherwise find common ground because white men see it as preferential treatment for white women and people of color. Better to struggle for transformative remedies that benefit the majority of the population, Fraser argues, than affirmative remedies that appear to advantage only a select few.[57] But the problem here is not affirmative action but the white citizen, who sees in affirmative action an attempt to restrict whites' unfettered access to the means of upward mobility. The backlash against affirmative action is an effort to preserve this access. It is the white citizen, not affirmative action, who holds back the promise for greater democracy. "Transformative remedies" that reject affirmative action inadvertently indulge the white citizen's intransigent demands. In this way, appeals to programs that promise to "universalize" benefits often surrender to the white imagination rather than subvert it.

Whiteness produces persistent effects of misrecognition as well as economic injustice, but it is first and foremost a political alliance between one class and a section of another class. It is a form of disciplinary power that organizes people into groups, distributes them according to a hierarchy, and allocates advantages to some and disadvantages to others, thereby shaping the way in which people make sense of the world. A focus on whiteness instead of culture and recognition illuminates the political nature of race. In so doing it shows that the redistribution-recognition dilemma is not as intractable as Fraser believes, since some of the greatest challenges to the unequal distribution of wealth in the United States have come from struggles for "recognition" by those denied full standing. Affirmative remedies that undermine the privileges of the white citizen do more than make surface adjustments to existing systems of injustice. By undermining the cross-class alliance they open up space for a radical democratic politics. The task, then, is not to undermine race per se but to undermine the *white citizen*, not just to recognize subordinated racial groups but also to refuse to recognize *whiteness*. Whether through affirmative or transformative means, the democratic task is to abolish the whiteness of citizenship.

The White Citizen in the Global Era

Sometimes, all that is solid melts into air. The racial order, a fixture in American life for over three hundred years, is evolving in response to changes in the political and economic structure begun in the early 1970s. These changes, generally referred to as globalization, raise questions for my argument. Will this century's problem still be the problem of the color line, or is globalization fundamentally transforming or even dissolving the racial order—and therefore the political significance of whiteness? If economic, political, and social trends continue, will there be a need to even worry about white citizenship in a global, diverse, hybrid society, much less abolish it? If not, is the multicultural and/or color-blind ideal more appropriate to our racial future after all?

Following Thomas Holt, I suggest there are two keys to answering these questions.[58] The first is immigration. One product of globalization in developed nations is a class of largely immigrant, low-paid, nonunionized, highly exploitable service and small-scale production workers. As these workers compete with native-born workers for scarce jobs, the stage is set for a clash that could very well assume a racial veneer. The argument that immigration breeds racial conflict, however, presumes that immigrants are of a different race simply due to their coming from a different part of the globe than Europe or Africa. Yet as I argued in chapter 1, race is a political rather than geographic or demographic product. Therefore, immigration by itself does not create a new racial dynamic. In fact, immigration has traditionally been an engine of assimilation, not racial distinction, as initial nativist anger eventually turns into acceptance and foreigners formerly scorned become full-fledged Americans—and white citizens.

Of course, immigration today is not entirely analogous to ethnic European assimilation in the *Herrenvolk* era. There is no longer, for example, an imperative for immigrants to become legally white. Immigrants today can become American citizens even as they preserve their ethnic identity.[59] Nevertheless, some scholars argue that the cultural pluralism of contemporary immigration is but a new "strategy of annexation" into whiteness that differs from earlier immigration only in that it reflects a different set of sensitivities demanded by a post-*Herrenvolk* world. This leads to the appearance of a wave of "multiracial" immigration, but as in the *Herrenvolk* era, these scholars argue, the crux of immigrant assimilation is still establishing social distance between one's own ethnic group and Black people.[60] As a result, it is doubtful that whites will become a minority anytime soon, according to sociologist George Yancey, for the same processes that whitened European immigrants are still at work in assimilating Latinos and Asians. As the antipode against which immigrants measure themselves, African Americans, meanwhile, continue to "experience a degree of alienation unlike that of other racial groups" and will therefore remain at the bottom of the racial hierarchy.[61] A bipolar order will persist as the white category expands to include Asians and Latinos (even if they prefer not to be referred to as "white" specifically), while Blackness remains the touchstone against which full assimilation is measured. This argument is not without its weaknesses. It downplays, for example, the historical experience of Mexican, Chinese, and Japanese peoples in the United States prior to contemporary immigration. Nevertheless, its points about the fluid nature of the white club and the alienation of African Americans are historically sound and should give pause to those who think the twenty-first century will be inevitably multiracial or "beyond race."

The second key to understanding the future of race is the increasing irrelevance of Black people as a group to the global economy. In the *Herrenvolk* era African Americans were central to production as slaves, sharecroppers, domestics, and industrial workers. In the global era, however, there is no economic role for the plurality of Black people. The likely outcome, Holt fears, is that some African Americans will succeed on an individual level but the majority will continue to endure poverty and oppression, only now due to economic irrelevance as much as explicit discrimination. "It is clear that although race may indeed do conceptual work in this economy, blacks-as-a-race have no economic role. Despite the dramatic rise in the number of middle-income blacks and, by historical measures, their visible integration into major institutions of the national life, one of the clearest consequences of the transformed economy has been the massive exclusion of blacks from the formal economy."[62]

The results of this may look strikingly new, in part. African Americans today are represented in American culture to an unprecedented extent, particularly in sports and entertainment. The "browning of mainstream commercial culture" touches nearly every consumer.[63] Apparently, Black people are increasingly central to the means of consumption even as they become disposable to the means of production.[64] Further, Vernon Jordan, Colin Powell, and Condoleeza Rice's presence as power brokers differs significantly from that of, say, Clarence Thomas. Thomas and the pantheon of higher-level Black public officials before him were traditionally appointed to positions "reserved" for Black people (such as ambassador to Liberia or a certain number of judgeships), providing African Americans with a modicum of representation without challenging white hegemony. Jordan, Powell, and Rice, however, by and large do not owe their elite positions to their race (although they may have benefited from affirmative action). The apparent unimportance of their

Blackness to their posts is historically unprecedented.[65] Yet despite these changes, some things will likely remain all too familiar, as the majority of Black people remain mired in economic irrelevance even as Black faces become a normal feature of public life.

A possible outcome of this combination of immigrant assimilation and Black superfluity could be the Latin Americanization of the racial order. As I argued in chapter 1, racial categories in Latin America tend to be more fluid than the rigid bipolar model of the United States. Rather than ancestry and the one-drop rule, the Latin American model typically associates race with class position and physical appearance. The result is a system of numerous racial gradations between white and Black that allow for social mobility among them, since wealth can "whiten" an otherwise dark person. Latin American migrants could bring this notion of race with them to the United States.[66] Combined with changes in the economic and social structure due to globalization, the result could be a racial hierarchy in which whites are generally on top and Black people are generally on bottom with a myriad of racial categories and hybrids in between, in which race becomes a relatively fluid term that designates class status, culture, and/or self-identification.[67]

So it appears that all that is solid does not necessarily vanish. Even if Latin Americanization occurs, "Racism . . . is never entirely new," as Holt reminds us. "Shards and fragments of its past incarnations are embedded in the new. Or, if we switch metaphors to an archaeological image, the new is sedimented onto the old, which occasionally seeps or bursts through."[68] Whether the nation becomes color blind, multicultural, transracial, hybrid, or *mestizaje*, racial hierarchy and white dominance will likely endure. Immigration may simply shift the color line to fold ever more ethnic groups into full citizenship at the expense of Black people, who remain at the bottom of the economic barrel. White resistance to policies that appear to threaten their favored status could result in a backlash. And left unchallenged, whiteness will still be the standard for full citizenship, the "browning" of American culture notwithstanding. Without a conscious political effort to overthrow it, the democratic problem of the white citizen will persist in the twenty-first century.

Unfortunately, the multicultural and color-blind ideals will not be equipped to deal with it. Multiculturalism and color blindness are means to contain political and social instability (particularly regarding race, culture, and ethnic nationalism) in an increasingly global and rapidly changing economy. As Slavoj Žižek points out, multiculturalism is the perfect cultural logic for a world in which capital is loyal to no country, religion, or race, yet people still are.[69] Tolerance, diversity, equality, and liberal democracy all form the basis of a new hegemonic ideal through which global capital functions. Such an ideal, he argues, must necessarily repudiate the most offensive forms of white supremacy and accommodate some sort of an integrated middle class. Yet it also discourages systematic change. As the new watchword of accumulation in the global era, multicultural "diversity" is not a radical ideal but a corporate imperative.[70]

Further, neither ideal challenges the passive conception of citizenship that is a legacy of racial standing. Even Fraser's social citizenship, which combines civil and political rights with the right to individual well-being, is ultimately more concerned with folding economic rights into citizenship than expanding participation in the public sphere.[71] All lack a participatory element that might fire the American political imagination in new ways. Thus, neither the color-blind nor the multicultural ideal represents a strategy for greater democracy. Both ideals present themselves as alternatives to a world of prejudice and xenophobia. They are that, but they are only that, because neither undermines the political imagination of the white citizen. Of course, not all multiculturalists want to produce a new cultural hegemony for global capital. Giroux explicitly hopes a new white identity can pave the way for a radical democracy, while social citizenship undoubtedly conflicts with globalization as it currently functions. Yet such aspirations are destined to be thwarted without a critique of the white democracy. In the absence of such a critique, color blindness and multiculturalism provide the surreptitious means by which the cross-class alliance persists.

As Nathan Glazer writes, we are all multiculturalists now.[72] One cannot open a newspaper, attend a conference, or listen to corporate and academic leaders without hearing of the need for diversity in the work-place, classroom, and boardroom. Unquestionably, this is a good thing. Yet it is not a project for greater democracy. Multiculturalism aims to achieve stability in a global economy. While this requires including people who were formerly excluded from the *Herrenvolk* democracy, it does not imply expanding democratic rights or deepening citizen participation in those affairs that affect ordinary people's lives.

The color-blind and multicultural ideals' acquiescence to whiteness is not so much a sign of their hypocrisy as it is proof of the determination of the white citizen to hold the cross-class alliance together in the post-*Herrenvolk* era. Whether through resistance to analyzing race in terms of power or through a rearticulation of whiteness as a culture that, properly purged of its racist features, deserves recognition with any other, the white citizen still lives, and has a will to live. The multicultural and color-blind ideals are not antinomies but flip sides of the same coin. By abandoning both we abandon the dispute between them, shifting the focus to the role of the white citizen in shaping the democratic imagination as well as in enforcing racial subordination. The radical democratic ideal, then, is neither the refusal of recognition of race nor the equal recognition of cultures or races but *the refusal of recognition of whiteness.* Such a refusal opens up space to create new forms of identity—for those who are white and those who are not—amidst a reinvigorated public sphere. Outlining the politics of the refusal or *abolition* of white democracy is the task of the final chapter.

CHAPTER 5

The Abolition-Democracy

I was in my car driving along the freeway when at a red light another car pulled alongside. A white woman was driving and on the passenger's side, next to me, was a white man. *"Malcolm X!"* he called out—and when I looked, he stuck his hand out of his car, across at me, grinning. "Do you mind shaking hands with a white man?" Imagine that! Just as the traffic light turned green, I told him, "I don't mind shaking hands with human beings. Are you one?"

—Malcolm X, *The Autobiography of Malcolm X*

One of the great stories about Malcolm X is how his views on white people changed after his pilgrimage to Mecca. While making his Hajj in 1964, he observed people of all colors living and worshipping Allah as equals, leading him to write in his journal that "the whites don't seem white."[1] He then realized it was indeed possible for there to be good "white" people.[2] As a result, he quickly abandoned the prejudice he held against whites when he was the spokesman for the Nation of Islam. Releasing his hatred, he began to judge people for what they did and said rather than who they were.

That, anyway, is the tale that inspired the postage stamp. The chance meeting with the white motorists would seem to confirm this rebirth from racist to civil rights champion. There is another way, however, to interpret this encounter. Certainly, Malcolm X underwent an extraordinary change in the last fifteen months of his life. But through it all he remained antiwhite. For example, a content analysis of his speeches found that, while he did begin to make favorable assertions about white people after his pilgrimage, over eighty percent of his references to whites were still negative.[3] He continued to be strongly critical of whites for their participation in the oppression of Black people;

he just came to allow for the possibility that they were not inherently racist. As he put it, "I haven't changed, I just see things on a broader scale."[4]

Malcolm X abandoned his belief that white people are devils by nature and came to believe that whites could potentially become human beings. Whiteness went from something one was to something one did. But this raises a question: if whites stopped acting like devils and started acting like humans, would they still be white? Malcolm did not have the language of social construction to help distinguish the political category of race from physical characteristics such as pale skin or hair that does not need a conk to be straight. His encounter with the white motorists, however, indicates that if he had had access to such language, the answer might very well have been no. After the Hajj, Malcolm X went from describing racial oppression as a conspiracy among whites to a system of white supremacy. Those who consent to the system (tacitly or expressly) remain devils in all but name, while those who resist it are human beings worthy of a handshake. The political challenge Malcolm raises with his handshake is how to turn "white people" into human beings. The process of becoming human, he implies, involves unbecoming white.[5]

In this final chapter I consider the implications of a political theory aimed at abolishing white citizenship. Borrowing a term from Du Bois, I call such a politics the *abolition-democracy*. Rooted in the spirit of the nineteenth-century abolitionists, the abolition-democracy is a politics committed to expanding freedom through the dissolution of whiteness. Its object, following Malcolm, is to make white citizens human beings through the elimination of their racial privileges. Drawing on utopian elements in Black radical political thought, the abolition-democracy seeks to directly challenge the status and privileges of whiteness, both to undermine racial discrimination and to expand democratic participation. Just as the original abolitionist movement paved the way for feminism's first wave, Reconstruction heralded the rise of organized labor, and the civil rights movement created political space for feminist, gay and lesbian, Chicano, and other movements, the abolition of white citizenship creates the potential to expand the American democratic imagination beyond the limits of liberalism.

The White Imagination Revisited

In this book I have argued that white democracy has not violated American ideals of equality, liberty, and citizenship so much as it has shaped them. I argued in chapter 2, for example, that whites in the *Herrenvolk* era rejected "social equality" because the term implied equal racial standing as much as it did the equalization of wealth. This has contributed to a conception of equality that is restricted to political rights and equal opportunity. A program like welfare is politically suspect in the white imagination because in redistributing wealth to both "undeserving people" and Black people (a distinction many whites barely bother to make), it appears as an unfair "handout" that violates the premise of individual effort and opportunity.[6] Thus, white citizenship has not simply reserved equal rights and opportunities for whites exclusively. It has also contributed to a narrow understanding of equality that conceives of social equality as illegitimate.

Whiteness also constrains the meaning of freedom. As David Roediger notes, a standing conception of citizenship tends to place mostly negative demands on the public sphere because liberty implies distinguishing oneself from a degraded status more than participating in those affairs that affect one's daily life.[7] Even the most minimal forms of citizen participation, therefore, suffice to denote standing. Accordingly, "negative" rights that protect one's status and property become more important than "positive" liberties such as substantive participation in politics or the right to the prerequisites for such participation (nutrition, shelter, health care, education, sufficient leisure time). Freedom in the white imagination is something to possess rather than an activity to practice. This passive conception of freedom tends to sustain a worldview of atomized, status-seeking persons who see in others a threat to individual liberty rather than a condition of it. As a result, citizenship becomes an identity that claims possession of significant political power but is generally disinclined to use it, particularly to challenge the structural inequalities built into a liberal capitalist system.

Of course, white privilege is not the only influence on American political ideals. Classical republicanism and liberalism, Enlightenment ideals, English common law, Puritan thought, Black freedom struggles, and other influences have all played roles in shaping the American democratic tradition.[8] Further, a negative conception of liberty and a formal conception of equality are hallmarks of nonracial liberalism as well as the white democracy. Nevertheless, in the United States the ideals of individual autonomy and equal opportunity were constructed against a backdrop of Black subordination and white advantage, and are so intertwined that they are not easily separated.

White citizenship, then, has left a lasting mark on the American democratic imagination. The democratic problem of the white citizen is not only that he or she has a material interest in excluding not-whites from the full fruits of democracy but that his or her very existence perpetuates a stunted conception of democracy. The white imagination is exclusive: it does not want to let new members into the polity, from American Indians to former slaves to Mexican immigrants to convicted felons. It promotes a negative conception of liberty: the individual is free to the extent that others do not interfere with her or him. It emphasizes standing: the object of democracy is less to participate in those affairs that affect one's daily life than to achieve a certain status and hold on to it. It is miserly: it casts a suspicious eye toward social programs that supply the prerequisites of participation, such as universal health care, a decent standard of living, and a good education, and it tends not to question private property and inequalities of wealth. It emphasizes individual success rather than class solidarity: the objective is to beat one's competition in the marketplace rather than challenge exploitation. Perhaps the most insidious aspect of the white imagination is that it presumes that the system of rights and representation established in the *Herrenvolk* and post–civil rights eras is the highest political form attainable. It assumes that the white citizen is free, when it is precisely the nature of his or her freedom that must be interrogated. In these ways, the white imagination sustains a narrow conception of democracy that inhibits more expansive and participatory visions.

The Utopian Element of Black Radical Political Thought

What is needed, then, is a political vision that exceeds the limits set by the white imagination. Unfortunately, contemporary democratic theory by and large has yet to meet this need because it is pervaded by a chastened conception of democracy that appears resigned to liberalism.[9] This is evident in that much of its intellectual energy is currently devoted to relatively modest proposals for procedures, practices, and programs that supplement liberal democratic institutions rather than challenge them. As Will Kymlicka and Wayne Norman note in their assessment of contemporary citizenship theory, "Most citizenship theorists either leave the question of how to promote citizenship unanswered or focus on 'modest' or 'gently and relatively unobtrusive ways' to promote civic virtues."[10] The appeal of "civic associations," which nearly all schools of thought in democratic theory endorse in one form or another, is a case in point. Jeffrey Isaac, for example, raises a powerful critique of the failure of political theory to come to grips with the recent changes sweeping the world, beginning with the fall of the Berlin Wall in 1989. Much of this failure has to do with a reflexive attachment to liberalism. Liberalism in itself, he argues, is insufficient to meet the needs and aspirations of humanity. As such, it must be supplemented with grassroots civic associations, or "oases in the desert" of liberal democracy, that can empower individuals and inculcate civic responsibility.

> It is in this light that we need to consider and to theorize other forms of democratic politics, other vehicles of democratic aspiration, not as replacements for the liberal democratic state but as adjuncts to it, ways of challenging the injustices to which it is insufficiently attentive and ways of promoting forms of exit, loyalty, and especially *voice* in a system increasingly beset by immobilism and sclerosis.[11]

Isaac proposes a "localist democracy" as an alternative, a regionally oriented, pragmatic, diffuse, and pluralist politics filled with civic associations that would flourish within the "admittedly unethical and unsatisfying framework of capitalism."[12] Isaac looks to the outer reaches of liberal democracy, yet even his vision is notable for its chastened view of the possibilities of democracy in the present era. Despite his critique of contemporary political theory, democratic theory in "dark times" apparently must still trade vision for pragmatism.

It seems utopianism is out of fashion these days. Yet a normative democratic theory needs a touch of utopia almost by definition. "Utopian" is not a word to scorn. Certainly, it can represent the hopelessly unrealistic, but it also describes political visions that go beyond the boundaries of conventional political thinking. The works of Carole Pateman and C. B. Macpherson on participatory democracy, for example, are so compelling in part because they refuse to limit themselves to a politics of the possible.[13] In their work, expanding citizens' participation in public affairs is a means to transform the structures of society as well as individuals' sense of their capacities. Yet as Emily Hauptmann has persuasively shown, deliberative democratic theory (which replaced participatory theory in the 1980s) has drawn much more modest conclusions about the possibilities of democratic participation in the contemporary era.[14] Deliberative democratic theorists claim to correct the excessive utopianism and simplistic nature of participatory theory, but their own theories lack a critical perspective and a transformative vision. Of course, pragmatism has a role in any attempt to theorize a more democratic society, but so does a politics that defines democracy in the most radical manner—as the ability of all persons to have a meaningful say in those affairs that affect their daily life—without worrying whether it is "realistic." The purpose of democratic theory is to imagine and seek the most democratic society possible, which implies reaching beyond liberal democracy and the modest aspirations of today's democratic theory.

The Black radical tradition is an important source to draw on in restoring the radical-utopian element in democratic theory and practice.

As Michael Dawson points out, Black radical thought, while not necessarily antiliberal, "cannot be confined within the boundaries of liberalism."[15] Its trenchant critique of white supremacy, its commitment to an international regard even while being rooted in a concern for the needs and desires of a specific community, and its expansive vision make it a wellspring of inspiration, knowledge, and philosophy for a twenty-first-century democratic theory. These utopian visions, or "freedom dreams" as Robin Kelley calls them, emerge from movements against white domination in particular. "Collective social movements are incubators of new knowledge," he asserts. Social movements against white supremacy "do what great poetry always does: transport us to another place, compel us to relive horrors and, more importantly, enable us to imagine a new society."[16] Rather than understanding democracy as something whites created and people of color sought to join, the Black radical tradition enables us to reinterpret American democracy as something that white citizens have contributed to yet compromised and that anticitizens have advanced. This is not to say that there is a single, coherent Black community that is inherently more moral or revolutionary than whites. My point is that the Black radical tradition, from abolitionism to nationalism to communism, has consistently challenged common notions about American democracy, exposed the limitations of the white political imagination, enabled new political visions, and shown the radical democratic potential of efforts against white citizenship. While examples of this tradition can be found in thinkers such as Martin Delany, James Baldwin, Angela Davis, Ella Baker, Malcolm X, Martin Luther King Jr., bell hooks, and others, I turn to W. E. B. Du Bois as a classic example.

In all of his writings Du Bois emphasizes the central role of Black people in history. Black self-activity, he argues, is the motor force of American freedom and culture: slaves won the Civil War in *Black Reconstruction*, invented modern American music in *The Souls of Black Folk*, and created the weekend in *Dusk of Dawn*. They even made John Brown.[17] Further, Du Bois consistently casts these achievements in radical-utopian terms. The Civil War was a "general strike" against slavery by the slaves, while the 1868 South Carolina state legislature was practically a dictatorship of the Black proletariat.[18]

This utopian strain informs his critique of race and democracy. For Du Bois, the central political task of the age is to abolish the color line. This means much more than the end of segregation; it is a call to transcend the white and dark worlds. As he argues in *Souls of Black Folk*, the striving of Black people is to overcome their double consciousness, but not by making the Black world supreme or by dissolving it into the white world. As with Hegel's spiral trajectory of history, the task is to forge the two antithetical worlds into a new polity.

> In this merging [the Negro] wishes neither of the older selves to be lost. He would not Africanize America, for America has too much to teach the world and Africa. He would not bleach his Negro soul in a flood of white Americanism, for he knows that Negro blood has a message for the world. He simply wishes to make it possible for a man to be both a Negro and an American, without being cursed and spit upon by his fellows, without having the doors of Opportunity closed roughly in his face.[19]

This is a call for neither assimilation nor separation. As David Levering Lewis argues, Du Bois rejects the integration-separation dichotomy "by affirming it in a permanent tension. Henceforth, the destiny of the race could be conceived as leading neither to assimilation nor separatism but to proud, enduring hyphenation."[20] Yet there is a deeper implication in this passage, and in Du Bois's life's work. By defending the Black world even as he calls for the abolition of the color line, Du Bois essentially calls for *the end of the white world*. As Arnold Rampersad argues, Du Bois understands the African American experience "as essentially a continuous political struggle with the white world."[21] For it is this world, Du Bois later writes, that "existed primarily, so far as I was concerned, to see with sleepless vigilance that I was kept within bounds."[22] The dark world, on the other hand, is the democratic antithesis to whiteness. In its preservation lies the hope of the world. "A belief in humanity," he writes, "is a belief in colored men."[23] The political problem for

Du Bois is not how to find a way for (the white) democracy to include Black people. Rather, *democracy should aspire to the dark world*, since the struggle for its freedom opens up political possibilities unimaginable to those tethered to the white world.

Du Bois hints at such possibilities in "Criteria of Negro Art," an article originally published in the NAACP's *Crisis* magazine in 1926. In it, he asks his largely Black readership, "What is the thing we are after?" He replies, "We want to be Americans, full-fledged Americans, with all the rights of other American citizens." This seems like an honorable demand for full civil and political rights, and indeed it is. But he continues:

> But is that all? Do we want simply to be Americans? Once in a while through all of us there flashes some clairvoyance, some clear idea, of what America really is. We who are dark can see America in a way that white Americans cannot. And seeing our country thus, are we satisfied with its present goals and ideals? . . . [P]ushed aside as we have been in America, there has come to us . . . a vision of what the world could be if it were really a beautiful world . . . a world where men know, where men create, where they realize themselves and where they enjoy life. It is that sort of a world we want to create for ourselves and for all America.[24]

This utopian imagination, borne of Black struggle, is one of the potential fruits of unshackling democratic politics from the bonds of whiteness. "We have within us as a race new stirrings," Du Bois maintains. "Stirrings of the beginning of a new appreciation of joy, of a new desire to create, of a new will to be."[25] The battle to abolish the white world, he suggests, goes beyond the inclusion of all persons into the polity. It is the struggle for human emancipation itself.[26]

Principles of the Abolition-Democracy

The term "abolition-democracy" is from *Black Reconstruction*. Du Bois uses it to refer to the Black and white abolitionists who led the "Reconstruction of Democracy" after the Civil War. The workers and small capitalists who formed the abolition-democracy firmly believed in democratic government, but also in the system of private property and in the American Dream.[27] But the abolition-democracy's significance went much deeper than these petty bourgeois aspirations, Du Bois argues. The abolition-democracy was revolutionary because in challenging the power of the former slave masters, it cut to the foundations of the nation's class system. While its professed aim was liberal democracy, the cataclysmic struggle it engendered opened up the possibility to create a radical or "industrial democracy." I borrow the term "abolition-democracy" for a contemporary political theory to evoke the expansive democratic potential of struggles against white citizenship.

Most historians date the origins of the American abolitionist movement at 1831, the year in which William Lloyd Garrison began publishing his newspaper *The Liberator*.[28] Resistance to slavery, of course, is as old as the institution itself, and antislavery organizations existed in the New World at least since the Revolutionary era. *The Liberator*, however, inaugurated a new wave of abolitionist activity that broke from the moderate, conciliatory, and procolonizationist politics of earlier antislavery societies. Garrison's paper argued that slavery was a sin and that slaves should be freed immediately and unconditionally, without compensation to slaveholders. It also railed against racial prejudice. The constitution of the New England Anti-Slavery Society (founded by Garrison in 1832), for example, calls for the immediate emancipation of slaves and declares that "a mere difference of complexion is no reason why any man should be deprived of any of his natural rights, or subjected to any political disability."[29] Garrison also believed that an antislavery society should welcome all religious, social, and political viewpoints. The only necessary principle of unity among abolitionists, he argued, is a commitment to immediate and unconditional emancipation.[30]

The abolitionists lectured and petitioned against slavery. They published newspapers and pamphlets, using them as organizing tools. They held meetings, conventions, antislavery bazaars, and sewing circles. They raised money, passed resolutions, organized vigilance committees against the Fugitive Slave Law, and participated in the Underground Railroad.

In at least one instance—John Brown's raid on Harpers Ferry—they organized armed rebellion against slavery. Abolitionists also deliberately challenged the nation's racial boundaries. Meetings flouted segregated seating customs. African Americans served in positions of leadership in antislavery organizations. White female agents of the American Anti-Slavery Society toured with Black male agents.[31] Financial support came from Northern Black communities and white settlements in western states like Ohio. Unquestionably, white paternalism and racial prejudice existed within the movement; nevertheless, abolitionism marked the first time white Americans collectively participated in efforts to abolish the color line.[32]

The abolitionists were vilified in the press, denounced from the pulpit, and attacked in the streets. Their meetings were broken up by mobs, their halls trashed, their printing presses thrown into rivers, and their speakers pelted with rotten vegetables, stones, snowballs, and brickbats—this in the North! Garrison himself was nearly lynched by a Boston mob in 1835. Yet by the late 1850s the North had come 'round to the abolitionist perspective. In 1848 the Free Soil Party opposed the expansion of slavery into the new territories; the new Republican Party would do the same a few years later. Chief Justice Roger Taney's opinion in *Dred Scott v. Sandford* (1857) infuriated the North rather than settled the slavery question as he intended. John Brown's 1859 assault on Harpers Ferry thrilled Northerners—just as his quick trial and summary execution outraged them. Garrison's abolitionist career began by dodging projectiles from angry mobs, but by 1864 he was meeting with President Lincoln at the White House.[33] A movement that began with just a few hundred people had managed to abolitionize half the nation and inspire a civil war that would clinch its principal demand of immediate and unconditional emancipation without compensation to the slave owner. It was a revolutionary movement.[34]

The abolitionists' principles and achievements make them an important, if underappreciated, source of a new democratic politics, for in the process of challenging slavery and racial prejudice they challenged white citizenship itself, thereby creating space for expanded democratic practices. There are three elements of abolitionist praxis that are particularly relevant for today: their model of the political actor as agitator, their emphasis on freedom, and their willingness to follow the radical implications of their demands.

The Abolitionist as Agitator

As historian Aileen Kraditor emphasizes, the radical abolitionists engaged in antislavery work as agitators rather than reformers.[35] The abolition of slavery, they argued, could not be achieved through normal political channels because the entire political system, from the parties to the federal government, served the interests of the slave power. The Garrisonians' foremost concern was to build a constituency, not to influence legislators, pass laws, or run candidates for office. They sought to build it by awakening consciences, encouraging free speech and debate, publishing propaganda, and refusing to sacrifice principle for political expediency. The abolitionist as agitator refused to compromise, for she believed that adherence to principle is itself the most expedient course.[36]

Reformist abolitionists urged the Garrisonians to be more "respectable" in their criticism of slavery. It is more effective, they argued, to win people over through cool, rational discourse than with fierce denunciations of slaveholders, the church, and the state for their complicity in slavery. The radicals replied that it is agitation, not reasoning, that gets results. As the Garrisonian Wendell Phillips states:

> The cause is not ours, so that we might, rightfully, postpone or put in peril the victory by moderating our demands, stifling our convictions, or filing down our rebukes, to gratify any sickly taste of our own, or to spare the delicate nerves of our neighbor. . . . The press, the pulpit, the wealth, the literature, the prejudices, the political arrangements, the present self-interest of the country, are all against us. God has given us no weapon but the truth, faithfully uttered, and addressed, with the old prophets' directness, to the conscience of the individual sinner. . . . We have facts for those who think, arguments for those who reason; but he who cannot be reasoned out of his prejudices must be laughed out of them.[37]

Phillips's insistence that "There are far more dead hearts to be quickened than confused intellects to be cleared up" is a powerful rejoinder to the belief that deliberation, reason, and the forceless force of the better argument is the best form of suasion.[38] The Garrisonians made the case for radicalness over respectability, principle over expedience, militancy over discipline, and volume over toned-down talk. Should the slave, they ask, expect anything less?

Many Northerners dismissed as unrealistic the Garrisonians' demand for immediate emancipation and the end of racial prejudice. The Garrisonians replied that limiting one's goals to what is "realistic" sets the sights of social change too low, while demanding the unattainable makes favorable compromise possible by making a reform-minded politician's demands seem reasonable. (Consider how Malcolm X's fiery statements made Martin Luther King's demands tenable to white moderates, who otherwise felt that King was going too far too fast.) Further, the call for immediate and unconditional emancipation was not just a demand but a means of struggle, for it opened the ears and eyes of the public. "We have never said that slavery would be overthrown by a single blow," Garrison once confessed. "That it ought to be, we shall always contend."[39] Agitation, the abolitionists show, is vital for democratic politics because in demanding the impossible one creates possibilities.

The Goal Is Freedom

Democracy is often understood as a political form driven by the desire for equality. Robert Dahl, for example, explains that democratization is an uneven and unsteady battle between the "logic of equality" (the desire to extend equal political rights to all members of a polity) and "the brute facts of inequality." Accordingly, he argues, the best way to counter these facts is to steadily extend democratic rights to excluded groups.[40] Inclusion is the means and equality the end.

Unquestionably, racial discrimination is a form of inequality. Yet it is notable that in two of the nation's most significant struggles against this "brute fact," equality served as neither political slogan nor final end. Slaves prayed for "the coming of the Lord," fought for jubilee, and renamed themselves "Freeman" after emancipation. Civil rights activists demanded "Freedom Now!," took Freedom Rides, and sang freedom songs during Freedom Summer. In both struggles, the slogan and the goal was freedom. Calls for "inclusion" or "diversity" were nonexistent. Cries for "equality" were not entirely absent but were clearly less common. It was not that equality was irrelevant, of course, but that it was assumed to be an implicit part of freedom. Indeed, as Richard King argues, since African Americans took it for granted that they were equal to whites, the debate over equality during the civil rights movement was largely "an argument among white people."[41]

This commitment to liberty was the touchstone of the abolitionist movement. Black abolitionists in particular insisted on freedom from bondage, freedom from color caste, and freedom from poverty. Abolitionists struggled for free speech in the face of local intimidation and federal censorship, elevated the Declaration of Independence above the Constitution in esteem, emphasized personal liberty, and resisted racial privileges.[42] Perhaps most importantly, abolitionists insisted that freedom means the ability to participate in public affairs. As the abolitionist Martin Delany explains, "No people can be free who themselves do not constitute an essential part of the *ruling element* of the country in which they live."[43]

This quest for participation is obscured when democracy is associated primarily with the "logic of equality." For this reason, an abolitionist-democratic politics seeks to emphasize participation by reasserting freedom as the basic ideal upon which democratic theory should rest. Of course, it appreciates the significance of equality, including equal political rights and the fair distribution of "social rights" such as universal health care, decent housing, adequate nutrition, and a minimum standard of living for all. But it insists that these must orbit around participation, for as Hannah Arendt argues, humans are not truly free until they have the option of participating in political debates and making decisions. "Men *are* free—as distinguished from their possessing the gift for freedom—as long as they act, neither before nor after; for to *be* free and to act are the same."[44] The abolition-democracy goes beyond equal rights and inclusion to embrace a concept of freedom as substantive participation in public affairs. The path to participation runs through the struggle against white citizenship.

Radical Implications

Marx sought to change the world through a "ruthless criticism of everything existing." He argued that theory must be ruthless in two senses. It must not be afraid of its own conclusions, however radical, and it must not be afraid of being in conflict with the powers that be.[45] The abolitionists followed Marx on both counts. They were not afraid to go where their radical conclusions took them, from women's suffrage to condemning the Constitution as a proslavery document to arguing for disunion to welcoming civil war. Abolitionists' radical views often extended beyond antislavery. Many experimented with diet (including vegetarianism), were early practitioners of alternative medicine, and were open to new forms of religious worship. Abolitionists even transformed the traditional Christian wedding ceremony, as when Theodore Weld and Angelina Grimké married without a minister and without Grimké promising to obey Weld.[46] Following the radical logic of their arguments sometimes required rejecting their own cherished beliefs, as when Abby Kelley, Stephen Foster, and William Garrison defended John Brown's raid despite their pacifism.[47] These Garrisonians had little desire to be "respectable" or to moderate their beliefs, since they were convinced that a moderate approach to antislavery often meant complicity with slavery. "I am for conciliation," Phillips explained, "but not for conciliating the slaveholder. Death to the system, and death or exile to the master, is the only motto."[48]

The abolitionists' radical crusade has several important implications for a contemporary abolitionist-democratic politics. It suggests that an attack on racial subordination raises the level of struggle against oppression in general. By undermining slavery the abolitionists challenged the entire political and economic order. Unlike trade unionism, prison reform, women's suffrage, temperance, or other reform movements of their day, the abolitionists' demand for unconditional emancipation with no compensation to slaveholders threatened the entire structure of the American state, which was dominated by the slave power. Attacking slavery melted the glue that kept the Union together. The abolitionists placed their fingers on the nation's fault line; through their agitation they pried the crack apart.[49] The lesson for today, as David Roediger points out, is that as the walls of racial oppression tumble, class rule is also shaken.[50]

Further, an abolitionist politics shows that expanding democracy is not just a matter of changing democratic procedures or norms but also of creating new institutions: integrated antislavery meetings; state legislatures supplemented by mass meetings of Black women, men, and children during Reconstruction; freedom schools in the back of beauty parlors during the civil rights movement; Black Panther parties for self-defense. These institutions offered new means of participation that went beyond voting and potentially beyond liberal democracy.[51] Civic education, deliberation, social rights, and civic associations are all important accoutrements of democracy, but by themselves or even taken together they remain within the limits to democratic participation set by liberalism. Expanding participation beyond these limits implies new institutions or the transformation of existing ones. This is a political challenge that requires conflict more than consensus, struggle more than agonism, and debate more than deliberation. Contemporary democratic theory has been reluctant to pursue these themes but the abolition-democracy turns politics toward them.

Strategy and Application

I have argued that vision is one of the principal weaknesses of contemporary democratic theory, but the lack of strategy is evident as well. Democratic theorists commonly preface their arguments for expanded democracy with a disclaimer that their model presupposes a diminishment of economic and social inequalities but provide no ideas for how to achieve this. William Connolly, for example, writes, "Agonal democracy presupposes a reduction in established economic inequalities, and this objective in turn requires a mobilization of public energies to promote it."[52] But the mobilization of such energies is precisely what a democratic theory is supposed to help achieve. Connolly's theory of greater democracy rests on reduced social and economic disparities, yet reduced disparities depend on greater democracy. This catch-22 reflects a lack of strategy. The abolition-democracy, on the other hand, is both means and end. Through its strategy of abolishing white citizenship, space is created for new forms of democratic participation and new political ideals.

An abolitionist-democratic strategy does not seek to build coalitions by downplaying racial tensions or to create class-based social programs that "transcend" race. Instead, it directly confronts policies and practices that sustain the cross-class alliance and thereby limit the democratic imagination of white citizens. Thus, policies such as busing and affirmative action are important not so much because they foster diversity but because they redistribute racially skewed education resources, countering whites' material interest in segregated schools and preferential access to elite universities. Similarly, policies that attack redlining redistribute housing wealth in a way that undermines whites' privileged access to the best homes, best neighborhoods, and lowest interest rates. An abolitionist-democratic strategy challenges neighborhood associations, often regarded as beacons of face-to-face democracy, when they serve as vehicles for gentrifying inner-city neighborhoods and driving out residents of color. It challenges parent-teacher associations when they seek to preserve racial segregation or tracking in schools. It challenges unions, such as teachers' or police officers' unions, when they place the interests of their members before the need to fight racial discrimination. It monitors the police to prevent racial profiling and arrest rates that disproportionately impact people of color. It monitors the courts to prevent biased juries, sentencing disparities, and racially skewed incarceration rates. For the reasons set out in chapter 4, it resists any attempts to resuscitate a "progressive white identity," in the classroom or elsewhere.

The abolition-democracy works for reparations to redistribute wealth unjustly accumulated by whites as a result of centuries of slavery and segregation. Yet as Robin Kelley argues, reparations are about "more than a paycheck and an apology." Equally important is the way in which any resources won in a reparations struggle would be distributed. There are few implications for democratic participation if reparations merely involve the government distributing checks to the victims and ancestors of slavery and segregation. If reparations are understood as "a means to mobilize African Americans to struggle for social change, self-transformation, and self-reliance," however, it raises important questions of democracy.[53] It suggests that the means of distribution are as important as the wealth distributed. It would also require a democratic structure so that ordinary people can determine for themselves how to spend the money. If reparations went to building autonomous Black institutions rather than individuals, for example, it would benefit the entire nation, not just the Black community, since it would involve creating democratic institutions in largely urban areas.[54]

In sum, an abolitionist-democratic strategy seeks to abolish explicit and normalized white advantages in housing, education, employment, asset accumulation, health, criminal justice, and politics, both because such preferences are morally wrong and because struggles against them point toward greater democratic possibilities. The radical potential of such a strategy is suggested by the historical impact of the Black freedom struggles on American democracy. The abolitionist movement inspired the first wave of feminism. Emancipation led to jubilee, then Reconstruction, then the rise of organized labor and the movement for an eight-hour day.[55] The civil rights movement imagined a "beloved community" and unleashed a flurry of social movements, from women's liberation to the student movement to Stonewall to Black and Brown and Red Power to the revolutionary underground. Black freedom struggles, whose ostensible purpose was to fulfill the "American Creed," quickly spilled over the containers of liberal democracy. An abolitionist-democratic politics seeks to do the same. It seeks to restore the radical-utopian and the action dimensions of democratic theory by imagining a world without whiteness. In so doing, it envisions a world free of oppression and domination in general. A democratic politics must be an abolitionist politics.

An abolitionist strategy has two potential weaknesses. Without a doubt, it is difficult to convince white citizens to surrender existing short-term privileges for the possibility of long-term gain. Privileged groups rarely give up their power voluntarily—especially when they no longer believe themselves to be privileged. But the difficulty of a task does not diminish its necessity. All social movements face difficulties that appear insurmountable at the onset. Conversely, it could be that the radical potential of an abolitionist-democratic politics, which advocates a social movement from below, is being undermined by diversity policies from above. University administrators vigorously defend affirmative action on campus and in court. Corporate executives hunt for employees who will diversify their workforce and expand their access to "ethnic markets." Federal attorneys prosecute violations of the civil rights acts. Republican presidents appoint African Americans to important posts and promise to channel funds through Black churches. Such elites hardly fit the model of abolitionist as agitator, yet they would seem to be doing this work. Ironically, the radical democratic potential of the abolition-democracy is possibly blunted more by these activities than by overt white racists. Of course, the eradication of discrimination is to be celebrated regardless of who carries it out. Nevertheless, the consequences of dismantling the cross-class alliance from above are potentially significant for democratic theory.

Many of these elites seem to assume that the cross-class alliance will wither away without serious repercussions. Yet it is unclear how the white working class—which depends on its racial status much more than elites—will react to the erosion of whiteness from above, particularly in difficult economic times. Normalized white advantage breeds dissatisfaction among both whites and not-whites, the latter because they continue to be discriminated against disproportionately, the former because they are advantaged *only* disproportionately. Given this, Jennifer Hochschild argues that we face two possible futures. Diversity policies could help the nation finally reach a "benign tipping point" in which enough African Americans occupy prominent positions that whites no longer resent their presence and Black people no longer feel unwanted. In this scenario whiteness would gradually fade from the political scene, making it nothing but a biologically inaccurate but politically innocuous description of physical difference. The other alternative is that white resistance could increase proportionately with Black progress, leading to greater racial conflict as whites attempt to preserve their privileges.[56] A third possibility is the abolition-democracy. Ultimately, whether the elite strategy from above, a white nationalist backlash, or the abolitionist strategy from below triumphs is uncertain, but for advocates of expanded democratic participation, I hope the choice among them is sufficiently clear.

In an essay titled "Black Man's Burden," John Killens asks his primarily Black audience:

> What are we going to do about these Europeans? . . . having liberated ourselves from them, politically, economically, socially, psychologically, culturally, how are we going to integrate them into the New World of Humanity, where racial prejudice will be obsolete, where the whiteness of their skin will not be held against them, but at the same time, will not afford them any special privileges? How are we going to teach them the meaning of some of the terms they themselves claim to have invented, but never practiced, as far as we were concerned; such terms as "democracy," "human dignity," and the "brotherhood of man"?[57]

The white citizen has been a Black burden throughout American history, but it has been a burden for democracy as well. As the editors of *Ebony* magazine put it in 1966, there is no "Negro problem" in the United States, but there is a white problem, and the solution to this problem lies "not in the Negro but in the white American and in the structure of the white community."[58] Today there is still the white problem—its expectations, its power, its solidarity, its imagination. Even after the civil rights movement, whiteness stands at the path to a more democratic society like a troll at the bridge. The political task, I have argued, is to chase the troll away, not to ignore it or invite it to the multicultural table.

An abolitionist-democratic theory provides the intellectual tools to scatter the troll. It identifies white citizenship and its "public and psychological wages" as key barriers to democratic participation. It emphasizes power rather than recognition, alienation rather than difference, privilege rather than exclusion. It suggests that the impulse for greater democracy lies neither in a color-blind society nor in granting equal worth to all races but in the vision of a world in which no one needs to be white. Such a world has the potential to overflow the containers of liberalism, carrying a new conception of democracy on its floodwaters. It is a politics based on a simple principle: No privilege held can compare to a world in which privilege does not exist.

Notes

Introduction

1. W. E. B. Du Bois, *Dusk of Dawn: An Essay toward an Autobiography of a Race Concept* (New Brunswick, NJ: Transaction, 1995), 29.

2. Mary G. Dietz, "Context Is All: Feminism and Theories of Citizenship," in *Dimensions of Radical Democracy: Pluralism, Citizenship, Community,* ed. Chantal Mouffe (London: Verso, 1992), 75.

3. Gunnar Myrdal, *An American Dilemma: The Negro Problem and Modern Democracy* (New York: Harper & Row, 1962), 4, 8.

4. Ibid., 24.

5. Rogers M. Smith, *Civic Ideals: Conflicting Visions of Citizenship in U.S. History* (New Haven: Yale University Press, 1997); "Beyond Tocqueville, Myrdal, and Hartz: The Multiple Traditions in America," *American Political Science Review* 87, no. 3 (1993): 549–66.

6. Smith, *Civic Ideals,* 6.

7. Ibid., 36.

8. Myrdal, *American Dilemma,* 48.

9. In a response to a critic, Smith acknowledges "political, economic, sociological, and psychological" linkages between liberalism, republicanism, and ascriptive systems, but he insists that logically they are contradictory. Reverting to the ideals/practices split, he writes, "[A]t the level of principle, the ideologies are contradictory in important ways: their connections are primarily at different levels of lived experience": response to Jacqueline Stevens, "Beyond Tocqueville, Please!" *American Political Science Review* 89, no. 4 (1995): 990–95. At the level of "logic," liberalism and racism do contradict each other. Yet it is the level

of "lived experience"—politics, economics, psychology, culture, and history—that counts. An emphasis on the lived experience of these traditions, Smith himself indicates, suggests a conclusion that democracy and racial oppression in the United States are mutually constitutive rather than contradictory.

10. Edmund Morgan, "Slavery and Freedom: The American Paradox," *Journal of American History* 59, no. 1 (1972): 5.

11. Edmund S. Morgan, *American Slavery, American Freedom: The Ordeal of Colonial Virginia* (New York: W. W. Norton, 1975), 4.

12. Derrick Bell and Preeta Bansal, "The Republican Revival and Racial Politics," *Yale Law Journal* 97, no. 8 (1988): 1609–21.

13. Pierre L. van den Berghe, *Race and Racism: A Comparative Perspective* (New York: Wiley and Sons, 1967), 78.

14. Leon F. Litwack, *North of Slavery: The Negro in the Free States, 1790–1860* (Chicago: University of Chicago Press, 1961), chapter 1; David Walker, *Appeal to the Coloured Citizens of the World but in Particular, and Very Expressly, to Those of the United States of America*, ed. Charles M. Wiltse (New York: Hill and Wang, 1965).

15. Stephen Steinberg, *Turning Back: The Retreat from Racial Justice in American Thought and Policy* (Boston: Beacon Press, 1995), chapter 1.

16. Daniel T. Rodgers, *Contested Truths: Keywords in American Politics Since Independence* (New York: Basic Books, 1987).

17. Mary G. Dietz, "Merely Combating the Phrases of This World: Recent Democratic Theory," *Political Theory* 26, no. 1 (1998): 112–39.

18. David R. Roediger, *Toward the Abolition of Whiteness* (London: Verso, 1994), 2–3.

19. Charles W. Mills, *Blackness Visible: Essays on Philosophy and Race* (Ithaca, NY: Cornell University Press, 1998). This is not to say that race is only a form of power. Race also refers to culture, which is created, in part, as a response to the injuries suffered at the hands of white supremacy. My concern in this book is to understand race first and foremost as a political system.

20. Van den Berghe, *Race and Racism*, 11.

21. James Baldwin, "On Being 'White' . . . And Other Lies," *Essence*, April 1984, 92.

22. Theodore Allen, *The Invention of the White Race*, vol. 1 (New York: Verso, 1994), 22.

23. Du Bois, *Dusk of Dawn*, 117.

24. David R. Roediger, *The Wages of Whiteness: Race and the Making of the American Working Class* (New York: Verso, 1991); W. E. B. Du Bois, *Black Reconstruction in America: 1860–1880* (New York: Atheneum, 1992), 700.

25. Cheryl Harris, "Whiteness as Property," *Harvard Law Review* 106, no. 8 (1993): 1707–91.

26. Ibid., 1744–45.

27. As Stanley Greenberg notes, a state racial apparatus becomes necessary only when one attempts to subdue a population in order to systematically appropriate its labor. The extermination of indigenous populations and the stealing of their lands, for example, may be aided by a racist ideology but it does not require a state racial apparatus—a regular army will suffice. Stanley B. Greenberg, *Race and State in Capitalist Development: Comparative Perspectives* (New Haven: Yale University Press, 1980), 30, 33.

28. Lerone Bennett Jr., *The Shaping of Black America: The Struggles and Triumphs of African-Americans, 1619 to the 1990s* (New York: Penguin, 1993), 146.

29. Judith N. Shklar, *American Citizenship: The Quest for Inclusion* (Cambridge: Harvard University Press, 1991), 9.

30. Greenberg, *Race and State*, 406.

31. Matthew Pratt Guterl, *The Color of Race in America 1900–1940* (Cambridge: Harvard University Press, 2001). Analyses that understand race as a discourse frequently fall in the same trap. A discursive analysis of race need not be overly idealist, particularly if it includes institutions as well as expressions, beliefs, and other language acts. Unfortunately, the tendency of discursive analyses of race is to overemphasize the impact of the history of ideas on the American racial order, such as the influence of eighteenth-century European anthropology or psychoanalytical themes of "impurity" and "dirt," rather than slavery, segregation, and class relations. For example, see *Anatomy of Racism*, ed. David Theo Goldberg (Minneapolis: University of Minnesota Press, 1990).

32. Michael C. Dawson, "A Black Counterpublic? Economic Earthquakes, Racial Agenda(s), and Black Politics," *Public Culture* 7, no. 1 (1994): 199. Guterl's own evidence suggests that Grant's ideas did not reflect the racial order. He notes that Grant, who previously paid little attention to African Americans in his books, rushed to embrace the Black-white racial binary as the white reading public lost interest in his books—because they were increasingly divorced from the way the white public understood race. Further, Guterl reports that Grant helped craft a "Racial Integrity Law" in Virginia in 1925 that entrenched the

"one-drop rule" as state law, but he apparently never proposed antimiscegenation legislation between "Nordics" and "Mediterraneans," even at the height of the popularity of his book on the degeneration of the so-called Nordic race, *The Passing of the Great Race*. Guterl, *Color of Race*, 37, 47–48.

33. Michel Foucault, *Discipline and Punish: The Birth of the Prison* (New York: Vintage, 1979), 220–21.

1. A Political Theory of Race

1. Dale Maharidge, *The Coming White Minority: California, Multiculturalism, and America's Future* (New York: Vintage, 1999).

2. U.S. Census Bureau, "Profiles of General Demographic Characteristics 2000: 2000 Census of Population and Housing," May 2001, http://www.census.gov/prod/cen2000/dp1/2kh00.pdf. For an excellent analysis of how the census reproduces race rather than simply counts it, see Melissa Nobles, *Shades of Citizenship: Race and the Census in Modern Politics* (Stanford: Stanford University Press, 2000).

3. Joseph L. Graves Jr., *The Emperor's New Clothes: Biological Theories of Race at the Millennium* (New Brunswick, NJ: Rutgers University Press, 2001); Stephen Jay Gould, *The Mismeasure of Man*, rev. and exp. ed. (New York: Norton, 1996); Ashley Montagu, *Man's Most Dangerous Myth: The Fallacy of Race*, 5th ed. (London: Oxford University Press, 1974). For a history of the science of race, see Jonathan Marks, *Human Biodiversity: Genes, Race, and History* (New York: Aldine de Gruyter, 1995), and Thomas F. Gossett, *Race: The History of an Idea in America* (New York: Schocken, 1965).

4. L. Luca Cavalli-Sforza, Paolo Menozzi, and Alberto Piazza, *The History and Geography of Human Genes* (Princeton: Princeton University Press, 1994), 19.

5. Tzvetan Todorov, *On Human Diversity: Nationalism, Racism, and Exoticism in French Thought* (Cambridge: Harvard University Press, 1993), 96.

6. Pierre L. van den Berghe, *Race and Racism: A Comparative Perspective* (New York: Wiley and Sons, 1967), 52. The South did away with its "intermediate" categories (such as mulatto and quadroon) in the 1920s as Jim Crow matured, when even port cities like New Orleans and Charleston eliminated the mulatto social distinction. F. James Davis, *Who Is Black? One Nation's Definition* (University Park: Pennsylvania State University Press, 1991), 57–58.

7. James M. Jones, *Prejudice and Racism* (New York: McGraw-Hill, 1972), 6, 117.

8. Herbert Blumer, "Race Prejudice as a Sense of Group Position," *The Pacific Sociological Review* 1, no. 1 (1958): 3–7.

9. Jeff Spinner, *The Boundaries of Citizenship: Race, Ethnicity, and Nationality in the Liberal State* (Baltimore: Johns Hopkins University Press, 1994), 191 n. 25. This quote ironically appears in a footnote whose stated purpose is to "clarify [his] definition of race."

10. Cheryl Harris, "Whiteness as Property," *Harvard Law Review* 106, no. 8 (1993): 1718.

11. "Fact Sheet," Association of MultiEthnic Americans (AMEA) Inc., 20 January 2001, http://www.ameasite.org/factsheet.pdf.

12. This point is made very well by Susan Bickford in "Anti-Anti-Identity Politics: Feminism, Democracy, and the Complexities of Citizenship," *Hypatia* 12, no. 4 (1997): 111–31.

13. Ivan Hannaford, *Race: The History of an Idea in the West* (Baltimore: Johns Hopkins University Press, 1996).

14. Hannah Arendt, "Imperialism, Nationalism, Chauvinism," *Review of Politics* 7, no. 4 (1945): 441–63; *Origins of Totalitarianism* (New York: Harcourt, 1973).

15. Carl N. Degler, *Neither Black Nor White: Slavery and Race Relations in Brazil and the United States* (Madison: University of Wisconsin Press, 1971). The "mulatto" category was socially significant in French-influenced port cities like New Orleans and Charleston, too, until Jim Crow.

16. Herbert S. Klein, *Slavery in the Americas: A Comparative Study of Virginia and Cuba* (Chicago: University of Chicago Press, 1967), 259.

17. American Anthropological Association, "Response to OMB Directive 15," *American Anthropological Association*, 4 December 1998, http://ameranthassn.org/ombdraft.htm.

18. Barbara Jeanne Fields, "Ideology and Race in American History," in *Region, Race, and Reconstruction: Essays in Honor of C. Vann Woodward*, ed. J. Morgan Kousser and James M. McPherson (New York: Oxford University Press, 1982); "Slavery, Race and Ideology in the United States of America," *New Left Review*, no. 181 (1990): 95–118.

19. Fields, "Ideology and Race," 151.

20. Davis, *Who Is Black?* Of course, what counts as an "African feature" is subject to debate. Are "Egyptian features," for example, African? Further, as already mentioned, in Latin American countries like Brazil, possessing "African

features" is necessary but not sufficient to determine Blackness; one's wealth (or lack of it) is also important.

21. The phrase is from Aristide R. Zolberg, "Moments of Madness," *Politics and Society* 2, no. 2 (1972): 183–207.

22. W. E. B. Du Bois, *Black Reconstruction in America: 1860–1880* (New York: Atheneum, 1992), 370.

23. Whether the South was capitalist or a distinct mode of production is still a matter of contention among historians. For arguments that modern slavery was part of capitalism, see Eric Williams, *Capitalism and Slavery* (New York: Capricorn, 1966); Orlando Patterson, *Slavery and Social Death: A Comparative Study* (Cambridge: Harvard University Press, 1982); David Roediger, "Precapitalism in One Confederacy: Genovese, Politics, and the Slave South," *New Politics*, n.s., 3, no. 3 (1991): 90–95; Noel Ignatiev, "Reply to Martin Glaberman," *Labour/Le Travail* 36 (1995): 215–16. For arguments that it was not, see Martin Glaberman, "Slaves and Proletarians: The Debate Continues," *Labour/Le Travail* 36 (1995): 209–14; and Elizabeth Fox-Genovese and Eugene D. Genovese, *The Fruits of Merchant Capitalism: Slavery and Bourgeois Property in the Rise and Expansion of Capitalism* (New York: Oxford University Press, 1983).

24. Du Bois, *Black Reconstruction*, 16.

25. Ibid., 390–91. Thomas Holt reduces these numbers a bit, but Du Bois's basic point remains. Thomas Holt, *Black over White: Negro Political Leadership in South Carolina during Reconstruction* (Urbana: University of Illinois Press, 1977), 35–38.

26. Du Bois, *Black Reconstruction*, 346.

27. Ibid., 708.

28. Ibid., 347.

29. Ibid., 700–701. The specific phrase "wages of whiteness" is from David R. Roediger, *The Wages of Whiteness: Race and the Making of the American Working Class* (New York: Verso, 1991).

30. Du Bois, *Black Reconstruction*, 695.

31. Ibid., 701.

32. W. E. B. Du Bois, "Marxism and the Negro Problem," in *W. E. B. Du Bois: A Reader*, ed. David Levering Lewis (New York: Henry Holt, 1995), 541. Originally published in the May 1933 edition of *The Crisis* magazine. See also chapter 4, "Of Work and Wealth," in *Darkwater: Voices from Within the Veil* (New York: Schocken, 1969); "The Negro and Communism," in *W. E. B. Du Bois: A Reader*, ed. Lewis; "The White Worker," chapter 2 in *Black Reconstruction*; and

Donald Nonini, "Du Bois and Radical Theory and Practice," *Critique of Anthropology* 12, no. 3 (1992): 293–318.

33. Karl Marx, *Capital*, vol. 1, ed. Frederick Engels (New York: International, 1967), chapter 13; Michel Foucault, *Discipline and Punish: The Birth of the Prison* (New York: Vintage, 1979), 137–39, 218–23.

34. This is the opposite phenomena documented by Foucault in *Discipline and Punish*, whose study of the panopticon and other techniques used in eighteenth- and nineteenth-century European prisons reveals a *decrease* in police manpower even as the reach of the police greatly expanded throughout the social body.

35. Du Bois, *Black Reconstruction*, 12. Hannah Arendt's argument that European imperialism was powered by an "alliance between mob and capital" is very similar in structure to Du Bois's. Arendt, *Origins of Totalitarianism*, 151–55.

36. Foucault, *Discipline and Punish*, 218, 137. In fact, in a footnote on page 314, Foucault notes that the disciplines he analyzes in *Discipline and Punish* could also have been taken from, among other things, slavery and colonization.

37. Foucault does not discuss race in his principal work on disciplinary power, instead ranking it as a form of "biopower" in the first volume of *The History of Sexuality* (New York: Vintage, 1990). Rather than ensuring relations of docility-utility, biopower regulates populations to ensure their propagation and growth, health, life expectancy, and longevity. Varieties of racism in the nineteenth and twentieth centuries such as eugenics, he argues, were justified by and related to discourses of sex and population—controlling and counting populations, rank ordering them, keeping them "pure," etc. (26, 54). Foucault is right to point out the regulatory aspects of eugenics and biological racist discourses, but the ultimate significance of race in the United States is to construct politically docile and economically useful individuals, particularly white individuals, in a democratic polity. For this reason I hold that race is more like a discipline than a form of biopower.

38. For a detailed analysis of the white race as a buffer control stratum, see Theodore Allen, *The Invention of the White Race*, vol. 1 (chapter 1) and vol. 2 (chapter 13) (New York: Verso, 1994, 1997). Allen distinguishes racial oppression from national or colonial oppression based on how each achieves social control: "In the system of racial oppression, social control depends upon the denial of the legitimacy of social distinctions within the oppressed group. In the system of national oppression, social control depends upon the acceptance and fostering of social distinctions within the oppressed group" (1:241).

39. I define the capitalist class broadly not so much as those who own the

means of production but those who exercise effective control over those means. "Capitalist class" thus describes one side of a social relationship rather than designating a group of people who own capital (though of course such ownership is a necessary, though not sufficient, part of such a description). Likewise, I broadly define "working class" as that side of the relationship that has little effective control over the means of production, including the pace and content of its work. This includes a good number of people whom sociologists and politicians generally consider middle class. See Michael Zweig, *The Working Class Majority: America's Best Kept Secret* (Ithaca, NY: Cornell University Press, 2000).

40. Noel Ignatiev and John Garvey, "Abolish the White Race—By Any Means Necessary," *Race Traitor*, no. 1 (1993): 1.

41. Andrew Hacker, *Two Nations: Black and White, Separate, Hostile, Unequal*, expanded and updated ed. (New York: Ballantine, 1995), 18. The "club" analogy is from Ignatiev and Garvey, "Abolish the White Race."

42. Noel Ignatiev, *How the Irish Became White* (New York: Routledge, 1995); Matthew Frye Jacobson, *Whiteness of a Different Color: European Immigrants and the Alchemy of Race* (Cambridge: Harvard University Press, 1998); Roediger, *Wages of Whiteness*.

43. Lerone Bennett Jr., *The Shaping of Black America: The Struggles and Triumphs of African-Americans, 1619 to the 1990s* (New York: Penguin, 1993), 225.

44. Throughout the text I will use the term "not-white" to refer to the antithetical category to whiteness. When referring to the specific peoples who have occupied this category at various points in history, I will use "people of color" or refer to the specific ethnic designation.

45. Pierre van den Berghe, *South Africa: A Study in Conflict* (Middletown, CT: Wesleyan University Press, 1965), 64.

46. Chapter 17 of *Black Reconstruction*, "The Propaganda of History," is a scathing critique of Reconstruction literature up to the 1930s.

47. David Levering Lewis, *W. E. B. Du Bois: The Fight for Equality and the American Century 1919–1963* (New York: Henry Holt, 2000), 256–65.

48. W. E. B. Du Bois, "A Negro Nation Within the Nation," in *A W. E. B. Du Bois Reader*, ed. Andrew G. Paschal (New York: Collier, 1971), 74. See also W. E. B. Du Bois, *The Autobiography of W. E. B. Du Bois: A Soliloquy on Viewing My Life from the Last Decade of Its First Century* (New York: International, 1968), 290–98.

49. Arnold Rampersad, *The Art and Imagination of W. E. B. Du Bois* (Cambridge: Harvard University Press, 1976), 235. Charles Lemert also points out that Du Bois wrote *Black Reconstruction* with the present in mind as much as the past: "The Race of Time: Du Bois and Reconstruction," *Boundary 2* 27, no. 3 (2000): 215–48.

50. Du Bois, *Black Reconstruction*, 706–7.

51. A refreshing exception to this is Lawrie Balfour's "Unreconstructed Democracy: W. E. B. Du Bois and the Case for Reparations," *American Political Science Review* 97, no. 1 (2003): 33–44.

52. W. E. B. Du Bois, *The Souls of Black Folk* (New York: Signet Classic, 1969), 45.

53. Ibid.

54. Adolph L. Reed Jr., *W. E. B. Du Bois and American Political Thought: Fabianism and the Color Line* (New York: Oxford University Press, 1997), 176. Reed develops this critique of Black intellectuals further in *Stirrings in the Jug: Black Politics in the Post-Segregation Era* (Minneapolis: University of Minnesota Press, 1999). For similar arguments see Rampersad, *Art and Imagination*, and Shamoon Zamir, *Dark Voices: W. E. B. Du Bois and American Thought, 1888–1903* (Chicago: University of Chicago Press, 1995). For an argument that the theme of double consciousness was not just unimportant but even contradictory to the bulk of Du Bois's work, see Routledge M. Dennis, "Du Bois's Concept of Double Consciousness: Myth and Reality," *Research in Race and Ethnic Relations* 9 (1996): 69–90.

55. Dickson D. Bruce Jr., "W. E. B. Du Bois and the Idea of Double Consciousness," *American Literature* 64, no. 2 (1992): 299–309.

56. Du Bois, *Souls*, 44.

57. Du Bois, *Darkwater*, 246.

58. Du Bois, *Souls*, 204.

59. See, for example, Robert Gooding-Williams, "Philosophy of History and Social Critique in *The Souls of Black Folk*," *Social Science Information* 26, no. 1 (1987): 99–114.

60. W. E. B. Du Bois, *Dusk of Dawn: An Essay toward an Autobiography of a Race Concept* (New Brunswick, NJ: Transaction, 1995), 134–35. These latter two worlds do not necessarily constitute different races; they can be social classes as well. In fact, he contends, racial segregation is the "modern counterpart" to the world's class structure. The same sort of division applies globally. When

writing about the world and imperialism in *Dusk of Dawn* and *Darkwater*, he refers to the white world (sometimes calling it the European world), which consists of the white worlds of North America and Europe, and the dark world, which includes Africans, Asians, Native Americans, and the African Diaspora. These two worlds are divided by a veil cast by colonialism, of which racism in the United States is a close cousin. For an application of the double consciousness concept applied internationally, see Paul Gilroy, *The Black Atlantic: Modernity and Double Consciousness* (Cambridge: Harvard University Press, 1993).

61. As Gavin Jones argues, Du Bois deliberately distinguishes between "white" and "American" in *Souls*, using terms like "white Americanism" rather than simply Americanism to imply that that which is "truly American" by definition contains an element of Blackness: "'Whose Line Is It Anyway?' W. E. B. Du Bois and the Language of the Color Line," in *Race Consciousness: African American Studies for the New Century*, ed. Judith Jackson Fossett and Jeffrey A. Tucker (New York: New York University Press, 1997).

62. Du Bois, *Dusk of Dawn*, 135.

63. Ibid., 136.

64. Ibid., 153.

65. Richard Wright, *White Man, Listen!* (Garden City, NY: Doubleday, 1957), 148.

66. Du Bois's analysis here is similar to Frantz Fanon's argument that colonialism is "a world cut in two" (colonizer and colonized) that does not just oppress the native; it *creates* the native, as well as the settler. Fanon, *The Wretched of the Earth* (New York: Grove Press, 1963), 36–40.

67. Thomas Holt, "The Political Uses of Alienation: W. E. B. Du Bois on Politics, Race, and Culture, 1903–1940," *American Quarterly* 42, no. 2 (1990): 301–23. See also Frank M. Kirkland, "Modernity and Intellectual Life in Black," *The Philosophical Forum* 24, nos. 1–3 (1992–93): 136–65.

68. Patterson, *Slavery and Social Death*.

69. Du Bois, *Dusk of Dawn*, 173–79.

70. Du Bois, *Darkwater*, vii. The entire chapter "Beauty and Death" is also based on the double consciousness metaphor.

71. Ibid., 130–32; Zamir, *Dark Voices*, 199–200.

72. Frederick Douglass, *Narrative of the Life of Frederick Douglass, An American Slave* (New York: Anchor, 1989), 37.

73. For a good summary of criticisms of the bipolar model, see Michael Omi

and Howard Winant, *Racial Formation in the United States: From the 1960s to the 1990s*, 2d ed. (New York: Routledge, 1994).

74. Linda Gordon, "On 'Difference,'" *Genders* 10 (1991): 91–111.

75. Linda Nicholson, *The Play of Reason: From the Modern to the Postmodern* (Ithaca, NY: Cornell University Press, 1999).

76. Neil Foley, *The White Scourge: Mexicans, Blacks, and Poor Whites in Texas Cotton Culture* (Berkeley: University of California Press, 1997), 41.

77. Foley reports that one member of the League of United Latin American Citizens, explaining why they expelled another member for having "married a Negress," complained, "An American mob would lynch him. But we are not given the same opportunity to form a mob and come clean": Ibid., 209–10.

78. Alexander Saxton, *The Indispensable Enemy: Labor and the Anti-Chinese Movement in California* (Berkeley: University of California Press, 1971); Ronald Takaki, *Strangers from a Different Shore: A History of Asian Americans* (Boston: Little, Brown, 1998).

79. Claire Jean Kim, "The Racial Triangulation of Asian Americans," *Politics and Society* 27, no. 1 (1999): 112. See also James W. Loewen, *The Mississippi Chinese: Between Black and White*, 2d ed. (Waveland, MS: Waveland Press, 1988).

80. The apparently perplexing problem of why immigrant cab drivers of color often refuse to pick up Black passengers in New York City indicates that it still does. Indeed, this problem is not so vexing from a bipolar lens: The cab drivers are staking their claim to Americanness through the time-honored practice of proving they are not Black. This holds even for cab drivers from Haiti, who share an immigrant's interest in distancing themselves from African Americans. Elisabeth Bumiller, "Cabbies Who Bypass Blacks Will Lose Cars, Guiliani Says," *New York Times*, 11 November 1999, A1; "They Keep On Passin' Me By," *The Source*, no. 125 (February 2000), 59–61; Vijay Prashad, *The Karma of Brown Folk* (Minneapolis: University of Minnesota Press, 2000).

81. Lawrie Balfour, "'A Most Disagreeable Mirror': Race Consciousness as Double Consciousness," *Political Theory* 26, no. 3 (1998): 347.

82. John Hartigan Jr., "Establishing the Fact of Whiteness," *American Anthropologist* 99, no. 3 (1997): 495–505; Hartigan, *Racial Situations: Class Predicaments of Whiteness in Detroit* (Princeton: Princeton University Press, 1999); Howard Winant, *Racial Conditions: Politics, Theory, Comparisons* (Minneapolis: University of Minnesota Press, 1994); Annalee Newitz and Matthew Wray, "What is 'White Trash'? Stereotypes and Economic Conditions of Poor Whites in the U.S.," *The*

Minnesota Review, n.s., 47 (1996): 57–72; *White Trash: Race and Class in America*, ed. Annalee Newitz and Matthew Wray (New York: Routledge, 1996). One of the dangers of this position, as Maurice Berger points out, is that it encourages the study of whiteness as a "me too" phenomenon that attempts to exempt poor whites from a critique of white privilege. Poor whites are undoubtedly exploited but this does not mean that they do not enjoy the benefits of whiteness. Unfortunately, as Berger writes, "The legacy of shared antipathy toward black people, a legacy that underscores the power of racism to cut across class, is far less important to many students of white trash than the need to examine the needs and struggles of another disfranchised group": Maurice Berger, *White Lies: Race and the Myths of Whiteness* (New York: Farrar, Straus, Giroux, 1999), 205.

83. For example, Foley argues that theories of eugenics were used by Texas elites to racialize poor whites as a "scourge" and to explain their poverty as the result of their own genetic deficiencies (Foley, *White Scourge*, 79). But blaming the poor for their poverty is a time-honored tradition of the rich. Poor-bashing, even to the point where the rich doubt whether the poor are of the same breed as themselves, is not racial. It is a class ideology, even if the discourse reflects the trappings of race. What *is* racial is that in spite of their snobbery, white elites still gave in to policies that granted one section of the poor a social and political status that was, in some aspects, equal to their own. What is also racial are the indignities and sacrifices poor whites endured for the small comforts of white citizenship.

84. Quoted in Werner Sollors, "How Americans Became White: Three Examples," in *Multi-America: Essays on Cultural Wars and Cultural Peace*, ed. Ishmael Reed (New York: Viking, 1997), 3.

85. Wright, *White Man, Listen!* 31.

86. Dana D. Nelson, *National Manhood: Capitalist Citizenship and the Imagined Fraternity of White Men* (Durham: Duke University Press, 1998).

87. Charles Mills, *The Racial Contract* (Ithaca, NY: Cornell University Press, 1997), 3.

88. W. E. B. Du Bois, "Apology," in *W. E. B. Du Bois: A Reader*, ed. Lewis, 215.

89. Linda Gordon, *The Great Arizona Orphan Abduction* (Cambridge: Harvard University Press, 1999), 97.

2. The Problem of the White Citizen

1. David Grimsted, *American Mobbing, 1828–1861: Toward Civil War* (New York: Oxford University Press, 1998), 4; Michael Feldberg, *The Turbulent Era:*

Riot and Disorder in Jacksonian America (New York: Oxford University Press, 1980), 5.

2. Leonard L. Richards, *"Gentlemen of Property and Standing": Anti-Abolitionist Mobs in Jacksonian America* (New York: Oxford University Press, 1970).

3. Edmund S. Morgan, *American Slavery, American Freedom: The Ordeal of Colonial Virginia* (New York: W. W. Norton, 1975), 154–57; Morgan, "Slavery and Freedom: The American Paradox," *Journal of American History* 59, no. 1 (1972): 16–18; Winthrop D. Jordan, *White over Black: American Attitudes Toward the Negro, 1550–1812* (New York: W. W. Norton, 1968), 44–98.

4. By "African" I refer to those persons brought from Africa (directly or indirectly) and their descendants, or those whose African ancestry was considered preeminent by their community. By "English" I refer to those who immigrated from Britain and their descendants, or those whose British ancestry was considered preeminent. The labels do not describe all settlers. The terms "Black" and "white" are inappropriate until around 1700.

5. Morgan, *American Slavery*, 233–34; George M. Fredrickson, *White Supremacy: A Comparative Study in American and South African History* (Oxford: Oxford University Press, 1981), 23–25.

6. Lerone Bennett Jr., *The Shaping of Black America: The Struggles and Triumphs of African-Americans, 1619 to the 1990s* (New York: Penguin, 1993), 53; Theodore Allen, *The Invention of the White Race*, 2 vols. (New York: Verso, 1994–97), vol. 2, chapter 7.

7. Eric Williams, *Capitalism and Slavery* (New York: Capricorn, 1966), chapter 1; Fredrickson, *White Supremacy*, 62–68.

8. Wilcomb E. Washburn, *The Governor and the Rebel: A History of Bacon's Rebellion in Virginia* (Chapel Hill: University of North Carolina Press, 1957).

9. Antimiscegenation laws, first written in the early 1660s, were a response to the significant number of relationships between African men and European women. Martha Hodes, *White Women, Black Men: Illicit Sex in the Nineteenth Century* (New Haven: Yale University Press, 1997), 28–31.

10. Morgan, *American Slavery*, 329–37. For similar arguments, see Allen, *Invention*; Allen, "They Would Have Destroyed Me: Slavery and the Origins of Racism," *Radical America* 9, no. 3 (1975): 41–63; Bennett, *Shaping*, chapter 3; T. H. Breen and Stephen Innes, *"Myne Owne Ground": Race and Freedom on Virginia's Eastern Shore, 1640–1676* (New York: Oxford University Press, 1980);

George M. Fredrickson, "Toward a Social Interpretation of the Development of American Racism," in *Key Issues in the Afro-American Experience*, vol. 1, ed. Nathan I. Huggins, Martin Kilson, and Daniel M. Fox (New York: Harcourt, 1971); Fredrickson, *White Supremacy*, chapter 2; Oscar Handlin and Mary F. Handlin, "Origins of the Southern Labor System," *William and Mary Quarterly*, 3rd series, no. 7 (1950): 199–222; and Gary B. Nash, "Red, White, and Black: The Origins of Racism in Colonial America," in *The Great Fear: Race in the Mind of America*, ed. Gary B. Nash and Richard Weiss (New York: Holt, Rinehart, and Winston, 1970). Allen and Bennett argue even more forcefully than Morgan that the emergence of racial oppression was a deliberate plan of the colonial ruling class in Virginia and that white people had to be taught to "worship their skin," as Bennett puts it.

11. Michel Foucault, *Discipline and Punish: The Birth of the Prison* (New York: Vintage, 1979), 194.

12. This position is a contested one. Some historians argue that perceptions of difference in color, culture, and religion held by the English toward Africans at least since the 1500s led the English to immediately distinguish themselves from Africans in a way they did not from other foreign peoples. These innate prejudices, they argue, marked Africans as permanently different and inassimilable into English civilization and led to the system of racial slavery and Black degradation. Thus, they contend, racism actually preceded slavery, not vice versa. This argument, however, falters on two grounds. First, it cannot explain what turns ethnocentrism, a common enough phenomena, into a system of racial oppression. Even if the English were prejudiced against Africans from the first contact for reasons of skin color, religion, or culture, it was by no means inevitable that this prejudice would lead to a social system of white domination and the creation of a white race. There is no reason why the English people's perception of difference from Africans, however strong, would inevitably drive them to group themselves in a single "race" with Spaniards, Germans, Russians, Poles, French, and even the hated Irish. Second, the documents colonial historians rely on to address the relationship between slavery and race were written by colonial elites. Thus, they say little about how poor Englishmen and -women saw Africans. It seems just as likely that the rash of laws between 1660 and 1690 designed to separate the poor into Black and white groups were passed because prejudice was waning among poor English and African colonists as it was due to innate racial prejudice. For statements of the "racism before slavery" perspective,

see Carl N. Degler, "Slavery and the Genesis of American Race Prejudice," *Comparative Studies in Society and History* 2, no. 1 (1959): 49–66; Jordan, *White over Black*, chapter 2; Alden T. Vaughan, "The Origins Debate: Slavery and Racism in Seventeenth-Century Virginia," *The Virginia Magazine of History and Biography* 97, no. 3 (1989): 311–54. For good overviews of the origins of slavery debate, see Allen, *Invention*, vol. 1; Vaughan, "The Origins Debate"; and Alexander Saxton, *The Rise and Fall of the White Republic* (London: Verso, 1990), chapter 1.

13. Most of the historians I rely upon, excluding Allen and possibly Bennett, share an essentialist conception of race. That is, they assume the biological preexistence of races, though the power or status of each race had yet to be determined in the colonies. My point, with Allen, is that power and status created the races themselves.

14. Quoted in William Sumner Jenkins, *Pro-Slavery Thought in the Old South* (Gloucester, MA: Peter Smith, 1960), 193.

15. Though Native Americans were considered something like a separate race by 1630 and many of the statutes that degraded Africans included Indians as well, most historiography concludes that anti-Indian attitudes and policies were less significant to the construction of white identity than anti-Black ones because Native Americans, while not considered "civilized" by English Americans, were still considered free, making them a poor counterpoint to white identity. Jill Lepore, for example, argues that an American identity (as distinct from an English identity) was constructed in the Jacksonian era through the image of the "free" Indian and against the image of the "slave" African. This conception of "Indianness" reflected white chauvinism, of course, and actual Indians continued to be killed and racially oppressed, yet Indianness was crucial to the formation of American identity in a way that Blackness was not. "The Indian" helped construct an ethnic *American* identity in the Jacksonian era and alleviated white Americans' inferiority complex in relation to England. "The African," on the other hand, helped construct a racial *white* identity. Jill Lepore, *The Name of War: King Philip's War and the Origins of American Identity* (New York: Alfred A. Knopf, 1998). Other historians, however, argue for a more central role for Indian–colonist relations in the history of racial formation, placing the West and the trope of conquest (the drawing of lines and the allocation of power and meaning to those lines) at the center of American history and racial formation rather than the South and slavery. See Patricia Nelson Limerick, *The Legacy of*

Conquest: The Unbroken Past of the American West (New York: W. W. Norton, 1987). The relevant implication here is that my account of the development of the white race is shaped by the historiography I rely upon. An analysis starting with Indian–settler relations rather than slave–citizen relations would not refute the association of white supremacy with democracy I make here, I suspect, but it might modify the model of racial formation I present.

16. Robert A. Margo, "The Labor Force in the Nineteenth Century," in *The Cambridge Economic History of the United States*, vol. 2, ed. Stanley L. Engerman and Robert E. Gallman (Cambridge: Cambridge University Press, 1996), 213.

17. Arthur M. Schlesinger Jr., *The Age of Jackson* (Boston: Little, Brown, 1953), 9.

18. Michael R. Haines, "The Population of the United States 1790–1920," in *Cambridge Economic History of the United States*, vol. 2, ed. Engerman and Gallman, 193–97.

19. David R. Roediger, *The Wages of Whiteness: Race and the Making of the American Working Class* (New York: Verso, 1991); Saxton, *White Republic*; Sean Wilentz, *Chants Democratic: New York City and the Rise of the American Working Class, 1788–1850* (New York: Oxford University Press, 1984).

20. Schlesinger, *Age of Jackson*, 306–21, 335.

21. Judith N. Shklar, *American Citizenship: The Quest for Inclusion* (Cambridge: Harvard University Press, 1991).

22. Martha May, "Bread before Roses: American Workingmen, Labor Unions, and the Family Wage," in *Women, Work, and Protest: A Century of Women's Labor History*, ed. Ruth Milkman (Boston: Routledge, 1985); David Roediger, "Gaining a Hearing for Black-White Unity: Covington Hall and the Complexities of Race, Gender, and Class," chapter 10 in *Toward the Abolition of Whiteness* (London: Verso, 1994), 131–33.

23. The abolitionist movement provides an excellent example of the reaction against—and defense of—women's efforts to participate in the political sphere. See Aileen S. Kraditor, *Means and Ends in American Abolitionism: Garrison and His Critics on Strategy and Tactics, 1834–1850* (Chicago: Elephant, 1989), especially chapter 3.

24. Shklar writes that the two things that distinguish American political thought from the rest of modern history are "the early establishment of representative democracy and the persistence of slavery": Judith N. Shklar, *A Life of Learning* (Washington, DC: American Council of Learned Societies, 1989), 16.

25. Judith Shklar, "Rights in the Liberal Tradition," in *The Bill of Rights and the Liberal Tradition*, The Colorado College Studies 28 (Colorado Springs: Colorado College, 1992), 34. In a similar vein, she argues that citizenship is constructed in terms of membership and exile and that those persons excluded from a polity are "internal exiles." Thus slaves were like refugees in refugee camps. Shklar, "Obligation, Loyalty, Exile," *Political Theory* 21, no. 2 (1993): 181–97.

26. Shklar, *American Citizenship*, 16.

27. Roediger, *Wages of Whiteness*, 47.

28. Pierre L. van den Berghe, *Race and Racism: A Comparative Perspective* (New York: Wiley and Sons, 1967), 18.

29. Quoted in George M. Fredrickson, *The Black Image in the White Mind: The Debate on Afro-American Character and Destiny, 1817–1914* (New York: Harper and Row, 1971), 63–64.

30. Shklar, *American Citizenship*, 28.

31. Roediger, *Wages of Whiteness*, 57, 108.

32. Jean H. Baker, *Affairs of Party: The Political Culture of Northern Democrats in the Mid-Nineteenth Century* (Ithaca, NY: Cornell University Press, 1983), 243–44. In an 1879 referendum on the "Chinese question," California voters favored total exclusion of the Chinese by a vote of 150,000 to 900, or 99.4 percent of the vote: Alexander Saxton, *The Indispensable Enemy: Labor and the Anti-Chinese Movement in California* (Berkeley: University of California Press, 1971), 139.

33. Leon F. Litwack, *North of Slavery: The Negro in the Free States, 1790–1860* (Chicago: University of Chicago Press, 1961), 74–93; Baker, *Affairs of Party*, 243–49.

34. Ian Haney-López similarly argues that immigration laws and cases that limited naturalization to whites also show how "citizenship easily serves as a proxy for race": *White by Law: The Legal Construction of Race* (New York: New York University Press, 1996).

35. One possible reason why Shklar does not make this connection between whiteness and citizenship is because she holds a biological conception of race: "And whether or not you choose your nationality is a very tricky question, but you are stuck with your race" ("Obligation, Loyalty, Exile," 185). Both, I assert, are tricky questions.

36. Noel Ignatiev, *How the Irish Became White* (New York: Routledge, 1995), 132.

37. This work toward earning one's whiteness began almost immediately upon arrival. As Malcolm X told Alex Haley as they witnessed the arrival of European immigrants at the airport, "By tomorrow night, they'll know how to say their first English word—*nigger*": *The Autobiography of Malcolm X* (New York: Ballantine, 1965), 459.

38. My account of Irish assimilation here relies primarily on Ignatiev, *How the Irish*. Complementary accounts can be found in Allen, *Invention*, vol. 1, chapters 7–8, and Roediger, *Wages of Whiteness*, chapter 7.

39. In *Age of Jackson*, 320–21, Schlesinger argues that the Democratic Party fought nativism because Democrats saw their struggle against monopoly as international. However, he does not explain how this internationalist impulse accommodated the official Democratic Party policy of white supremacy and virulent anti-Black prejudice.

40. Ignatiev, *How the Irish*, 2.

41. *Dred Scott v. Sandford*, 60 U.S. 393 (1856); Don Fehrenbacher, *The Dred Scott Case: Its Significance in American Law and Politics* (New York: Oxford University Press, 1978).

42. David Roediger, "The White Question," *Race Traitor*, no. 1 (1993): 104–7.

43. This sense of superiority among white laborers was likely an ambiguous one. As George Rawick suggests, it may have had as much to do with a certain longing for a lost way of life that was unattached to the clock, less sexually repressed, and closer to nature as it did with revulsion toward such a life and those who (supposedly) lived it. He writes, "The Englishman met the West African as a reformed sinner meets a comrade of his previous debaucheries. The reformed sinner very often creates a pornography of his former life. He must suppress even his knowledge that he had acted that way or even that he wanted to act that way": George P. Rawick, *From Sundown to Sunup: The Making of the Black Community* (Westport, CT: Greenwood, 1972), 132.

44. Rogers M. Smith, "Beyond Tocqueville, Myrdal, and Hartz: The Multiple Traditions in America," *American Political Science Review* 87, no. 3 (1993): 549–66.

45. Alexis de Tocqueville, *Democracy in America*, trans. George Lawrence, ed. J. P. Mayer (New York: Anchor, 1969), 17.

46. Ibid., 12.

47. Tocqueville's conception of race was not a biological one. He resisted the growing trend in his day to associate particular physical and mental capabilities

with particular races. Emphasizing an older usage of the term, Tocqueville considered a "race" a group of people distinguished by their kind and level of civilization more than by any commonly shared genotypical or phenotypical traits. In effect, race was national character. James T. Schleifer, *The Making of Tocqueville's "Democracy in America"* (Chapel Hill: University of North Carolina Press, 1980), 62–72. So, for example, in his notebooks he speaks of French and English Canadians as two distinct races and Indians as yet another, and in *Democracy* he compares the Anglo-American race with the Spanish and French races. Alexis de Tocqueville, *Journey to America*, trans. George Lawrence, ed. J. P. Mayer (New Haven: Yale University Press, 1960), 39; *Democracy in America*, 408–13.

48. He says little directly about the white or Anglo-American race, presumably because it is the subject of the rest of the book. The white race in *Democracy* is almost always only invoked in contrast to African and Native Americans. It is rarely explicitly considered and when it is, it is usually in one of two ways: as oppressors or as a more powerful people and thus more intelligent in matters of trade, resource extraction, industry, culture, and governance. See, e.g., Tocqueville, *Democracy in America*, 334.

49. Ibid., 30.

50. Ibid., 28; Harry Liebersohn, "Discovering Indigenous Nobility: Tocqueville, Chamisso, and Romantic Travel Writing," *American Historical Review* 99, no. 3 (1994): 746–66.

51. Tocqueville, *Democracy in America*, 318.

52. Ibid., 340.

53. Comte de Arthur Gobineau, *The Inequality of Human Races*, trans. Adrian Collins (New York: H. Fertig, 1967). Tocqueville taunts Gobineau's views in a letter to him: "I am sure that Julius Caesar, if he had had the time, would have willingly written a book to show that the savages he met in Britain were not of the same human race as the Romans, and that while the latter were destined by nature to dominate the world, the former were fated to vegetate in an obscure corner" (Alexis de Tocqueville, *On Democracy, Revolution, and Society: Selected Writings*, ed. John Stone and Stephen Mennell [Chicago: University of Chicago Press, 1980], 321).

54. Fredrickson, *Black Image*, 6–27. Colonization was a movement for the forced deportation of free Black people to Africa until slavery eventually died out and all ex-slaves were removed from the United States. The abolitionists

succeeded in discrediting colonization by the mid-1830s, though it had a brief revival just before the Civil War among Republicans like Lincoln.

55. Many works on *Democracy in America* or Tocqueville in general, however, pay little attention to his thoughts on race and slavery, including Jack Lively, *The Social and Political Thought of Alexis de Tocqueville* (Oxford: Clarendon, 1962); Whitney Pope, *Alexis de Tocqueville: His Social and Political Theory* (Beverly Hills: Sage, 1986); and Marvin Zetterbaum, *Tocqueville and the Problem of Democracy* (Stanford: Stanford University Press, 1967). Further, Tocqueville's chapter on the "Three Races" of America was omitted from most abridged editions of *Democracy* in the 1950s and 1960s. For a discussion of this kind of abridging, see James L. Colwell, "The Calamities which They Apprehend: Tocqueville on Race in America," *Western Humanities Review* 21 (1967): 93–100.

56. For arguments that Tocqueville was negrophobic or racist, see Fredrickson, *Black Image*; Richard Resh, "Alexis de Tocqueville and the Negro," *Journal of Negro History* 48 (October 1963): 251–59; and Stephen Frederick Schneck, "Habits of the Head: Tocqueville's America and Jazz," *Political Theory* 17, no. 4 (1989): 638–62. For arguments that Tocqueville should be read as essentially antiracist, see Liebersohn, "Discovering Indigenous Nobility," and popular accounts such as Andrew Hacker, *Two Nations: Black and White, Separate, Hostile, Unequal*, expanded and updated ed. (New York: Ballantine, 1995), and Sven Lindqvist, *The Skull Measurer's Mistake and Other Portraits of Men and Women Who Spoke Out Against Racism*, trans. by Joan Tate (New York: New Press, 1997). For a good discussion of race and democracy in the America Tocqueville visited, see Harry W. Fritz, "Racism and Democracy in Tocqueville's America," *Social Science Journal* 13, no. 3 (1976): 65–75.

57. Baker, *Affairs of Party*, 253.

58. Tocqueville, *Democracy in America*, 356.

59. For a similar interpretation of Tocqueville, see Margaret Kohn, "The Other America: Tocqueville and Beaumont on Race and Slavery," *Polity* 35, no. 2 (2000): 169–93.

60. Tocqueville, *Democracy in America*, 252–53 n. 4. As I pointed out in the previous section, the Pennsylvania legislature revoked the right of Black males to vote in 1838, a few years after Tocqueville's visit.

61. Ibid., 357.

62. Ibid., 343.

63. Tocqueville, *Journey to America*, 106.

64. W. E. B. Du Bois, *The Gift of Black Folk* (Boston: Stratford, 1924), 139.

65. Alexis de Tocqueville, *Report on the Abolition of Slavery in the French Colonies* (Westport, CT: Negro Universities Press, 1970).

66. Tocqueville, *Democracy in America*, 342.

67. Ibid., 343.

68. Ibid., 341.

69. Evelyn Nakano Glenn, *Unequal Freedom: How Race and Gender Shaped American Citizenship and Labor* (Cambridge: Harvard University Press, 2002); Catherine A. Holland, *The Body Politic: Foundings, Citizenship, and Difference in the American Political Imagination* (New York: Routledge, 2001); Dana D. Nelson, *National Manhood: Capitalist Citizenship and the Imagined Fraternity of White Men* (Durham: Duke University Press, 1998).

70. Carole Pateman, *The Sexual Contract* (Stanford: Stanford University Press, 1988).

71. Linda K. Kerber, *No Constitutional Right to be Ladies: Women and the Obligations of Citizenship* (New York: Hill and Wang, 1998).

72. Hodes, *White Women, Black Men*; Julie Novkov, "Racial Constructions: The Legal Regulation of Miscegenation in Alabama, 1890–1934," *Law and History Review* 20 (2002), http://www.historycooperative.org/journals/lhr/20.2/novkov.html.

73. Kerber, *No Constitutional Right*, xx.

74. Patricia Hill Collins, *Fighting Words: Black Women and the Search for Justice* (Minneapolis: University of Minnesota Press, 1998), 15–16.

75. The terms "civil death" and "social death" derive from Cheryl I. Harris, "Finding Sojourner's Truth: Race, Gender, and the Institution of Property," *Cardozo Law Review* 18, no. 2 (1996): 309–409, and Orlando Patterson, *Slavery and Social Death: A Comparative Study* (Cambridge: Harvard University Press, 1982), respectively.

76. Harris, "Finding Sojourner's Truth," 321.

77. Ibid., 312.

78. Dana Frank, "White Working-Class Women and the Race Question," *International Labor and Working-Class History* 54 (fall 1998): 80–102; Evelyn Brooks Higginbotham, "African-American Women's History and the Metalanguage of Race," *Signs* 17, no. 2 (1992): 251–74.

79. Frank, "White Working-Class Women," 85.

80. Barbara Hilkert Andolsen, *"Daughters of Jefferson, Daughters of Bootblacks": Racism and American Feminism* (Macon, GA: Mercer University Press, 1986); Angela Y. Davis, *Women, Race & Class* (New York: Vintage, 1983); Paula Giddings, *When and Where I Enter: The Impact of Black Women on Race and Sex in America* (New York: William Morrow, 1984); Louise Michele Newman, *White Women's Rights: The Racial Origins of Feminism in the United States* (New York: Oxford University Press, 1999).

81. Aileen Kraditor, *The Ideas of the Woman Suffrage Movement, 1890–1920* (New York: Columbia University Press, 1965), 168.

82. Shklar, *American Citizenship*, 60–61; Kraditor, *Ideas of Woman Suffrage*, 252–53; Gretchen Ritter, "Gender and Citizenship after the Nineteenth Amendment," *Polity* 32, no. 3 (2000): 345–75. The Nineteenth Amendment technically covered Black women but it was an empty victory for most, as they were prevented from exercising their new right by the same tests, taxes, and terrors that had kept Black men from voting since the rise of Jim Crow.

83. Paula Baker, "The Domestication of Politics: Women and American Political Society, 1780–1920," *American Historical Review* 89, no. 3 (1984): 620–47.

84. Marilyn Frye, "On Being White: Toward a Feminist Understanding of Race and Race Supremacy," in her *The Politics of Reality: Essays in Feminist Theory* (Freedom, CA: The Crossing Press, 1983), 127.

85. Ibid., 114.

86. Harris, "Finding Sojourner's Truth," 336.

87. Kimberlé Williams Crenshaw, "Beyond Racism and Misogyny: Black Feminism and 2 Live Crew," in *Words That Wound: Critical Race Theory, Assaultive Speech, and the First Amendment*, ed. Mari J. Matsuda et al. (Boulder, CO: Westview Press, 1993); Kimberlé Crenshaw, "Demarginalizing the Intersection of Race and Sex: A Black Feminist Critique of Antidiscrimination Doctrine, Feminist Theory, and Antiracist Politics," *University of Chicago Legal Forum* 139 (1989): 139–67.

88. Collins, *Fighting Words*, 211.

89. This is not to say that this focus is the most appropriate in all contexts. For an example of a useful critique of white male citizenship specifically, see Nelson, *National Manhood*.

90. Higginbotham, "African-American Women's History," 274.

91. bell hooks, *Ain't I a Woman: Black Women and Feminism* (Boston: South End, 1981), 122.

92. Frank, "White Working-Class Women."

93. Tocqueville, *Democracy in America*, 35, 347–48, 375–76; *Journey to America*, 269.

94. Roediger, *Wages of Whiteness*, 13.

95. Sheldon Wolin, *Politics and Vision* (Boston: Little, Brown, 1961).

96. W. E. B. Du Bois, *Black Reconstruction in America: 1860–1880* (New York: Atheneum, 1992), 12.

97. Ibid., 700–701.

98. Ibid., 183.

99. Nancy Fraser, *Unruly Practices: Power, Discourse, and Gender in Contemporary Social Theory* (Minneapolis: University of Minnesota Press, 1989), chapters 7 and 8.

100. Du Bois, *Black Reconstruction*, 184. As Jennifer Hochschild has shown, the American Dream still dominates the American political imagination and it continues to be intimately connected to and challenged by race because white and Black Americans still see each other as barriers to each other's success: *Facing Up to the American Dream: Race, Class, and the Soul of the Nation* (Princeton: Princeton University Press, 1995).

101. Du Bois, *Black Reconstruction*, 700–701.

102. James Baldwin, *The Fire Next Time* (New York: Dell, 1963), 115.

103. In making this argument I do not want to imply that wiping away white privilege makes a utopian kingdom inevitable. The primary weakness of Du Bois's argument is that it assumes that without the wages of whiteness, there would be little else to prevent the crystallization of a politically conscious working class that could fight capital not just for reforms but for basic changes in the system. But class always operates in the context of other relationships that, while inevitably related to class, are not reducible to it. There is certainly a tendency toward class consciousness and labor unity in the processes of capitalist production, as Marx shows, but it is not inevitable. It is but one tendency among many, and it is often not the strongest. Class unity and consciousness, like democracy, are ultimately political products borne of vision, struggle, compromise, and hope. Nevertheless, though there are no sure paths to a more democratic society, Du Bois's gift to theory is his analysis of white wages

and the cross-class alliance and how their abolition is one of the most important prerequisites of such a society.

3. The Peculiar Dilemma of Whiteness

1. Quoted in George Fredrickson, *The Black Image in the White Mind: The Debate on Afro-American Character and Destiny, 1817–1914* (New York: Harper and Row, 1971), 61.

2. John F. Kennedy Jr., "Interview with George Wallace," *George* 1, no. 1 (1995): 178–87.

3. In 1995 the average income for Black families in Alabama was $19,786; for white families it was $37,040: Southern Education Foundation, *Miles to Go: A Report on Black Students and Postsecondary Education in the South* (Atlanta: Southern Education Foundation, 1998). In 2002, 26.1 percent of non-Hispanic white Alabamans twenty-five years and older had a bachelor's degree compared to 12.2 percent of Black Alabamans: U.S. Bureau of the Census, "Table 14. Educational Attainment of People 18 Years and Over, by Age, Sex, Race, and Hispanic Origin, for the 25 Largest States: March 2002," http://www.census.gov/population/www/socdemo/education/ppl-169.html.

4. Anthony W. Marx, *Making Race and Nation: A Comparison of South Africa, the United States, and Brazil* (Cambridge: Cambridge University Press, 1998), 14–15. Marx's argument is a strong challenge to Benedict Anderson's theory of nation-making, which holds that nations are the result of the unification of peoples through an "imagined community": *Imagined Communities: Reflections on the Origin and Spread of Nationalism* (London: Verso, 1983). Nations may be created if formerly disparate groups "imagine" themselves as members of the same nation, but Marx counters that nations are just as likely built upon the exclusion and oppression of others.

5. Evelyn Nakano Glenn, *Unequal Freedom: How Race and Gender Shaped American Citizenship and Labor* (Cambridge: Harvard University Press, 2002).

6. Stanley Greenberg, *Race and State in Capitalist Development: Comparative Perspectives* (New Haven: Yale University Press, 1980), 26–27.

7. John W. Cell, *The Highest Stage of White Supremacy: The Origins of Segregation in South Africa and the American South* (Cambridge: Cambridge University Press, 1982), 18. Cell argues that white supremacy is an umbrella term that refers to several different forms of domination, including genocide on the frontier, racial slavery, and segregation. By "highest stage of white supremacy" he does not mean that segregation is the worst form of racial oppression, only the

most sophisticated. Segregation was a moderate option chosen over and against more severe forms of racial terror. It represented the political middle rather than the extreme.

8. C. Vann Woodward, *The Strange Career of Jim Crow* (New York: Galaxy, 1957), 93.

9. Greenberg, *Race and State*, 140. The same can be said of labor unions in the *Herrenvolk* era. While unions in theory should be expansive and nonrestrictive, in practice they sacrificed these qualities to accommodate prevailing white sentiment and promote an exclusionary industrial unionism. Job undercutting, for example, was not prevented through open unionism but by erecting racial barriers around certain jobs, effectively creating a job reserve system for whites. Ibid., 284–85.

10. Martin Luther King Jr., *Why We Can't Wait* (New York: Mentor, 1964), chapter 6. Greenberg could find no instance in which management in Alabama firms chose to desegregate their workplace or break down job discrimination due to cost calculations, market pressures, or feelings of justice. "Change came only when black civil rights organizations grew impatient with southern employment practices or, more often, when changes in law or federal policy forced it": Greenberg, *Race and State*, 231.

11. While I assume that the dissolution of the *Herrenvolk* by the civil rights movement is permanent, numerous scholars have noted uncanny similarities between the aftermath of Reconstruction and the post–civil rights era today. My argument that the civil rights movement stands as a watershed in American democracy should be read with this warning in mind: we can go back. See, for example, Robin D. G. Kelley, *Yo' Mama's DisFUNKtional! Fighting the Culture Wars in Urban America* (Boston: Beacon Press, 1997); and Philip A. Klinkner with Rogers M. Smith, *The Unsteady March: The Rise and Decline of Racial Equality in America* (Chicago: University of Chicago Press, 1999).

12. Kimberlé Williams Crenshaw, "Color-blind Dreams and Racial Nightmares: Reconfiguring Racism in the Post–Civil Rights Era," in *Birth of a Nation 'hood: Gaze, Script, and Spectacle in the O. J. Simpson Case*, ed. Toni Morrison and Claudia Brodsky Lacour (New York: Pantheon, 1997).

13. Peggy MacIntosh, "White Privilege and Male Privilege: A Personal Account of Coming to See Correspondences Through Work in Women's Studies," Working Paper no. 189 (Wellesley College Center for Research on Women, 1988), 1–2.

14. My periodization here is similar to Omi and Winant's, who hold that,

with the exception of Reconstruction, the United States was a racial dictatorship from 1607 to 1965 and a system of racial hegemony afterward. It is also similar to Shelby Steele's division of American history into the eras of white racism (i.e., the *Herrenvolk*) and white guilt (i.e., the post–civil rights era), in which whites and American institutions go to great lengths (such as affirmative action and diversity policies) to prove they are *not* racist. The continuity between these two eras for Omi and Winant and Steele alike is that both are driven by white interests. Michael Omi and Howard Winant, *Racial Formation in the United States: From the 1960s to the 1990s*, 2d ed. (New York: Routledge, 1994), 66–67; Shelby Steele, "The Age of White Guilt and the Disappearance of the Black Individual," *Harper's Magazine* 305, no. 1830 (2002): 33–42. This periodization is not meant to deny other pivotal points in American racial history but to emphasize what pre–civil rights eras held in common—a society in which all those defined as white were socially and politically superior to all those defined as Black—and contrast it with the color-blind democracy, in which all individuals are officially equal regardless of race.

15. Karl Marx, "On the Jewish Question," in Karl Marx and Frederick Engels, *Collected Works*, vol. 3 (New York: International, 1975), 153.

16. Michel Foucault, *The History of Sexuality*, vol. 1, *An Introduction* (New York: Vintage, 1990).

17. Lewis R. Gordon, *Bad Faith and Antiblack Racism* (Atlantic Highlands, NJ: Humanities Press, 1995); Peniel E. Joseph, "'Black' Reconstructed: White Supremacy in Post Civil Rights America," *The Black Scholar* 25, no. 4 (1995): 52–55. A shining example of this consequence is that efforts to eliminate affirmative action have been redefined by their proponents as "civil rights initiatives."

18. My distinction between standing and normalization is not meant to imply that normalizing practices are exclusive to the post–civil rights era or that standing belongs only to the *Herrenvolk* age. The residues of white standing continue to operate in racial profiling, redlining, and "driving while Black." Likewise, Du Bois always understood that the basis of white power is not so much its official backing by the state as it is the fact that the white world's domination appears—especially to whites—as the normal condition of society. "The present attitude and action of the white world is not based solely upon rational, deliberate intent. It is a matter of conditioned reflexes; of long followed habits, customs and folkways; of subconscious trains of reasoning and

unconscious nervous reflexes": W. E. B. Du Bois, *Dusk of Dawn: An Essay toward an Autobiography of a Race Concept* (New Brunswick, NJ: Transaction, 1995), 171–72. My point is not so much that normalization is a "new form" of racism that has replaced an "old form" but that the shift from the *Herrenvolk* to the color-blind democracy has been accompanied by a change in the general means by which racial power operates.

19. Cheryl Harris, "Whiteness as Property," *Harvard Law Review* 106, no. 8 (1993): 1713–14.

20. Ibid., 1721.

21. Dalton Conley, *Being Black, Living in the Red: Race, Wealth, and Social Policy in America* (Berkeley: University of California Press, 1999), 28.

22. Harris, "Whiteness as Property," 1715.

23. The following analysis is suggested by Immanuel Wallerstein's work on the meaning of the bourgeoisie in history. Immanuel Wallerstein, "The Bour-geois(ie) as Concept and Reality," in Etienne Balibar and Immanuel Wallerstein, *Race, Nation, Class: Ambiguous Identities* (London: Verso, 1991).

24. Lawrie Balfour, "'A Most Disagreeable Mirror': Race Consciousness as Double Consciousness," *Political Theory* 26, no. 3 (1998): 347.

25. Carol M. Swain, *The New White Nationalism in America: Its Challenge to Integration* (Cambridge: Cambridge University Press, 2002).

26. I assume that participation is at the heart of proposals for a more radical, deliberative, communicative, agonal, stronger, or deeper democracy. There are significant differences among these models of democracy. Further, democratic theory has other concerns, such as a more equitable distribution of wealth, the educative effects of participation, and the expansion of individual rights to include "social" or welfare rights. Nevertheless, whether through citizenship, civic associations, workplace democracy, councils, collectives, communes, delib-erative spaces, or coalitions, democratic theory is defined by the quest, in some manner, to go beyond the limits of citizen participation under existing liberal democracies. In order to avoid confusion between this objective and the phi-losophy of participatory democracy associated with Carole Pateman, C. B. Macpherson, and others, I will generally refer to "democratic participation" instead of "participatory democracy."

27. Judith N. Shklar, *American Citizenship: The Quest for Inclusion* (Cambridge: Harvard University Press, 1991), 30.

28. Ibid., 94.

29. See, for example, Seyla Benhabib, "Toward a Deliberative Model of Democratic Legitimacy," in *Democracy and Difference: Contesting the Boundaries of the Political*, ed. Seyla Benhabib (Princeton: Princeton University Press, 1996).

30. The phrase is from Seyla Benhabib, "Judith Shklar's Dystopic Liberalism," *Social Research* 11, no. 2 (1994): 477–88.

31. Benjamin Barber, *Strong Democracy* (Berkeley: University of California Press, 1984).

32. Robert A. Dahl, *On Democracy* (New Haven: Yale University Press, 1998); Jürgen Habermas, *The Inclusion of the Other: Studies in Political Theory* (Cambridge: MIT Press, 1998); David Held, *Models of Democracy*, 2d ed. (Stanford: Stanford University Press, 1996).

33. Michael Walzer, *On Tolerance* (New Haven: Yale University Press, 1997).

34. *Democracy and Difference*, ed. Benhabib; William E. Connolly, *Identity\ Difference: Democratic Negotiations of Political Paradox* (Ithaca, NY: Cornell University Press, 1991).

35. William E. Connolly, *The Ethos of Pluralization* (Minneapolis: University of Minnesota Press, 1995), xiv–xv.

36. Ibid., 197.

37. Ibid., 180.

38. Ibid., xv.

39. William E. Connolly, "Pluralism, Multiculturalism and the Nation-State: Rethinking the Connections," *Journal of Political Ideologies* 1, no. 1 (1996): 61, italics in original.

40. Connolly, *Ethos of Pluralization*, 180.

41. Ibid., 184.

42. Ibid., 113.

43. Ibid., 129.

44. Ruy Teixeira and Joel Rogers, *America's Forgotten Majority: Why the White Working Class Still Matters* (New York: Basic Books, 2000). See also Richard D. Kahlenberg, *The Remedy: Class, Race, and Affirmative Action* (New York: Basic Books, 1996).

45. George Lipsitz, *The Possessive Investment in Whiteness: How White People Profit from Identity Politics* (Philadelphia: Temple University Press, 1998); Michael K. Brown, *Race, Money, and the American Welfare State* (Ithaca, NY: Cornell University Press, 1999); Robert C. Lieberman, *Shifting the Color Line: Race and the American Welfare State* (Cambridge: Harvard University Press, 1998).

46. Derrick Bell, *Faces at the Bottom of the Well: The Permanence of Racism* (New York: Basic Books, 1992). Scholars have documented the white self-interest principle at work in the most surprising of places, such as President Bill Clinton's 1997 Initiative on Race and Al Gore's failed strategy to win the electoral votes in Florida in his 2000 presidential campaign. See Claire Jean Kim, "Managing the Racial Breach: Clinton, Black-White Polarization, and the Race Initiative," *Political Science Quarterly* 117, no. 1 (2002): 55–79; and Howard Gillman, *The Votes That Counted: How the Court Decided the 2000 Election* (Chicago: University of Chicago Press, 2001).

47. I deliberately add "as it relates to white identity" because I do not mean to suggest that modifying dominant identities will result in their dissolution in all cases. Arguments for the abolition of other identities require a separate justification from the one presented here.

48. Iris Marion Young, *Justice and the Politics of Difference* (Princeton: Princeton University Press, 1990), 66, 74–75.

49. Ibid., 37–38.

50. Ibid., 43. She defines a social group as "a collective of persons differentiated from at least one other group by cultural forms, practices, or way of life."

51. Ibid., 91.

52. Ibid. Further, Young points out that at times justice requires *inequality*. Echoing Marx, she writes, "A politics of difference argues that equality as the participation and inclusion of all groups sometimes requires different treatment for oppressed or disadvantaged groups. To promote social justice, I argue, social policy should sometimes accord special treatment to groups" (158).

53. Ronald Beiner, "Why Citizenship Constitutes a Theoretical Problem in the Last Decade of the Twentieth Century," in *Theorizing Citizenship*, ed. Ronald Beiner (Albany: State University of New York Press, 1995); Chantal Mouffe, "Feminism, Citizenship, and Radical Democratic Politics," in *Feminists Theorize the Political*, ed. Judith Butler and Joan W. Scott (New York: Routledge, 1992); Nancy Fraser, *Justice Interruptus: Critical Reflections on the "Postsocialist" Condition* (New York: Routledge, 1997), chapter 8.

54. Lani Guinier, *The Tyranny of the Majority: Fundamental Fairness in Representative Democracy* (New York: Free Press, 1994), 103.

55. Ibid.

56. Ibid., 15.

57. Ibid., 137–42.

58. Ibid., 93–94.

59. For criticisms of the problems in implementing Guinier's proposals, see Mark A. Graber, "Conflicting Representations: Lani Guinier and James Madison on Electoral Systems," *Constitutional Commentary* 13, no. 3 (1996): 291–307; Pamela S. Karlan, "Democracy and Dis-Appointment," *Michigan Law Review* 93, no. 6 (1995): 1273–96; and John L. Safford, "John C. Calhoun, Lani Guinier, and Minority Rights," *PS: Political Science* 28, no. 2 (1995): 211–16.

60. Guinier, *Tyranny of the Majority*, 112.

4. The Failure of Multiculturalism and Color Blindness

1. Jim Walsh, "Illegals Target of Crackdown by Chandler Police," *Arizona Republic*, 31 July 1997, B2; Hector Tobar, "An Ugly Stain on a City's Bright and Shining Plan," *Los Angeles Times*, 28 December 1998, A1. The lawsuit was settled in February 1999. The city of Chandler paid $400,000 and enacted a new policy preventing city police from enforcing federal immigration laws. Janie Magruder, "$400K Settles Roundup Suit in Chandler," *Arizona Republic*, 11 February 1999, A1.

2. Monica Davis, "Chandler Diversity Worth Celebrating, Festival Officials Say," *Arizona Republic*, 21 January 1999, East Valley sec.

3. Michael H. Hunt, *Ideology and U.S. Foreign Policy* (New Haven: Yale University Press, 1987).

4. Thomas Borstelmann, *The Cold War and the Color Line: American Race Relations in the Global Arena* (Cambridge: Harvard University Press, 2002); Mary L. Dudziak, "Desegregation as a Cold War Imperative," *Stanford Law Review* 41, no. 1 (1988): 61–120; Philip A. Klinkner with Rogers M. Smith, *The Unsteady March: The Rise and Decline of Racial Equality in America* (Chicago: University of Chicago Press, 1999), chapters 7 and 8; John David Skrentny, "The Effect of the Cold War on African American Civil Rights: America and the World Audience, 1945–1968," *Theory and Society* 27, no. 2 (1998): 237–85.

5. Lawrence Bobo, James R. Kluegel, and Ryan A. Smith, "Laissez-Faire Racism: The Crystallization of a 'Kinder, Gentler' Anti-Black Ideology," Russell Sage Foundation, June 1996, http://epn.org/sage/rsbobo1.html; Aldon D. Morris, *The Origins of the Civil Rights Movement: Black Communities Organizing for Change* (New York: Free Press, 1984).

6. This phenomenon of the Black middle class choosing its racial interests over its class interests was so strong that Du Bois in 1953 was confident that whatever happened in the struggle for racial equality, the Black middle class

would be compelled to follow the Black working class rather than lead it or break away from it. W. E. B. Du Bois, "Negroes and the Crisis of Capitalism in the United States," *Monthly Review* 41, no. 1 (1989): 27–35. For an opposing perspective, see E. Franklin Frazier, *Black Bourgeoisie* (Glencoe, IL: Free Press, 1957).

7. Melvin L. Oliver and Thomas M. Shapiro, *Black Wealth/White Wealth: A New Perspective on Racial Inequality* (New York: Routledge, 1995).

8. William Julius Wilson, *The Declining Significance of Race: Blacks and Changing American Institutions* (Chicago: University of Chicago Press, 1978).

9. Some color-blind advocates argue against racial classification of any kind, claiming that even this practice ultimately subverts a color-blind society. For them, race is a myth that is perpetuated by any public acknowledgment of it. Racial classification is racist and must be eliminated because even with the best of intentions it ends up perpetrating the power of race rather than undermining it. Yehudi O. Webster, *The Racialization of America* (New York: St. Martin's Press, 1992).

10. In an extreme instance of this logic, Dinesh D'Souza actually calls for the repeal of the 1964 Civil Rights Act, claiming that its antidiscrimination provisions should apply only to the public sector and that any private business or institution should be free to discriminate as it pleases, since ethnocentrism is universal and natural. Dinesh D'Souza, *The End of Racism* (New York: Free Press, 1995), 544–45.

11. *Plessy v. Ferguson*, 163 U.S. 537 (1896) (Harlan, J., dissenting). The phrase "separate but equal" is actually from Harlan's dissent, not the majority opinion.

12. *Plessy v. Ferguson*, 559.

13. Neil Gotanda, "A Critique of 'Our Constitution is Color-Blind,'" *Stanford Law Review* 44, no. 1 (1991): 1–68.

14. Stephan Thernstrom and Abigail Thernstrom, *America in Black and White: One Nation, Indivisible* (New York: Simon & Schuster, 1997). The book received a great deal of attention in the press, particularly after Abigail Thernstrom challenged President Bill Clinton for his support for affirmative action at a President's Initiative on Race forum in December 1997.

15. Ibid., 95.

16. Ibid., 529.

17. Ibid., 534. This shift in blame from white privilege to Black deficiency is a common theme in conservative arguments regarding race. For Charles Murray and Richard Herrnstein, the Black-white gap in various social indicators is due

to genetic differences that debilitate African Americans. For Dinesh D'Souza, racial inequality is due to the cultural pathologies of African Americans. The Thernstroms' historical approach steers clear of either sort of explanation, yet their conclusions stack up in a familiar pile: the discriminations the dark world endures are fundamentally of its own doing. Richard J. Herrnstein and Charles Murray, *The Bell Curve: Intelligence and Class Structure in American Life* (New York: Free Press, 1994); D'Souza, *End of Racism*.

18. Stephen Steinberg, "Up from Slavery: The Myth of Black Progress," *New Politics*, n.s., 7, no. 1 (1998): 69–81.

19. Paul M. Sniderman and Edward G. Carmines, *Reaching Beyond Race* (Cambridge: Harvard University Press, 1997), 4, italics in original.

20. Jim Sleeper, *Liberal Racism* (New York: Viking, 1997), 143.

21. Kimberlé Williams Crenshaw, "Color-blind Dreams and Racial Nightmares: Reconfiguring Racism in the Post–Civil Rights Era," in *Birth of a Nation 'hood: Gaze, Script, and Spectacle in the O. J. Simpson Case*, ed. Toni Morrison and Claudia Brodsky Lacour (New York: Pantheon, 1997), 100.

22. George Lipsitz, "The Possessive Investment in Whiteness: Racialized Social Democracy and the 'White' Problem in American Studies," *American Quarterly* 47, no. 3 (1995): 381.

23. John Tomlinson, *Cultural Imperialism* (Baltimore: Johns Hopkins University Press, 1991), 7.

24. Amy Gutmann, "Introduction," in Charles Taylor et al., *Multiculturalism: Examining the Politics of Recognition*, ed. Amy Gutmann (Princeton: Princeton University Press, 1994), 5.

25. Charles Taylor, "The Politics of Recognition," in Taylor et al., *Multiculturalism*, ed. Gutmann.

26. Charles Taylor, *Hegel and Modern Society* (Cambridge: Cambridge University Press, 1979), 11.

27. Taylor, "The Politics of Recognition," 34.

28. Ibid., 26–27.

29. J. A. May, "The 'Master-Slave' Relation in Hegel's *Phenomenology of Spirit* and in the Early Marx: A Study in One Aspect of the Philosophical Foundations of Marxism," *Current Perspectives in Social Theory* 5 (1984): 225–66.

30. K. Anthony Appiah, "Race, Culture, Identity: Misunderstood Connections," in K. Anthony Appiah and Amy Gutmann, *Color Conscious: The Political Morality of Race* (Princeton: Princeton University Press, 1996), 92.

31. Taylor, "The Politics of Recognition," 26.

32. Ibid., 59–60.

33. See, for example, Appiah, "Race, Culture, Identity"; Amelie Oksenberg Rorty, "The Hidden Politics of Cultural Identification," *Political Theory* 22, no. 1 (1994): 152–66; Sasja Tempelman, "Construction of Cultural Identity: Multiculturalism and Exclusion," *Political Studies* 47, no. 1 (1999): 17–31; and Thomas L. Dumm, "Strangers and Liberals," *Political Theory* 22, no. 1 (1994): 167–75. See also the numerous edited collections on multiculturalism that include Taylor's essay, including *Campus Wars: Multiculturalism and the Politics of Difference*, ed. John Arthur and Amy Shapiro (Boulder: Westview, 1995); *Multiculturalism: A Critical Reader*, ed. David Theo Goldberg (Cambridge: Blackwell, 1994); and *Theorizing Multiculturalism: A Guide to the Current Debate*, ed. Cynthia Willett (Cambridge: Blackwell, 1998).

34. Taylor himself acknowledges this. He implies that his model of recognition applies to the situation of Black people in the United States in several places in "The Politics of Recognition" (26, 36, 38, 65). In his review of Will Kymlicka's *Multicultural Citizenship* (*American Political Science Review* 90, no. 2 [1996]: 408), however, he acknowledges that African Americans do not fit into his cultural model.

35. Linda Nicholson, *The Play of Reason: From the Modern to the Postmodern* (Ithaca, NY: Cornell University Press, 1999), 135.

36. Orlando Patterson, *Slavery and Social Death: A Comparative Study* (Cambridge: Harvard University Press, 1982).

37. It is possible to interpret misrecognition itself as a form of power, and Taylor indeed does say that misrecognition can be a form of oppression. But the focus of misrecognition is on the demeaning images the misrecognized have had forced on them (and in some ways have internalized) by the powers that be, not the social relations that enable one group to (mis)recognize another.

38. Taylor, "The Politics of Recognition," 70.

39. Further, it is quite possible to do so without appealing to poststructuralism (which is not meant to imply that I oppose such appeals). The basis for such an analysis lies in Hegel's master-slave dialectic, from which the concept "recognition" originates. See, for example, Leonard Cassuto, "Frederick Douglass and the Work of Freedom: Hegel's Master-Slave Dialectic in the Fugitive Slave Narrative," *Prospects* 21, ed. Jack Salzman (1996): 229–59; David Brion Davis, *The Problem of Slavery in the Age of Revolution: 1770–1823* (Ithaca,

NY: Cornell University Press, 1975), 560–64; and May, "The 'Master-Slave' Relation."

40. I exclude from the following critique works on whiteness by scholars such as Neil Foley, Ian Haney-López, Cheryl Harris, bell hooks, Noel Ignatiev, Matthew Frye Jacobsen, David Roediger, and Alexander Saxton, as well as other important works such as Toni Morrison's *Playing in the Dark: Whiteness and the Literary Imagination* (Cambridge: Harvard University Press, 1992). These scholars are more interested in critiquing whiteness than in discovering a usable past in its name and thus have much to offer. Roediger locates the origins of this sort of inquiry in African American scholarship and terms it "critical studies of whiteness" to distinguish it from the field of "whiteness studies" I criticize here. *Black On White: Black Writers on What It Means to Be White*, ed. David R. Roediger (New York: Schocken, 1998). For an overview of the literature on whiteness and the debates surrounding it, see Peter Kolchin, "Whiteness Studies: The New History of Race in America," *Journal of American History* 89, no. 1 (2002): 154–73.

41. Henry A. Giroux, "White Noise: Toward a Pedagogy of Whiteness," in *Race-ing Representation: Voice, History, and Sexuality*, ed. Kostas Myrsiades and Linda Myrsiades (Lanham, MD: Rowman & Littlefield, 1998).

42. Ibid., 42. Ruth Frankenberg poses a similar dilemma: "At this time in U.S. history, whiteness as a marked identity is explicitly articulated mainly in terms of the 'white pride' of the far right. In a sense, this produces a discursive bind for that small subgroup of white women and men concerned to engage in antiracist work: if whiteness is emptied of any content other than that which is associated with racism or capitalism, this leaves progressive whites apparently without a genealogy" (Ruth Frankenberg, *White Women, Race Matters: The Social Construction of Whiteness* [Minneapolis: University of Minnesota Press, 1993], 232).

43. Giroux, "White Noise," 43.

44. For similar approaches to whiteness, see *The Minnesota Review* 47 (fall 1996: The White Issue); *Becoming and Unbecoming White: Owning and Disowning a Racial Identity*, ed. Christine Clark and James O'Donnell (Westport, CT: Bergin & Garvey, 1999); *Whiteness: A Critical Reader*, ed. Mike Hill (New York: New York University Press, 1997); AnnLouise Keating, "Interrogating 'Whiteness,' (De)Constructing 'Race,'" *College English* 57, no. 8 (1995): 901–18; Beverly Daniel Tatum, "Teaching White Students about Racism: The Search for White Allies and the Restoration of Hope," *Teachers College Record* 95, no. 4 (1994):

462–76; George Yudice, "Neither Impugning nor Disavowing Whiteness Does a Viable Politics Make," in *After Political Correctness*, ed. Christopher Newfield and Ronald Strickland (Boulder: Westview, 1995).

45. Joe L. Kincheloe and Shirley R. Steinberg, "Addressing the Crisis of Whiteness: Reconfiguring White Identity in a Pedagogy of Whiteness," in *White Reign: Deploying Whiteness in America*, ed. Joe L. Kincheloe, Shirley R. Steinberg, Nelson M. Rodriguez, and Ronald E. Chennault (New York: St. Martin's Press, 1998), 12. One should note that they offer no such vision in their book, either.

46. Ibid.

47. Ibid., 23.

48. Kincheloe and Steinberg even demur in defining whiteness itself, falsely claiming that "no one at this point really knows exactly what whiteness is," as if African American scholars and others have not been criticizing it for years. Giroux claims it is possible to construct a white identity without essentializing whiteness (as if the main problem with whiteness is its essentialism), but it is his own logic that is essentializing. Because Blackness contains a content independent of relations of subordination, Giroux assumes that whiteness must have one, too. He does not consider that it might be possible for a Black culture to survive without a white one or that whites might someday identify themselves other than racially. Kincheloe and Steinberg, "The Crisis of Whiteness," 4; Giroux, "White Noise," 70–71.

49. Adam Cornford, "'Colorless All-Color': Notes on White Culture," *Bad Subjects* 33 (September 1997), http://eserver.org/bs/33/cornford.html; David Carroll Cochran, *The Color of Freedom: Race and Contemporary American Liberalism* (Albany, NY: SUNY Press, 1999), 106.

50. Albert Murray, *The Omni-Americans: Some Alternatives to the Folklore of White Supremacy* (New York: Da Capo, 1990).

51. Cochran, *Color of Freedom*, 62.

52. Nancy Fraser, *Justice Interruptus: Critical Reflections on the "Postsocialist" Condition* (New York: Routledge, 1997), 22.

53. For a similar argument, see Iris Marion Young, "Unruly Categories: A Critique of Nancy Fraser's Dual Systems Theory," in *Theorizing Multiculturalism*, ed. Willett, 51.

54. Robin D. G. Kelley, "'But a Local Phase of a World Problem': Black History's Global Vision, 1883–1950," *Journal of American History* 86, no. 3 (1999): 1045–77.

55. Lawrence Blum, "Recognition, Value, and Equality: A Critique of Charles Taylor's and Nancy Fraser's Accounts of Multiculturalism," in *Theorizing Multiculturalism*, ed. Willett.

56. The only expressly political element I find in Fraser's conception of recognition and redistribution in *Justice Interruptus* is her suggestion that redistribution might involve "subjecting investment to democratic decision-making": Fraser, *Justice Interruptus*, 15.

57. Ibid., 34, 38.

58. Thomas C. Holt, *The Problem of Race in the Twenty-First Century* (Cambridge: Harvard University Press, 2000).

59. According to the Naturalization Act of 1790, naturalization was limited to "free white persons." This led to numerous court cases in which people from Turkey, Mexico, Japan, and elsewhere tried to prove they were white and therefore fit for citizenship. Post–Civil War legislation made it possible for people of African descent to naturalize as well, but due to a strong desire not to identify with Blackness, no immigrant seeking American citizenship sought to do so by demonstrating their African heritage. The significance of this point will be evident below. Ian Haney-López, *White by Law: The Legal Construction of Race* (New York: New York University Press, 1996).

60. Jonathan W. Warren and Frances Winddance Twine, "White Americans, the New Minority? Non-Blacks and the Ever-Expanding Boundaries of Whiteness," *Journal of Black Studies* 28, no. 2 (1997): 200–218; "Discussion: Other Races," *Race Traitor*, no. 6 (1996): 32–42.

61. George Yancey, *Who is White? Latinos, Asians, and the New Black/Nonblack Divide* (Boulder: Lynne Rienner, 2003), 4.

62. Holt, *Problem of Race*, 102.

63. Leon E. Wynter, *American Skin: Pop Culture, Big Business, and the End of White America* (New York: Crown, 2002).

64. Holt, *Problem of Race*, 108–9.

65. This raises the question as to whether Powell, Thomas, or other Black elites are or could be white, given my definition of race as a political category of privilege. I believe the answer is no. Whiteness is the enjoyment or expectation of racial privilege in a democratic polity. Powell, Rice, Jordan, and Thomas enjoy significant class status and political power, but they do not enjoy or have a reasonable expectation of enjoying racial privilege.

66. This argument is suggested by Linda Gordon in *The Great Arizona Orphan Abduction* (Cambridge: Harvard University Press, 1999), 96–105.

67. Or as Orlando Patterson suggests, these influences could be absorbed in some parts of the country while other regions (particularly those with concentrated Black populations, such as the South and the Midwest), more or less retain a bipolar notion of race: "Race by the Numbers," *New York Times*, 8 May 2001, A27.

68. Holt, *Problem of Race*, 20.

69. Slavoj Žižek, "Multiculturalism, Or, the Cultural Logic of Multinational Capitalism," *New Left Review*, no. 225 (1997): 28–51.

70. For example, the Supreme Court received a record number of amicus curiae briefs on behalf of the University of Michigan in its successful defense of affirmative action in *Grutter v. Bollinger*, 539 U.S. (2003) and *Gratz v. Bollinger*, 539 U.S. (2003). At least forty briefs came from Fortune 500 corporations such as General Motors, Microsoft, Coca-Cola, and Dow Chemical. Stephanie A. Crockett, "Fortune 500 Companies Back University of Michigan Affirmative Action Program," *BET.com*, 10 February 2003, http://www.bet.com/articles/1,,c1gb5447-6183,00.html; "Affirmative Action Cases Get More Support from Businesses," *The University of Michigan News and Information Services*, 31 May 2001, http://www.umich.edu/~newsinfo/Releases/2001/May01/r053101e.html. Yet while diversity may be good business, confronting white privilege is decidedly not. As a vice president for human resources in one company told a journalist, "Diversity is good business [but as for] sitting people down and trying to unearth their racial inclinations, I don't think it's healthy": David K. Shipler, *A Country of Strangers: Blacks and Whites in America* (New York: Alfred A. Knopf, 1997), 539.

71. Nancy Fraser and Linda Gordon, "Contract versus Charity: Why Is There No Social Citizenship in the United States?" in *The Citizenship Debates: A Reader*, ed. Gershon Shafir (Minneapolis: University of Minnesota Press, 1998); T. H. Marshall, *Class, Citizenship, and Social Development: Essays by T. H. Marshall*, ed. Seymour Martin Lipset (Chicago: University of Chicago Press, 1964).

72. Nathan Glazer, *We Are All Multiculturalists Now* (Cambridge: Harvard University Press, 1997).

5. The Abolition-Democracy

1. "Malcolm X's Writings Offer Insights," *New York Times*, 8 March 2002, A17.

2. Malcolm X puts the term "white" in scare quotes himself when he refers to white Muslims in his letters from Mecca. See Malcolm X, "Letters

from Abroad," in *Malcolm X Speaks: Selected Speeches and Statements*, ed. George Breitman (London: Secker & Warburg, 1965), 60.

3. Raymond Rodgers and Jimmie N. Rogers, "The Evolution of the Attitude of Malcolm X Toward Whites," *Phylon* 44, no. 2 (1983): 108–15.

4. Quoted in ibid., 114.

5. Of course, Malcolm X's primary concern was not whites but the condition of Black people in the United States. Nevertheless, he knew that this condition could not be resolved without confronting "white-ism." See Malcolm X, "God's Judgment of White America," in Malcolm X, *The End of White World Supremacy*, ed. Imam Benjamin Karim (New York: Arcade, 1971), 130.

6. Martin Gilens, *Why Americans Hate Welfare: Race, Media, and the Politics of Antipoverty Policy* (Chicago: University of Chicago Press, 2000).

7. David R. Roediger, *The Wages of Whiteness: Race and the Making of the American Working Class* (New York: Verso, 1991), 60.

8. Bernard Bailyn, *The Ideological Origins of the American Revolution* (Cambridge: Harvard University Press, 1967); Lerone Bennett Jr., *The Shaping of Black America: The Struggles and Triumphs of African-Americans, 1619 to the 1990s* (New York: Penguin, 1993).

9. For similar criticisms of democratic theory, see Mary G. Dietz, "Merely Combating the Phrases of this World: Recent Democratic Theory," *Political Theory* 26, no. 1 (1998): 112–39; and Monique Deveaux, "Agonism and Pluralism," *Philosophy and Social Criticism* 25, no. 4 (1999): 1–22.

10. Will Kymlicka and Wayne Norman, "Return of the Citizen: A Survey of Recent Work on Citizenship Theory," in *Theorizing Citizenship*, ed. Ronald Beiner (Albany: State University of New York Press, 1995), 301. Kymlicka and Norman challenge the very relevance of modern theories of citizenship, given their timidity and their refusal to seriously challenge liberal rights.

11. Jeffrey C. Isaac, *Democracy in Dark Times* (Ithaca, NY: Cornell University Press, 1998), 11–12, italics in original.

12. Jeffrey C. Isaac, "Intellectuals, Marxism, and Politics," *New Left Review*, n.s., no. 2 (2000): 111–15.

13. C. B. Macpherson, *The Real World of Democracy* (Oxford: Clarendon, 1966); Macpherson, *The Life and Times of Liberal Democracy* (New York: Oxford University Press, 1977); Carole Pateman, *Participation and Democratic Theory* (Cambridge: Cambridge University Press, 1970).

14. Emily Hauptmann, "Can Less Be More? Leftist Deliberative Democrats' Critique of Participatory Democracy," *Polity* 33, no. 3 (2001): 397–421.

15. Michael C. Dawson, "A Black Counterpublic? Economic Earthquakes, Racial Agenda(s), and Black Politics," *Public Culture* 7, no. 1 (1994): 204.

16. Robin D. G. Kelley, *Freedom Dreams: The Black Radical Imagination* (Boston: Beacon, 2002), 8–9. See also Peniel E. Joseph, "Waiting till the Midnight Hour: Reconceptualizing the Heroic Period of the Civil Rights Movement, 1954–1965," *Souls* 2, no. 2 (2000): 6–17.

17. In *John Brown*, Du Bois shows how the values, experiences, struggles, and resistance of Black people profoundly shaped Brown. W. E. B. Du Bois, *John Brown* (New York: International, 1987). As William Cain argues, Du Bois essentially portrays Brown as a symbol of Black achievement. William E. Cain, "Violence, Revolution, and the Cost of Freedom: John Brown and W. E. B. Du Bois," *Boundary 2* 17, no. 1 (1990): 305–30.

18. W. E. B. Du Bois, *Black Reconstruction in America: 1860–1880* (New York: Atheneum, 1992), chapters 4 and 10.

19. W. E. B. Du Bois, *The Souls of Black Folk* (New York: Signet Classic, 1969), 45–46.

20. David Levering Lewis, *W. E. B. Du Bois: Biography of a Race, 1868–1919* (New York: Henry Holt, 1993), 281.

21. Arnold Rampersad, *The Art and Imagination of W. E. B. Du Bois* (Cambridge: Harvard University Press, 1976), 98.

22. W. E. B. Du Bois, *Dusk of Dawn: An Essay toward an Autobiography of a Race Concept* (New Brunswick, NJ: Transaction, 1995), 135.

23. W. E. B. Du Bois, *Darkwater: Voices from Within the Veil* (New York: Schocken, 1969), 49.

24. W. E. B. Du Bois, "Criteria of Negro Art," in *W. E. B. Du Bois: A Reader*, ed. David Levering Lewis (New York: Henry Holt, 1995), 509–10.

25. Ibid., 510.

26. Lou Turner, "The Young Marx's Critique of Civil Society, and the Self-Limiting Emancipation of Black Folk: A Post–Los Angeles Reconstruction," *Humanity and Society* 19, no. 4 (1995): 91–107. Du Bois's own democratic imagination was a mixture of bourgeois liberalism, Fabian socialism, Black nationalism, and an uncritical appreciation for Stalin and Mao. Adolph L. Reed Jr., *W. E. B. Du Bois and American Political Thought: Fabianism and the Color Line* (New York: Oxford University Press, 1997); W. E. B. Du Bois, *The Autobiography of W. E. B. Du Bois: A Soliloquy on Viewing My Life from the Last Decade of Its First Century* (New York: International, 1968). It is a combination that, however strange it seems now, was not so unusual in the first half of the twentieth

century. He claimed a lifelong affinity for "industrial democracy" but typical of early-twentieth-century socialists, his conception of it was bureaucratic and overly concerned with economic efficiency. For example, in 1958 Du Bois defined socialism as "a disciplined economy and political organization in which the first duty of a citizen is to serve the state": W. E. B. Du Bois, "Message to the Accra Conference," in *An ABC of Color* (New York: International, 1989), 209. Notably, democracy and freedom do not figure in this definition. As Reed points out, Du Bois never expressed any concern about the contradiction between socialism as a form of rationalized, bureaucratic, centralized planning and as the expansion of democracy into all spheres of social life. Despite this, Du Bois's political thought remains important for democratic theory because of his insistence that the democratic potential of undermining the color line goes beyond achieving civil rights to creating space for a more radically emancipatory politics.

27. Du Bois, *Black Reconstruction*, 595, 184.

28. Aileen S. Kraditor, *Means and Ends in American Abolitionism: Garrison and His Critics on Strategy and Tactics, 1834–1850* (Chicago: Elephant, 1989). I freely admit that my heroic account of the original abolitionist movement below is essentially Garrisonian and that it downplays political and religious differences within the movement between Garrison and anti-Garrisonians, between radicals and reformists, and between major figures such as Garrison, Frederick Douglass, and John Brown. Garrison and his followers believed that American society was thoroughly immoral and that slavery was but the worst of many sins. Thus, they welcomed a fundamental change in American ideology and institutions and did not shrink from radical demands, including the dissolution of the Union. Reformist abolitionists, on the other hand, believed American society was fundamentally good except for slavery. They wanted to end slavery while leaving Northern society otherwise intact. My discussion of the abolitionists in this chapter, unless otherwise noted, refers to the radical wing of the movement rather than the reformist wing because the Garrisonians, unlike the reformists, enunciated a radical political vision that went beyond the limits of liberal democracy. Kraditor argues that there were four factions of abolitionism: Garrisonians, anti-Garrisonians, radicals, and reformists. While there was considerable overlap between the Garrisonians and the radicals and the anti-Garrisonians and the reformists, they were not completely coterminous. For the purposes of this chapter, however, I consider the Garrisonians and the radicals to be synonymous.

29. Constitution of the New England Anti-Slavery Society, in *The Abolitionists: A Collection of Their Writings*, ed. Louis Ruchames (New York: G. P. Putnam's Sons, 1963), 33.

30. This led him, for example, to welcome debate in the American Anti-Slavery Society (formed in 1833) on women's equality, a debate that resulted in a split in 1840 between the radical Garrisonian wing and the more conservative wing, which left to form the American and Foreign Anti-Slavery Society.

31. For example, Abby Kelley and Frederick Douglass's speaking tour in Rhode Island in 1841. See Dorothy Sterling, *Ahead of Her Time: Abby Kelley and the Politics of Antislavery* (New York: W. W. Norton, 1991), 139–44.

32. My argument implies that abolitionism was not a predominantly white movement, as it is often portrayed, but essentially a Black movement that welcomed anyone willing to join its cause. Benjamin Quarles identifies much of the free Black population in the North as abolitionist and notes that the initial support, financial and otherwise, to Garrison's *Liberator* and other abolitionist projects came from the Black community. For white abolitionists, commitment to antislavery politics required them to confront Black people as human beings. This process was not free of prejudice or patronizing attitudes—even Garrison was known to lecture free Blacks on the need to appear morally upright. Yet this confrontation was a necessary part of whites making themselves a part of a Black freedom struggle. Benjamin Quarles, *Black Abolitionists* (New York: Da Capo, 1969).

33. Lincoln would later confess that he personally was "only an instrument" in the antislavery struggle and that "The logic and moral power of Garrison and the antislavery people of the country and the army have done it all." See Henry Mayer, *All on Fire: William Lloyd Garrison and the Abolition of Slavery* (New York: St. Martin's Griffin, 1998), 568.

34. Herbert Aptheker argues that the abolitionist movement contained all the elements of a revolutionary movement, including a radical vision, strategy, organization, revolutionary consciousness, "class cohesiveness," martyrs, armed struggle, and civil war: *Abolitionism: A Revolutionary Movement* (Boston: Twayne, 1989).

35. This section follows Kraditor's excellent analysis of agitation in the abolitionist movement in *Means and Ends*, chapters 2 and 7.

36. Ibid., 213.

37. Wendell Phillips, "Philosophy of the Abolition Movement," in *On Civil Rights and Freedom*, ed. Louis Filler (New York: Hill and Wang, 1965), 35–36.

Similarly, Frederick Douglass once spoke, "At a time like this, scorching irony, not convincing argument, is needed. O! had I the ability, and could I reach the nation's ear, I would, to-day, pour out a fiery stream of biting ridicule, blasting reproach, withering sarcasm, and stern rebuke. For it is not light that is needed, but fire; it is not the gentle shower but thunder. We need the storm, the whirlwind, and the earthquake": Douglass, "What to the Slave Is the Fourth of July?" 5 July 1852, Archives of American Public Address, http://douglass.speech.nwu.edu/doug_a10.htm.

38. Phillips, "Philosophy of the Abolition Movement," 36; Kimberly K. Smith, *The Dominion of Voice: Riot, Reason, and Romance in Antebellum Politics* (Lawrence: University of Kansas Press, 1999).

39. Quoted in Kraditor, *Means and Ends*, 29.

40. Robert A. Dahl, *On Democracy* (New Haven: Yale University Press, 1998).

41. Richard H. King, *Civil Rights and the Idea of Freedom* (Athens: University of Georgia Press, 1996), 14.

42. Eric Foner, *The Story of American Freedom* (New York: W. W. Norton, 1998), 84–94.

43. Quoted in ibid., 88, italics in original. Similarly, Richard King argues that there were four meanings of freedom in the civil rights movement: as individual rights; as autonomy, or the ability to govern oneself; as collective deliverance, or liberation from external control; and as participation, or the right to participate in public affairs, including voting, nightly mass meetings, demonstrations, and other means of deliberation and decision making. King, *Civil Rights and the Idea of Freedom*, 26–28.

44. Hannah Arendt, "What Is Freedom?" in *Between Past and Future* (New York: Penguin, 1968), 153, italics in original.

45. Karl Marx, "Letters from *Deutsch-Französische Jahrbücher*," in Karl Marx and Frederick Engels, *Collected Works*, vol. 3 (New York: International, 1975), 142.

46. Sterling, *Ahead of Her Time*, 62.

47. Ibid., 325–26.

48. Wendell Phillips, "The State of the Country," in *The Lesson of the Hour: Wendell Phillips on Abolition and Strategy*, ed. Noel Ignatiev (Chicago: Kerr, 2001), 136.

49. Aptheker, *Abolitionism*, 105.

50. David R. Roediger, *Toward the Abolition of Whiteness* (London: Verso, 1994), 66.

51. Elsa Barkley-Brown, "Negotiating and Transforming the Public Sphere: African American Political Life in the Transition from Slavery to Freedom," *Public Culture* 7, no. 1 (1994): 107–46; Aldon D. Morris, *The Origins of the Civil Rights Movement: Black Communities Organizing for Change* (New York: Free Press, 1984); Bobby Seale, *Seize the Time: The Story of the Black Panther Party and Huey P. Newton* (New York: Black Classic, 1997).

52. William E. Connolly, *Identity\Difference: Democratic Negotiations of Political Paradox* (Ithaca, NY: Cornell University Press, 1991), 212.

53. Kelley, *Freedom Dreams*, 128–29.

54. For an example of this, see Kelley's account of the "Black Manifesto" in ibid., 120–23.

55. Karl Marx, *Capital*, vol. 1, ed. Frederick Engels (New York: International, 1967), 284; Roediger, *Toward the Abolition of Whiteness*, 66.

56. Jennifer L. Hochschild, *Facing Up to the American Dream: Race, Class, and the Soul of the Nation* (Princeton: Princeton University Press, 1995).

57. John O. Killens, "Black Man's Burden," in *The White Problem in America*, ed. editors of *Ebony* (Chicago: Johnson, 1966), 165.

58. *The White Problem in America*, ed. editors of *Ebony*, 1.

Index

abolition, xix, xxii, 67, 80–81, 84–87, 89, 92–93, 118, 123, 143

abolition-democracy, xxiii, xxvi; definition of, 126, 133–34; and participation, 138–39; radicalness of, 139–40; strategy of, 141–45

abolitionist movement, 62, 134–40, 142; abolitionists as agitators, 136–37, 143; as Black movement, 187n; radical vs. reformist, 186n

affirmative action, 61, 75, 85–86, 117, 120, 141, 143

African Americans: agency of, 53; as anticitizens, 43–44, 47, 54–55; colonial Virginia, 34–37; and democratic ideals, xiii, xxiii; free, 7; and globalization, 120; and immigration, 45, 119–20; middle class, 20, 23–24, 99, 176n; migration of, 98; progress of, 102–3, 143–44; and Reconstruction, 10–12; subordination of, xiv, xv; Tocqueville on, 49–50; and and whiteness, xxii, 18, 42, 62; women, 56, 58–59. *See also* Blackness; working class, Black

alienation, 20, 23

Allen, Theodore, xviii, 38

American Creed, xiii, xvi

American dilemma, xiii, xvi

anticitizens, 43–44, 55, 58, 131

antimiscegenation laws, 54–56, 59

Arendt, Hannah, 7, 138, 153n

Asian Americans, 2, 17, 27–28, 119, 163n

assimilation, 5, 27, 45–46, 119

Bacon's rebellion, 35–36

Baldwin, James, xviii, xix, 62

Balfour, Lawrie, 28, 75

Bansal, Preeta, xv

Bell, Derrick, xv, 86

Bennett, Lerone, 17

bipolarity, 9, 25–28, 30, 70

Black radical political thought, 130–33

Black world. *See* dark world

Joel Olson is assistant professor of political science at Northern Arizona University.